TEENAGE MUTANT NINJA TURTLES

CHASING PHANTOMS ▷ VOLUME 16

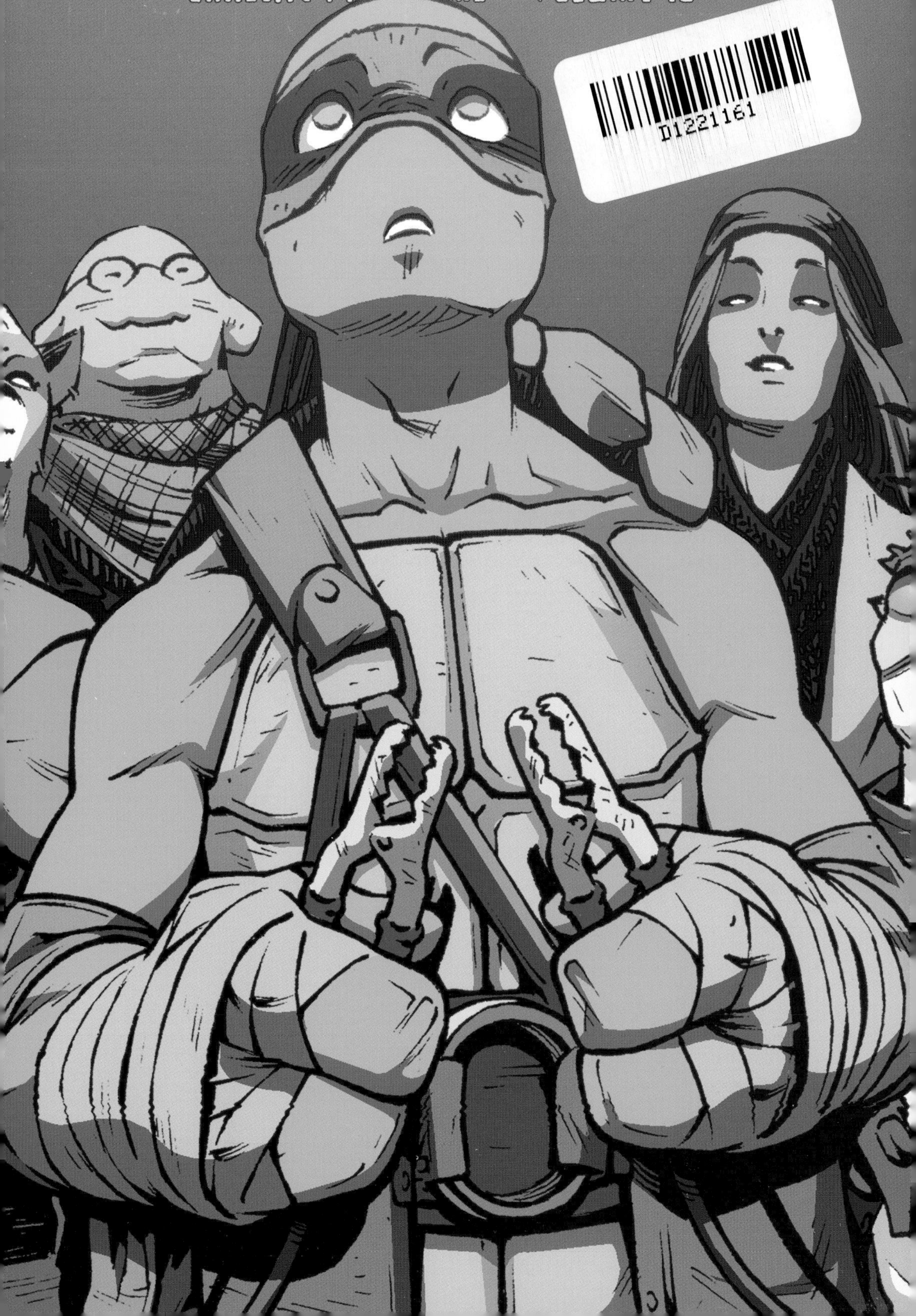

nickelodeon™

Special thanks to Joan Hilty & Linda Lee for their invaluable assistance.

For international rights, contact **licensing@idwpublishing.com**

ISBN: 978-1-63140-859-5

20 19 18 17   1 2 3 4

IDW®
www.IDWPUBLISHING.com

Ted Adams, CEO & Publisher • Greg Goldstein, President & COO • Robbie Robbins, EVP/Sr. Graphic Artist • Chris Ryall, Chief Creative Officer • David Hedgecock, Editor-in-Chief • Laurie Windrow, Senior Vice President of Sales & Marketing • Matthew Ruzicka, CPA, Chief Financial Officer • Lorelei Bunjes, VP of Digital Services • Jerry Bennington, VP of New Product Development

Facebook: facebook.com/idwpublishing • Twitter: @idwpublishing • YouTube: youtube.com/idwpublishing
Tumblr: tumblr.idwpublishing.com • Instagram: instagram.com/idwpublishing

Originally published as TEENAGE MUTANT NINJA TURTLES issues #61–65.

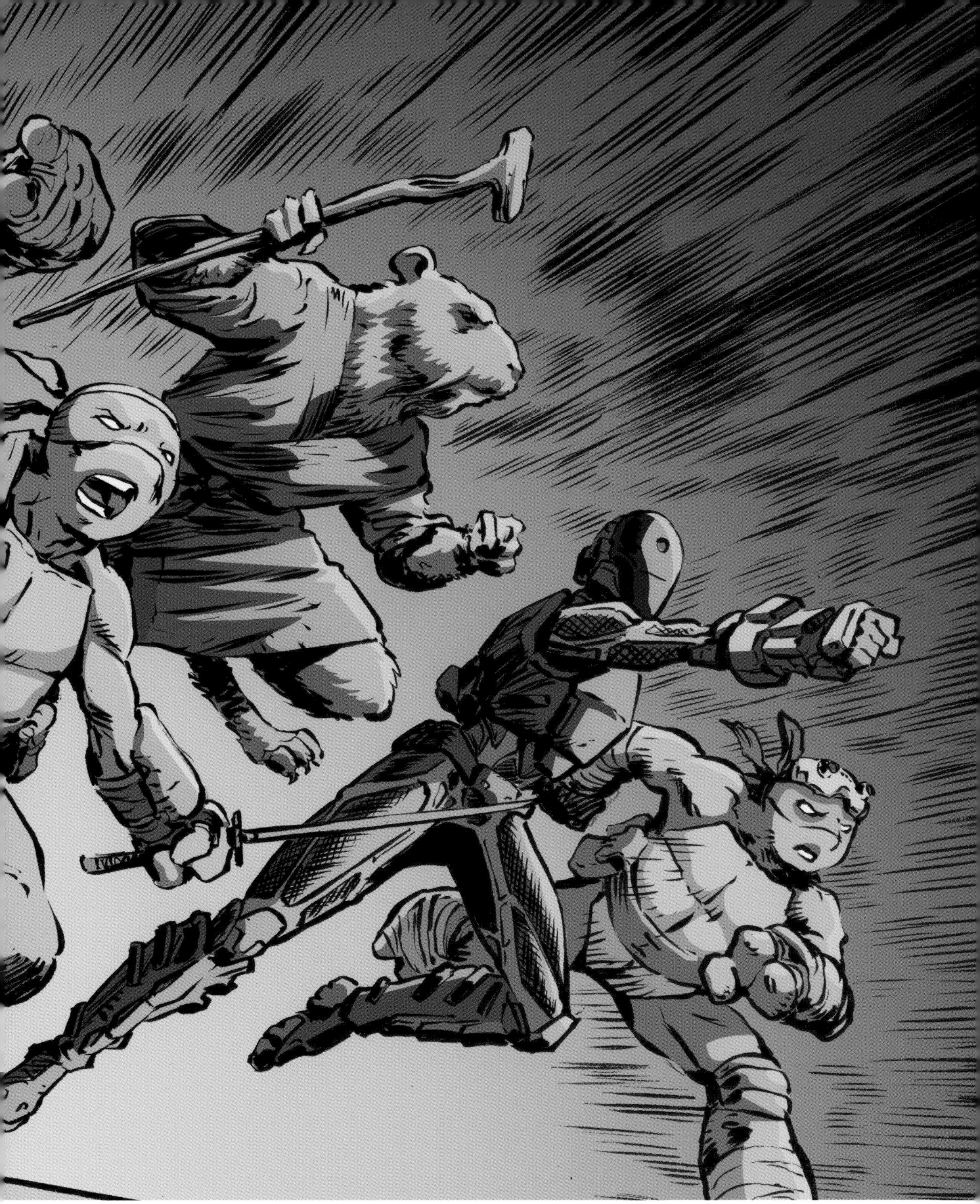

Story by Kevin Eastman, Bobby Curnow, and Tom Waltz

Script by Tom Waltz

Art by Dave Wachter and Mateus Santolouco (Ch. 5)

Colors by Ronda Pattison

Series Edits by Bobby Curnow

Letters and Production by Shawn Lee

Cover by Dave Wachter

Collection Edits by Justin Eisinger & Alonzo Simon

Publisher Ted Adams

Based on characters created by Peter Laird and Kevin Eastman

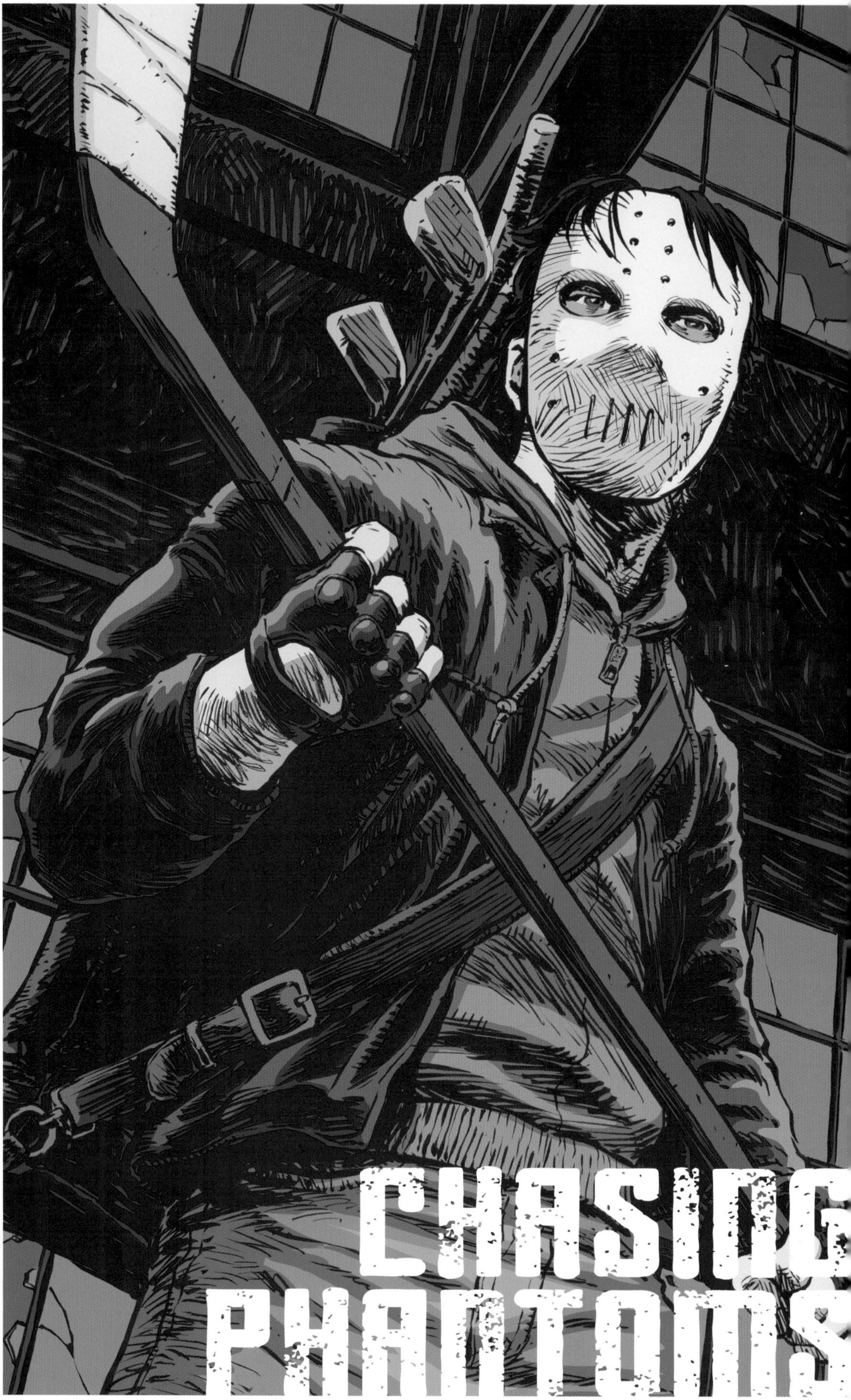
CHASING
PHANTOMS

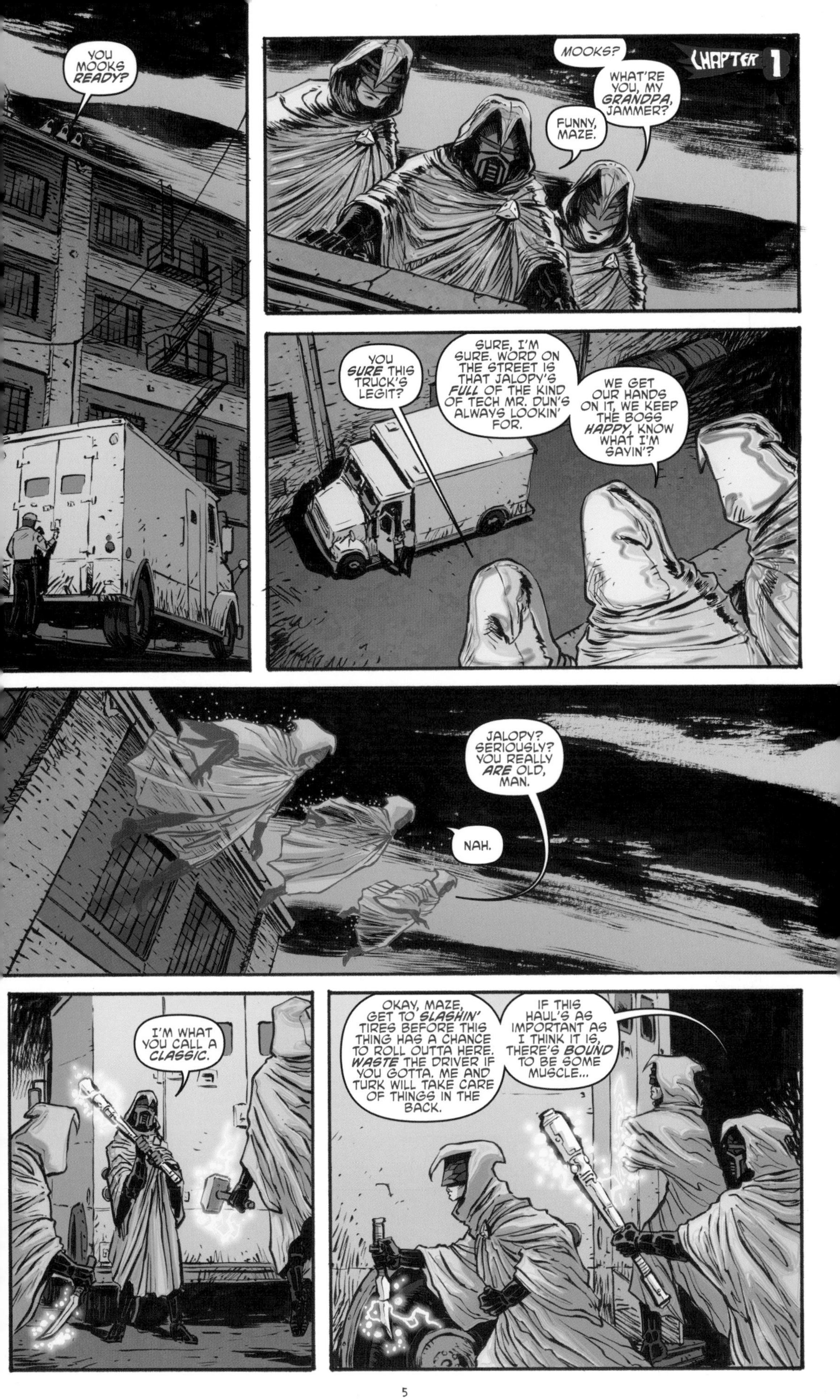
YOU MOOKS READY?
MOOKS?
WHAT'RE YOU, MY GRANDPA, JAMMER?
FUNNY, MAZE.
CHAPTER 1
YOU SURE THIS TRUCK'S LEGIT?
SURE, I'M SURE. WORD ON THE STREET IS THAT JALOPY'S FULL OF THE KIND OF TECH MR. DUN'S ALWAYS LOOKIN' FOR.
WE GET OUR HANDS ON IT, WE KEEP THE BOSS HAPPY, KNOW WHAT I'M SAYIN'?
JALOPY? SERIOUSLY? YOU REALLY ARE OLD, MAN.
NAH.
I'M WHAT YOU CALL A CLASSIC.
OKAY, MAZE, GET TO SLASHIN' TIRES BEFORE THIS THING HAS A CHANCE TO ROLL OUTTA HERE. WASTE THE DRIVER IF YOU GOTTA. ME AND TURK WILL TAKE CARE OF THINGS IN THE BACK.
IF THIS HAUL'S AS IMPORTANT AS I THINK IT IS, THERE'S BOUND TO BE SOME MUSCLE...

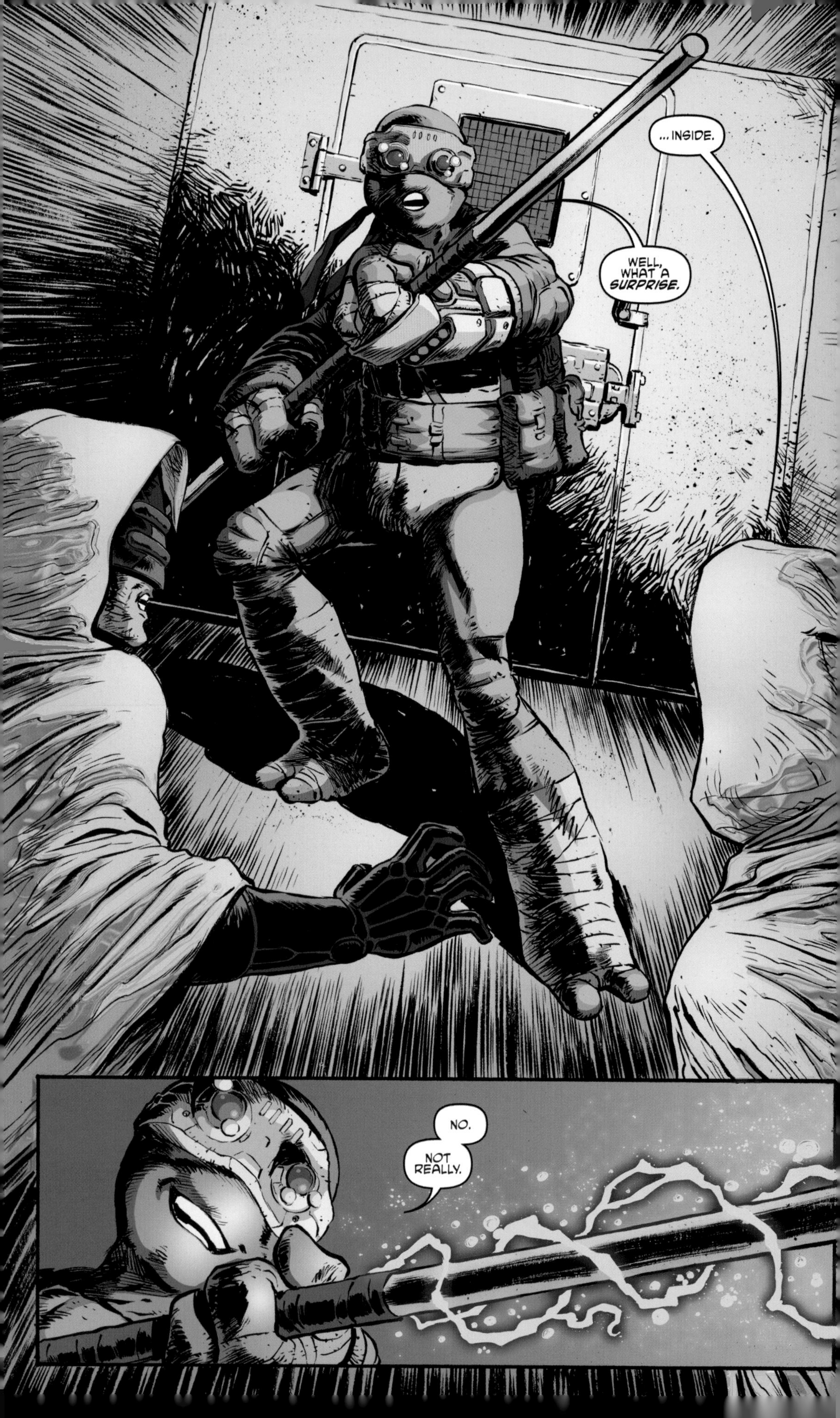
...INSIDE.
WELL, WHAT A SURPRISE.
NO.
NOT REALLY.

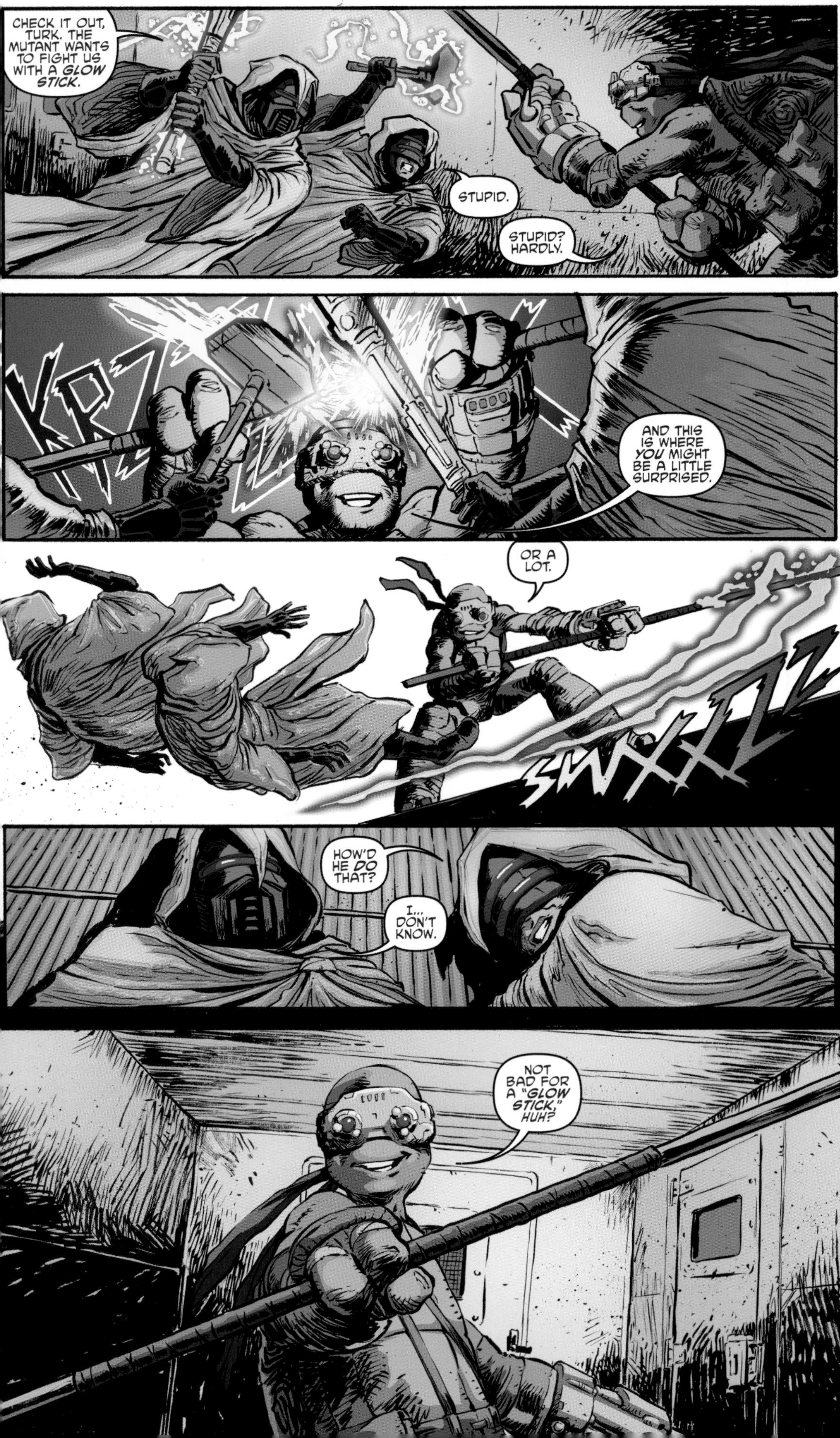
CHECK IT OUT, TURK. THE MUTANT WANTS TO FIGHT US WITH A GLOW STICK.
STUPID.
STUPID? HARDLY.
KRZZ
AND THIS IS WHERE YOU MIGHT BE A LITTLE SURPRISED.
OR A LOT.
SWXXZZ
HOW'D HE DO THAT?
I... DON'T KNOW.
NOT BAD FOR A "GLOW STICK," HUH?

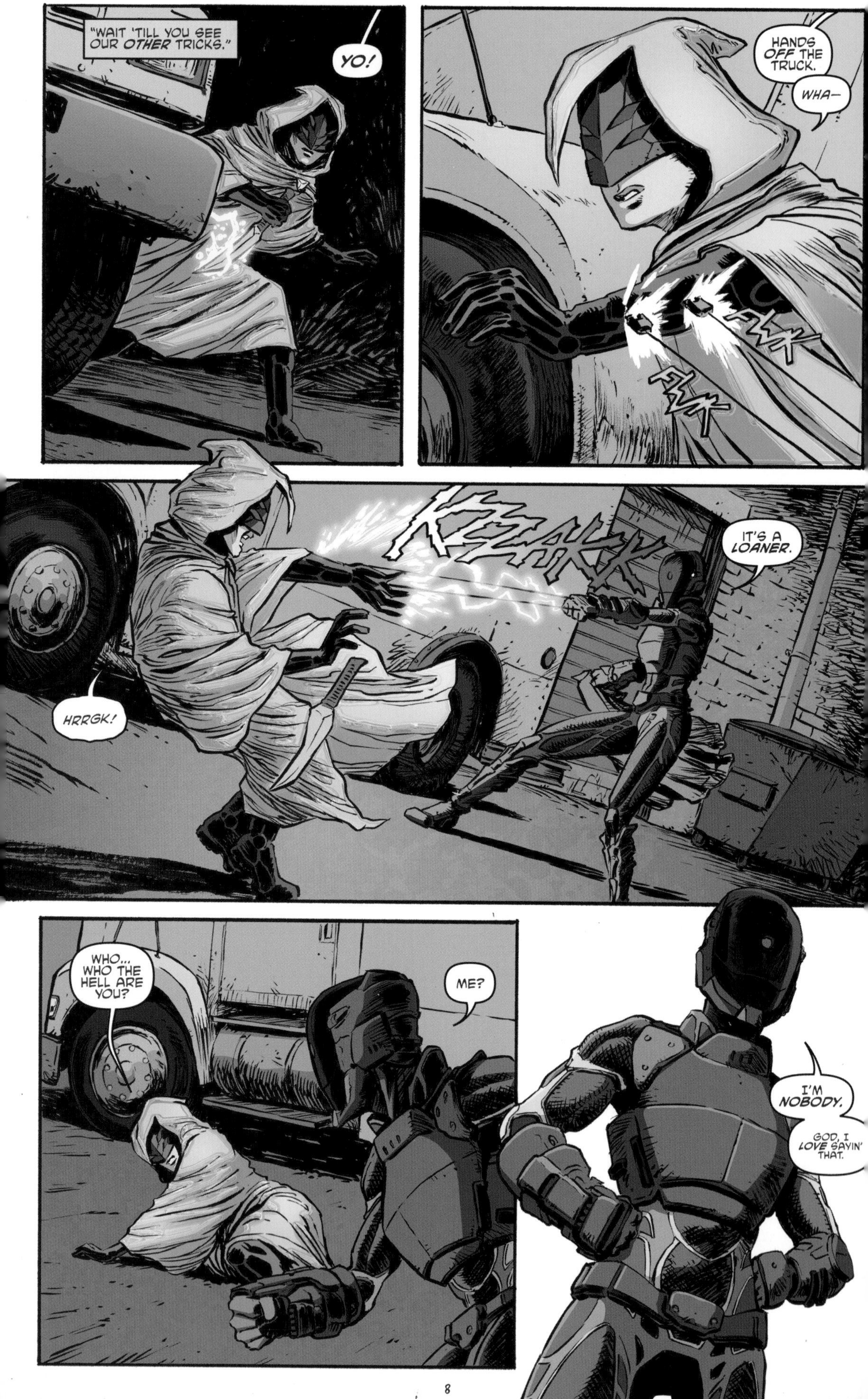
"WAIT 'TILL YOU SEE OUR OTHER TRICKS."
YO!
HANDS OFF THE TRUCK.
WHA—
FWK
FWK
KZZAKK
IT'S A LOANER.
HRRGK!
WHO... WHO THE HELL ARE YOU?
ME?
I'M NOBODY.
GOD, I LOVE SAYIN' THAT.

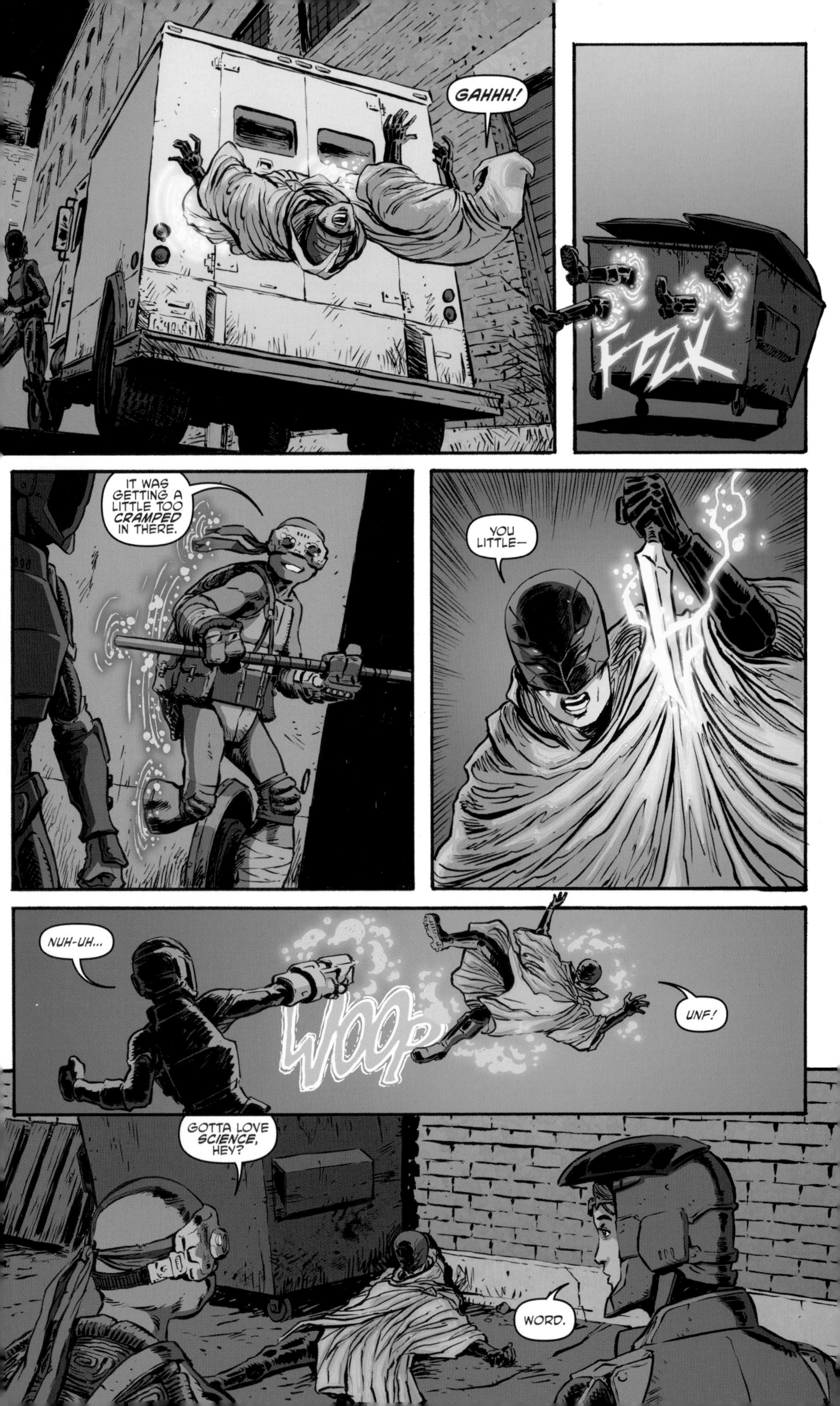
GAHHH!
FZZK
IT WAS GETTING A LITTLE TOO CRAMPED IN THERE.
YOU LITTLE—
NUH-UH...
WOOP
UNF!
GOTTA LOVE SCIENCE, HEY?
WORD.

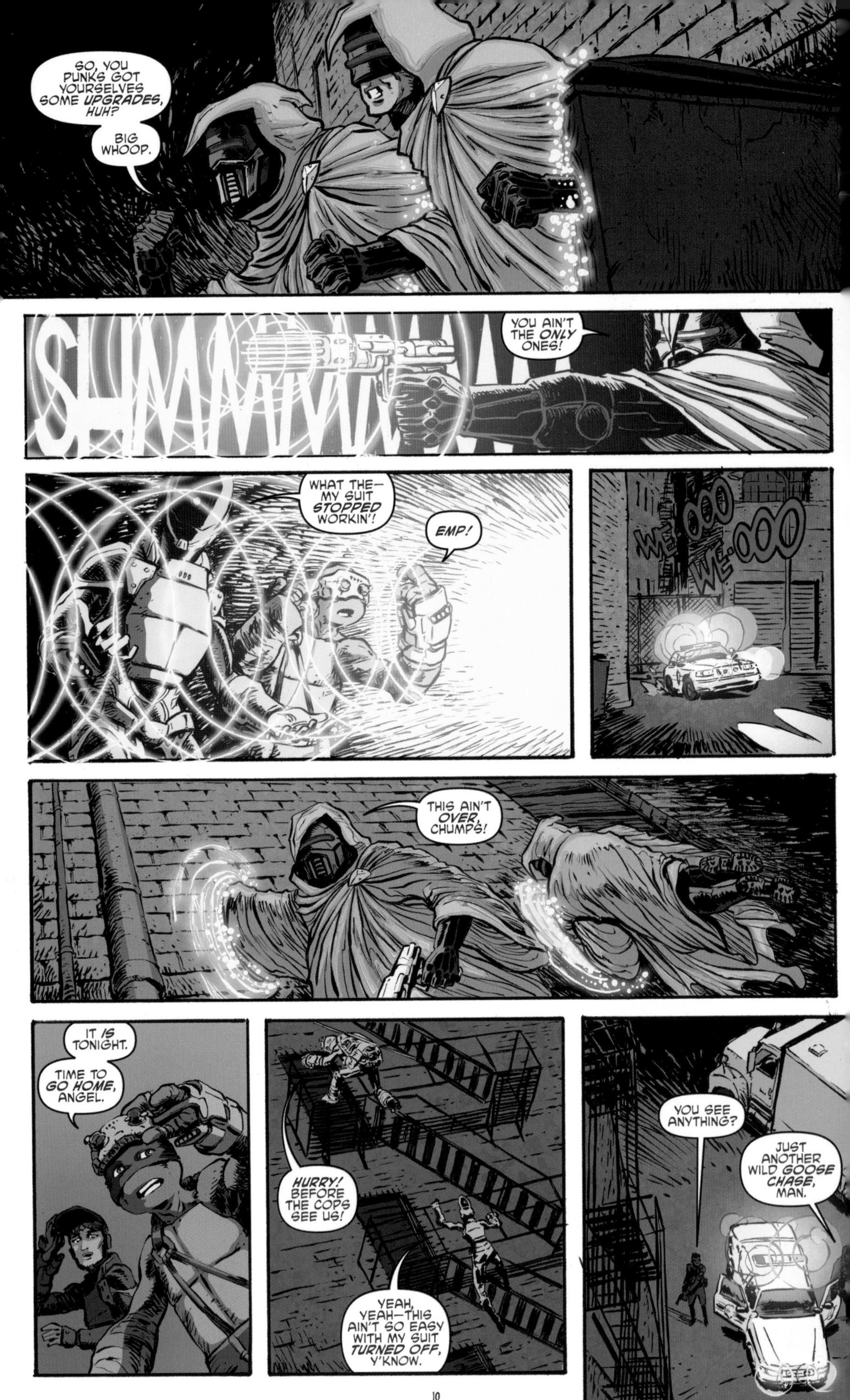
SO, YOU PUNKS GOT YOURSELVES SOME UPGRADES, HUH?
BIG WHOOP.
SHMMMMMM
YOU AIN'T THE ONLY ONES!
WHAT THE— MY SUIT STOPPED WORKIN'!
EMP!
WE-OOO
WE-OOO
THIS AIN'T OVER, CHUMPS!
IT IS TONIGHT.
TIME TO GO HOME, ANGEL.
HURRY! BEFORE THE COPS SEE US!
YEAH, YEAH—THIS AIN'T SO EASY WITH MY SUIT TURNED OFF, Y'KNOW.
YOU SEE ANYTHING?
JUST ANOTHER WILD GOOSE CHASE, MAN.

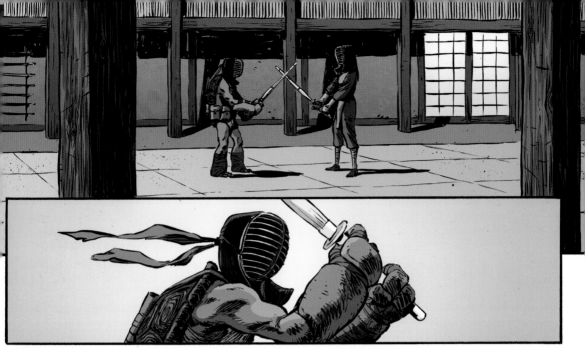

UNF!

KRAK

HYAH!

VERY *GOOD*, JENNIKA. YOU MET MY *KATSUGI MEN* WITH *DEBANA WAZA*.

I CAN TELL YOU'VE BEEN *TRAINING* WITH MASTER SPLINTER.

OW.

THANK YOU, *CHUNIN*, BUT IT WAS A FORTUNATE COUNTER ON MY PART, *NOTHING MORE.*

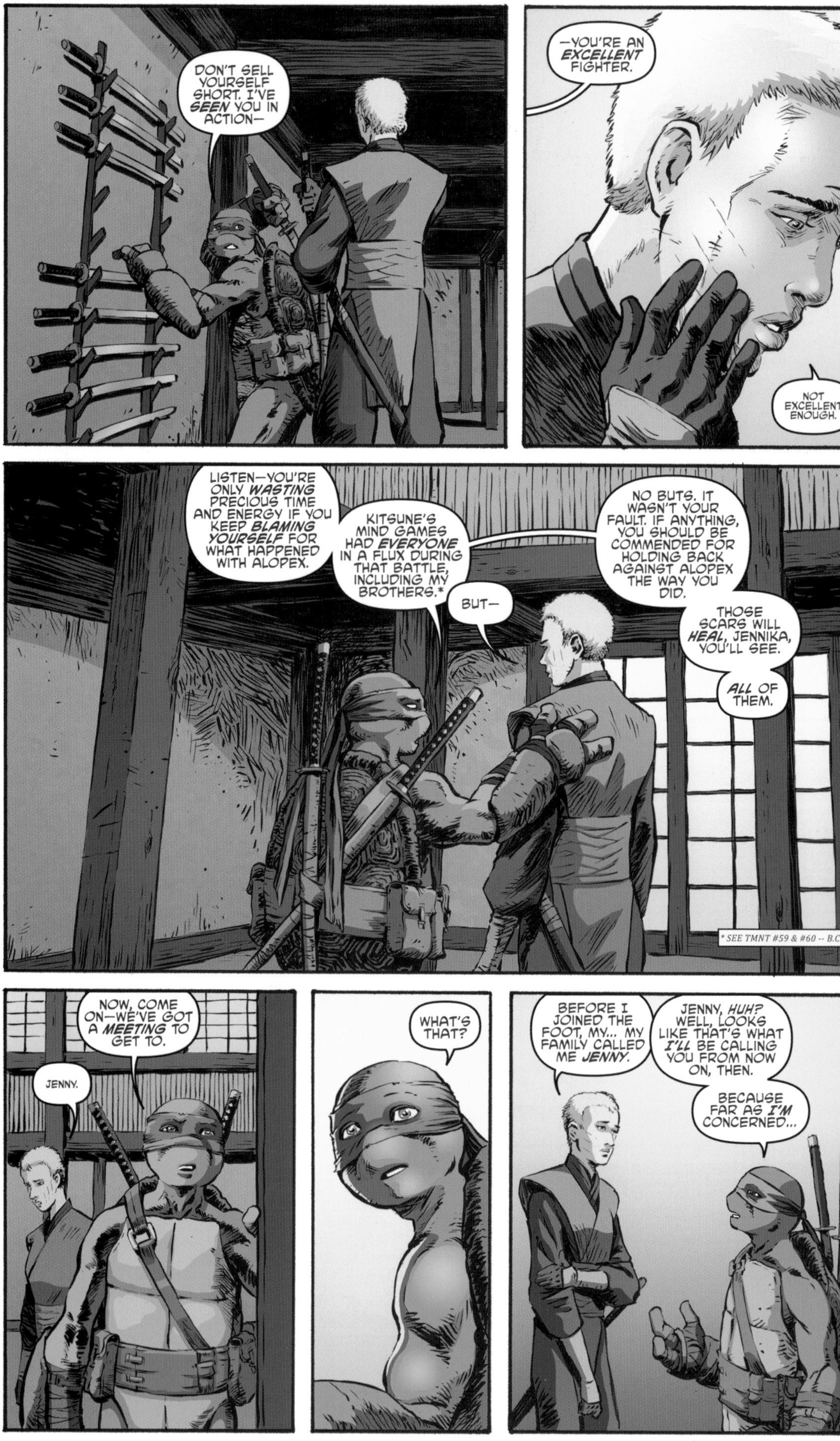

DON'T SELL YOURSELF SHORT. I'VE SEEN YOU IN ACTION—
—YOU'RE AN EXCELLENT FIGHTER.
NOT EXCELLENT ENOUGH.
LISTEN—YOU'RE ONLY WASTING PRECIOUS TIME AND ENERGY IF YOU KEEP BLAMING YOURSELF FOR WHAT HAPPENED WITH ALOPEX.
KITSUNE'S MIND GAMES HAD EVERYONE IN A FLUX DURING THAT BATTLE, INCLUDING MY BROTHERS.*
BUT—
NO BUTS. IT WASN'T YOUR FAULT. IF ANYTHING, YOU SHOULD BE COMMENDED FOR HOLDING BACK AGAINST ALOPEX THE WAY YOU DID.
THOSE SCARS WILL HEAL, JENNIKA, YOU'LL SEE.
ALL OF THEM.
* SEE TMNT #59 & #60 -- B.C.
NOW, COME ON—WE'VE GOT A MEETING TO GET TO.
JENNY.
WHAT'S THAT?
BEFORE I JOINED THE FOOT, MY... MY FAMILY CALLED ME JENNY.
JENNY, HUH? WELL, LOOKS LIKE THAT'S WHAT I'LL BE CALLING YOU FROM NOW ON, THEN.
BECAUSE FAR AS I'M CONCERNED...

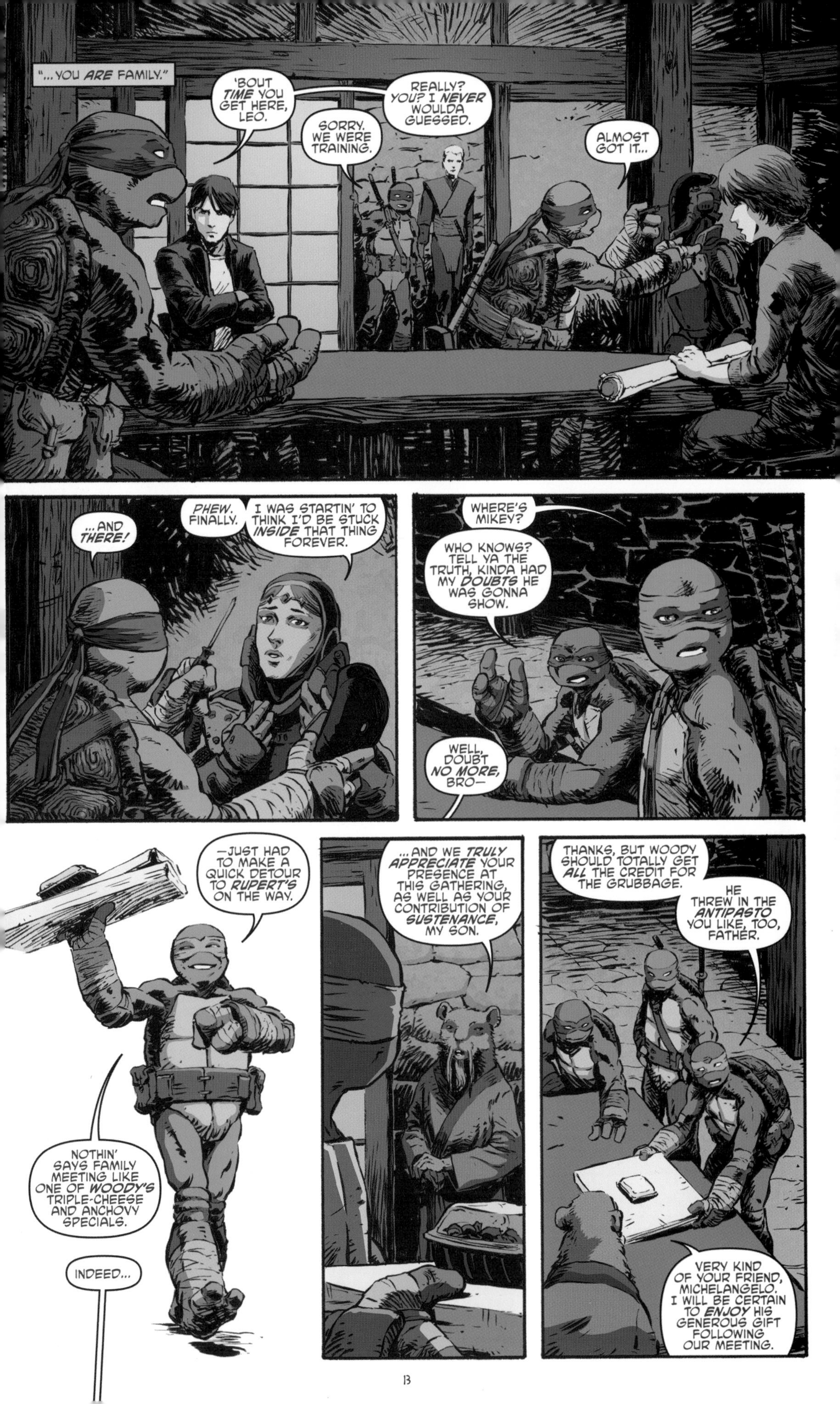
"...YOU ARE FAMILY."
'BOUT TIME YOU GET HERE, LEO.
REALLY? YOU? I NEVER WOULDA GUESSED.
SORRY. WE WERE TRAINING.
ALMOST GOT IT...
...AND THERE!
PHEW. FINALLY.
I WAS STARTIN' TO THINK I'D BE STUCK INSIDE THAT THING FOREVER.
WHERE'S MIKEY?
WHO KNOWS? TELL YA THE TRUTH, KINDA HAD MY DOUBTS HE WAS GONNA SHOW.
WELL, DOUBT NO MORE, BRO—
—JUST HAD TO MAKE A QUICK DETOUR TO RUPERT'S ON THE WAY.
NOTHIN' SAYS FAMILY MEETING LIKE ONE OF WOODY'S TRIPLE-CHEESE AND ANCHOVY SPECIALS.
INDEED...
...AND WE TRULY APPRECIATE YOUR PRESENCE AT THIS GATHERING, AS WELL AS YOUR CONTRIBUTION OF SUSTENANCE, MY SON.
THANKS, BUT WOODY SHOULD TOTALLY GET ALL THE CREDIT FOR THE GRUBBAGE.
HE THREW IN THE ANTIPASTO YOU LIKE, TOO, FATHER.
VERY KIND OF YOUR FRIEND, MICHELANGELO. I WILL BE CERTAIN TO ENJOY HIS GENEROUS GIFT FOLLOWING OUR MEETING.

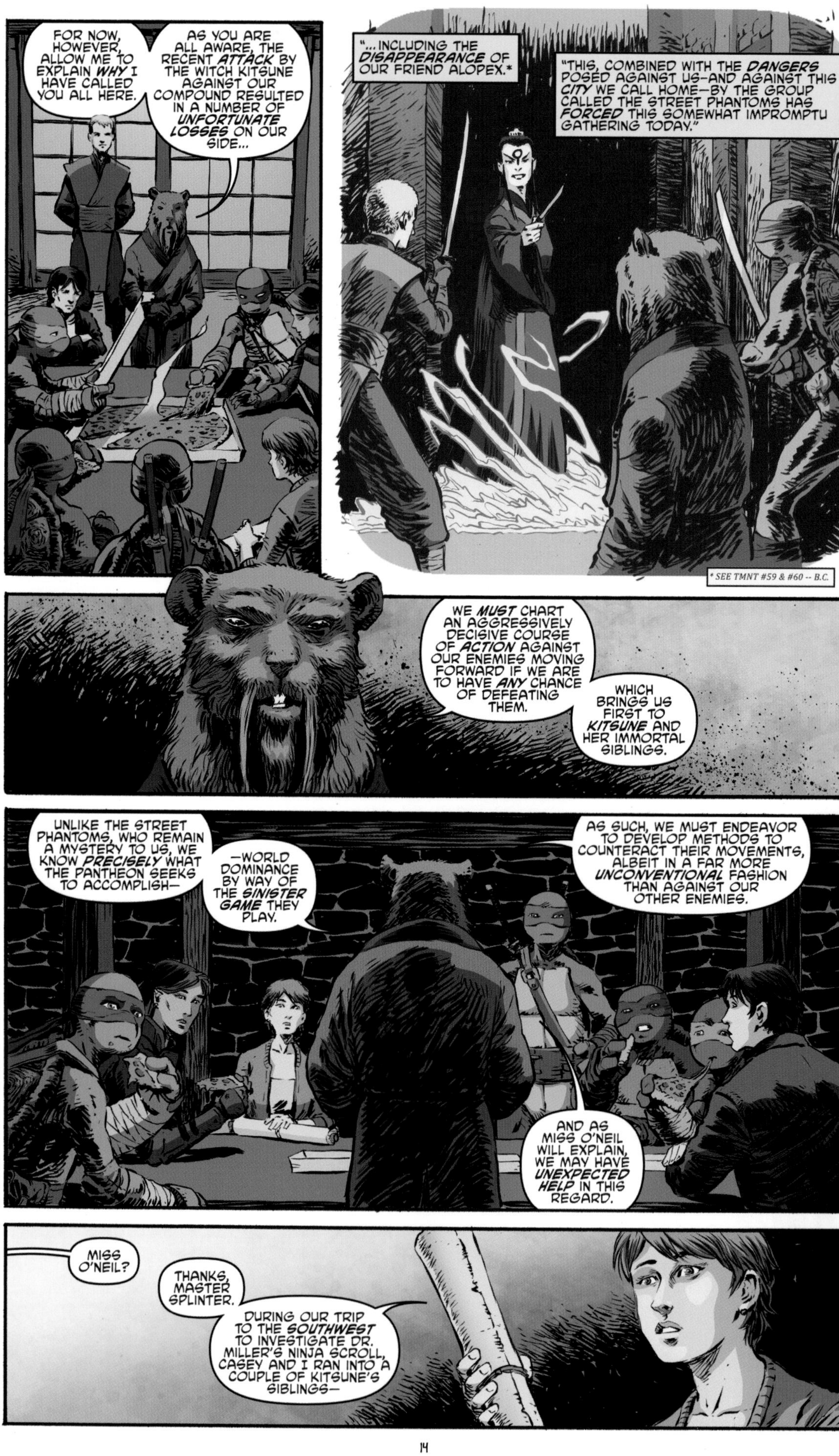
FOR NOW, HOWEVER, ALLOW ME TO EXPLAIN WHY I HAVE CALLED YOU ALL HERE.
AS YOU ARE ALL AWARE, THE RECENT ATTACK BY THE WITCH KITSUNE AGAINST OUR COMPOUND RESULTED IN A NUMBER OF UNFORTUNATE LOSSES ON OUR SIDE...
"...INCLUDING THE DISAPPEARANCE OF OUR FRIEND ALOPEX.*
"THIS, COMBINED WITH THE DANGERS POSED AGAINST US—AND AGAINST THIS CITY WE CALL HOME—BY THE GROUP CALLED THE STREET PHANTOMS HAS FORCED THIS SOMEWHAT IMPROMPTU GATHERING TODAY."
* SEE TMNT #59 & #60 -- B.C.
WE MUST CHART AN AGGRESSIVELY DECISIVE COURSE OF ACTION AGAINST OUR ENEMIES MOVING FORWARD IF WE ARE TO HAVE ANY CHANCE OF DEFEATING THEM.
WHICH BRINGS US FIRST TO KITSUNE AND HER IMMORTAL SIBLINGS.
UNLIKE THE STREET PHANTOMS, WHO REMAIN A MYSTERY TO US, WE KNOW PRECISELY WHAT THE PANTHEON SEEKS TO ACCOMPLISH—
—WORLD DOMINANCE BY WAY OF THE SINISTER GAME THEY PLAY.
AS SUCH, WE MUST ENDEAVOR TO DEVELOP METHODS TO COUNTERACT THEIR MOVEMENTS, ALBEIT IN A FAR MORE UNCONVENTIONAL FASHION THAN AGAINST OUR OTHER ENEMIES.
AND AS MISS O'NEIL WILL EXPLAIN, WE MAY HAVE UNEXPECTED HELP IN THIS REGARD.
MISS O'NEIL?
THANKS, MASTER SPLINTER.
DURING OUR TRIP TO THE SOUTHWEST TO INVESTIGATE DR. MILLER'S NINJA SCROLL, CASEY AND I RAN INTO A COUPLE OF KITSUNE'S SIBLINGS—

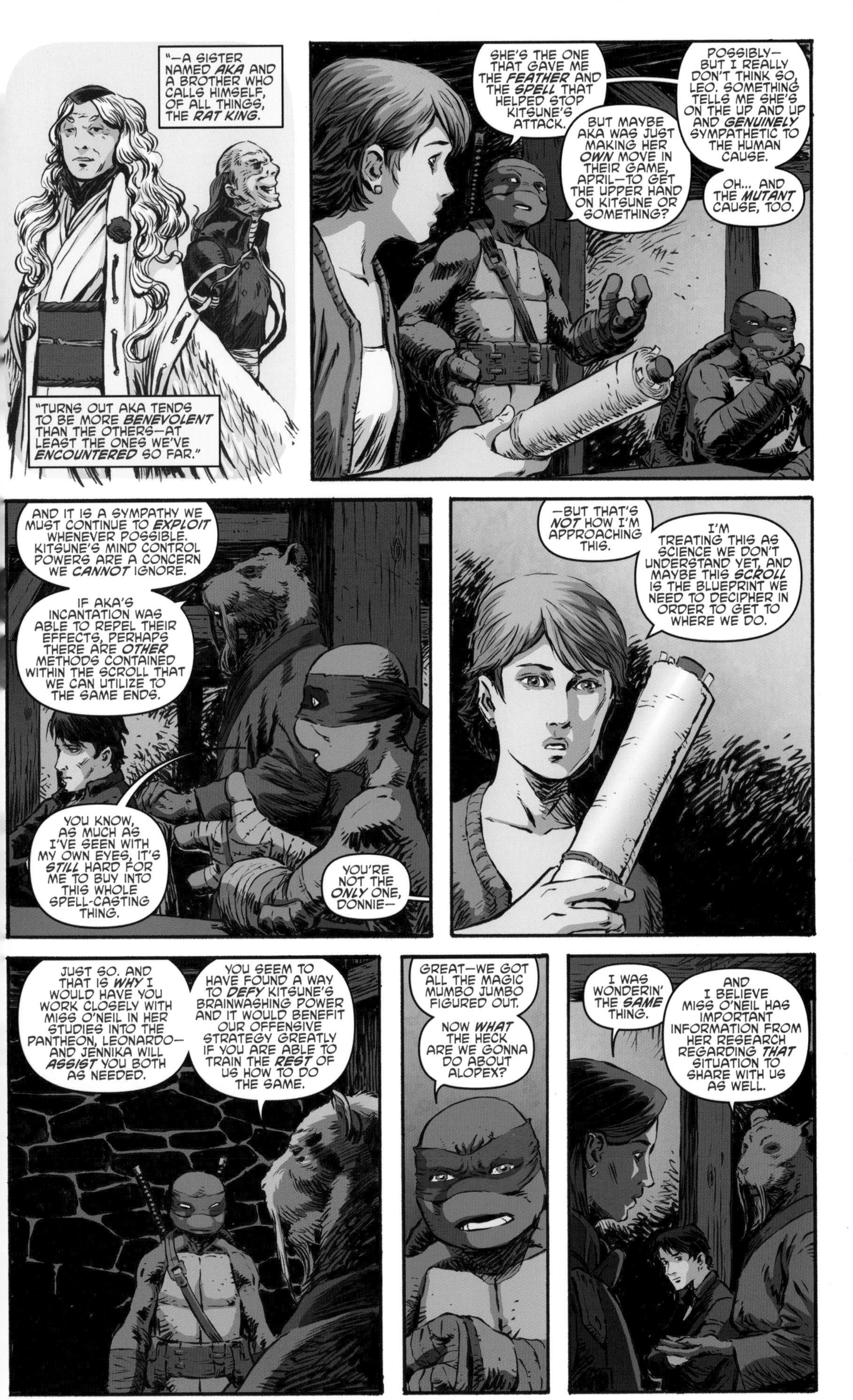
"—A SISTER NAMED AKA AND A BROTHER WHO CALLS HIMSELF, OF ALL THINGS, THE RAT KING.
"TURNS OUT AKA TENDS TO BE MORE BENEVOLENT THAN THE OTHERS—AT LEAST THE ONES WE'VE ENCOUNTERED SO FAR."
SHE'S THE ONE THAT GAVE ME THE FEATHER AND THE SPELL THAT HELPED STOP KITSUNE'S ATTACK.
BUT MAYBE AKA WAS JUST MAKING HER OWN MOVE IN THEIR GAME, APRIL—TO GET THE UPPER HAND ON KITSUNE OR SOMETHING?
POSSIBLY—BUT I REALLY DON'T THINK SO, LEO. SOMETHING TELLS ME SHE'S ON THE UP AND UP AND GENUINELY SYMPATHETIC TO THE HUMAN CAUSE.
OH... AND THE MUTANT CAUSE, TOO.
AND IT IS A SYMPATHY WE MUST CONTINUE TO EXPLOIT WHENEVER POSSIBLE. KITSUNE'S MIND CONTROL POWERS ARE A CONCERN WE CANNOT IGNORE.
IF AKA'S INCANTATION WAS ABLE TO REPEL THEIR EFFECTS, PERHAPS THERE ARE OTHER METHODS CONTAINED WITHIN THE SCROLL THAT WE CAN UTILIZE TO THE SAME ENDS.
YOU KNOW, AS MUCH AS I'VE SEEN WITH MY OWN EYES, IT'S STILL HARD FOR ME TO BUY INTO THIS WHOLE SPELL-CASTING THING.
YOU'RE NOT THE ONLY ONE, DONNIE—
—BUT THAT'S NOT HOW I'M APPROACHING THIS.
I'M TREATING THIS AS SCIENCE WE DON'T UNDERSTAND YET, AND MAYBE THIS SCROLL IS THE BLUEPRINT WE NEED TO DECIPHER IN ORDER TO GET TO WHERE WE DO.
JUST SO. AND THAT IS WHY I WOULD HAVE YOU WORK CLOSELY WITH MISS O'NEIL IN HER STUDIES INTO THE PANTHEON, LEONARDO—AND JENNIKA WILL ASSIST YOU BOTH AS NEEDED.
YOU SEEM TO HAVE FOUND A WAY TO DEFY KITSUNE'S BRAINWASHING POWER AND IT WOULD BENEFIT OUR OFFENSIVE STRATEGY GREATLY IF YOU ARE ABLE TO TRAIN THE REST OF US HOW TO DO THE SAME.
GREAT—WE GOT ALL THE MAGIC MUMBO JUMBO FIGURED OUT.
NOW WHAT THE HECK ARE WE GONNA DO ABOUT ALOPEX?
I WAS WONDERIN' THE SAME THING.
AND I BELIEVE MISS O'NEIL HAS IMPORTANT INFORMATION FROM HER RESEARCH REGARDING THAT SITUATION TO SHARE WITH US AS WELL.

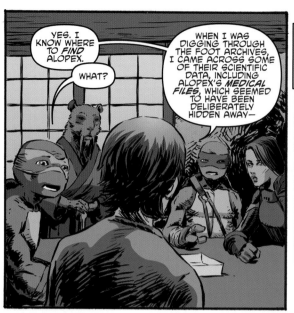

YES. I KNOW WHERE TO *FIND* ALOPEX.

WHAT?

WHEN I WAS DIGGING THROUGH THE FOOT ARCHIVES, I CAME ACROSS SOME OF THEIR SCIENTIFIC DATA, INCLUDING ALOPEX'S *MEDICAL FILES*, WHICH SEEMED TO HAVE BEEN DELIBERATELY HIDDEN AWAY—

"—TURNS OUT THE SCIENTISTS WHO MUTATED HER ALSO *MICRO-CHIPPED* HER DURING THE PROCESS. SOMEBODY—I'M GUESSING KITSUNE—DIDN'T WANT ALOPEX TO BE FOUND WHEN SHE LEFT THE FOOT.

"ANYWAY, I PUNCHED THE INFO INTO ONE OF THEIR TRACKING COMPUTERS AND IT LOOKS LIKE SHE'S HEADING *NORTHWEST*... AND FAST."

ALASKA.

HUH?

ALOPEX TOLD ME SHE'S FROM *ALASKA*. THAT'S WHERE THE FOOT CAPTURED HER BEFORE THEY, YOU KNOW... *CHANGED* HER.

I BET SHE'S FEELIN' *ASHAMED* BY EVERYTHING THAT'S HAPPENED AND PROBABLY TRYIN' TO GET AS *FAR AWAY* AS SHE CAN BECAUSE OF IT.

BUT THAT'S *BULL!* STINKIN' KITSUNE HAD HER ALL *SCREWED UP*, JUST LIKE THE REST OF US. IT WASN'T HER FAULT.

NO, MY SON, IT WAS NOT, AND WE WILL NOT ABANDON ALOPEX NOW IN HER TIME OF CONFUSION.

THAT IS WHY I WOULD HAVE YOU—AND MISS ANGEL, IF SHE IS WILLING—GO TO OUR LOST FRIEND AND *BRING* HER HOME.

WILLING? YOU KIDDIN'? *WHEN* DO WE START?

NOT *SOON* ENOUGH.

PERHAPS *SOONER* THAN YOU THINK, RAPHAEL—

—I HAVE TASKED ONE OF OUR *BEST PILOTS* TO SPEED YOU ON YOUR WAY JUST AS SOON AS YOU ARE BOTH READY. TIME IS OF THE ESSENCE.

ALOPEX IS *FAMILY* AND AN INTEGRAL PART OF THIS CLAN AND SHE MUST BE RETURNED TO US QUICKLY.

HER WARRIOR SKILLS WILL BE *VITAL* TO OUR SUCCESS IN THE *MULTIPLE CONFLICTS* WE FACE.

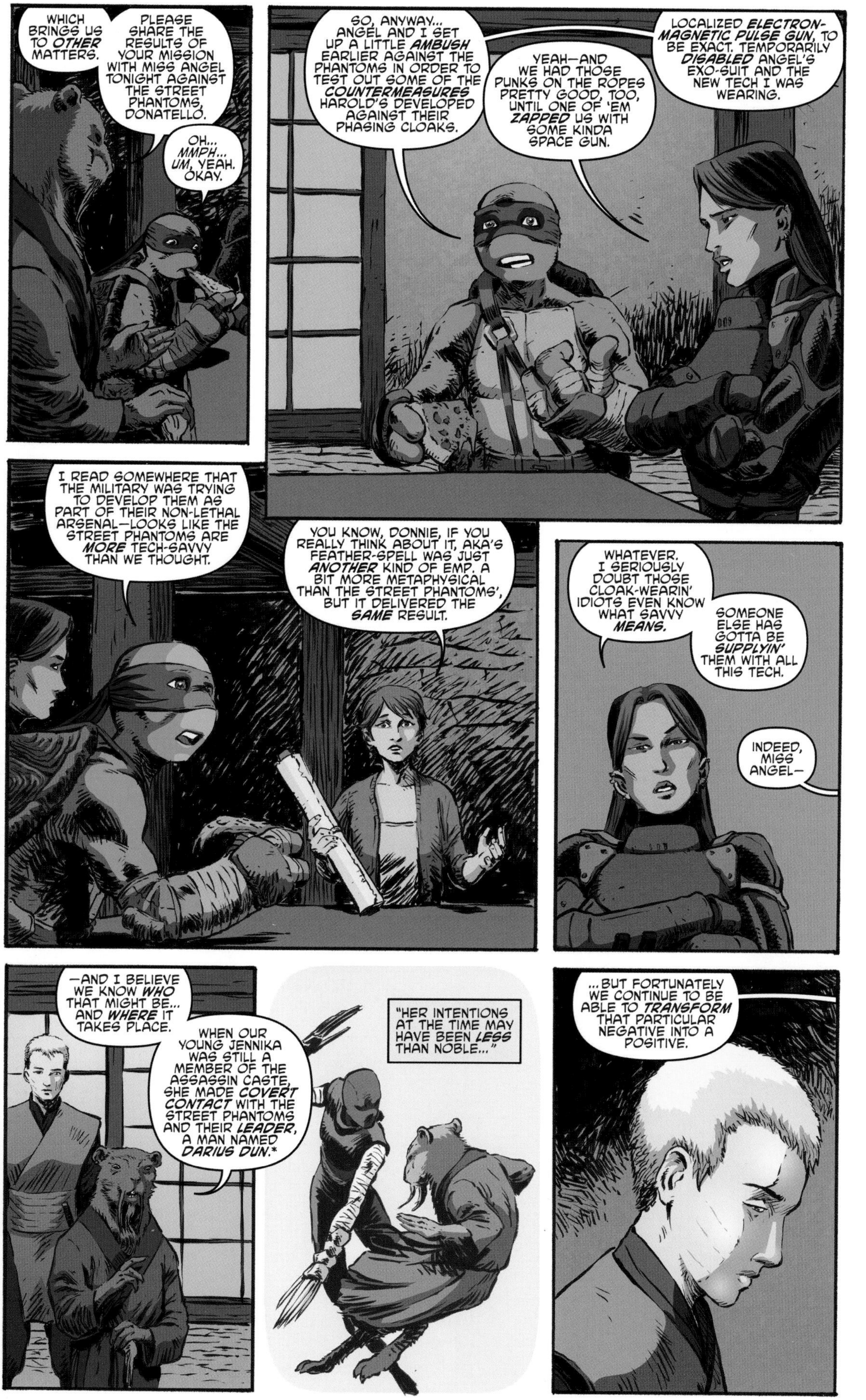
WHICH BRINGS US TO OTHER MATTERS.
PLEASE SHARE THE RESULTS OF YOUR MISSION WITH MISS ANGEL TONIGHT AGAINST THE STREET PHANTOMS, DONATELLO.
OH... MMPH... UM, YEAH. OKAY.
SO, ANYWAY... ANGEL AND I SET UP A LITTLE AMBUSH EARLIER AGAINST THE PHANTOMS IN ORDER TO TEST OUT SOME OF THE COUNTERMEASURES HAROLD'S DEVELOPED AGAINST THEIR PHASING CLOAKS.
YEAH—AND WE HAD THOSE PUNKS ON THE ROPES PRETTY GOOD, TOO, UNTIL ONE OF 'EM ZAPPED US WITH SOME KINDA SPACE GUN.
LOCALIZED ELECTRON-MAGNETIC PULSE GUN, TO BE EXACT. TEMPORARILY DISABLED ANGEL'S EXO-SUIT AND THE NEW TECH I WAS WEARING.
I READ SOMEWHERE THAT THE MILITARY WAS TRYING TO DEVELOP THEM AS PART OF THEIR NON-LETHAL ARSENAL—LOOKS LIKE THE STREET PHANTOMS ARE MORE TECH-SAVVY THAN WE THOUGHT.
YOU KNOW, DONNIE, IF YOU REALLY THINK ABOUT IT, AKA'S FEATHER-SPELL WAS JUST ANOTHER KIND OF EMP. A BIT MORE METAPHYSICAL THAN THE STREET PHANTOMS', BUT IT DELIVERED THE SAME RESULT.
WHATEVER. I SERIOUSLY DOUBT THOSE CLOAK-WEARIN' IDIOTS EVEN KNOW WHAT SAVVY MEANS.
SOMEONE ELSE HAS GOTTA BE SUPPLYIN' THEM WITH ALL THIS TECH.
INDEED, MISS ANGEL—
—AND I BELIEVE WE KNOW WHO THAT MIGHT BE... AND WHERE IT TAKES PLACE.
WHEN OUR YOUNG JENNIKA WAS STILL A MEMBER OF THE ASSASSIN CASTE, SHE MADE COVERT CONTACT WITH THE STREET PHANTOMS AND THEIR LEADER, A MAN NAMED DARIUS DUN.*
"HER INTENTIONS AT THE TIME MAY HAVE BEEN LESS THAN NOBLE..."
...BUT FORTUNATELY WE CONTINUE TO BE ABLE TO TRANSFORM THAT PARTICULAR NEGATIVE INTO A POSITIVE.

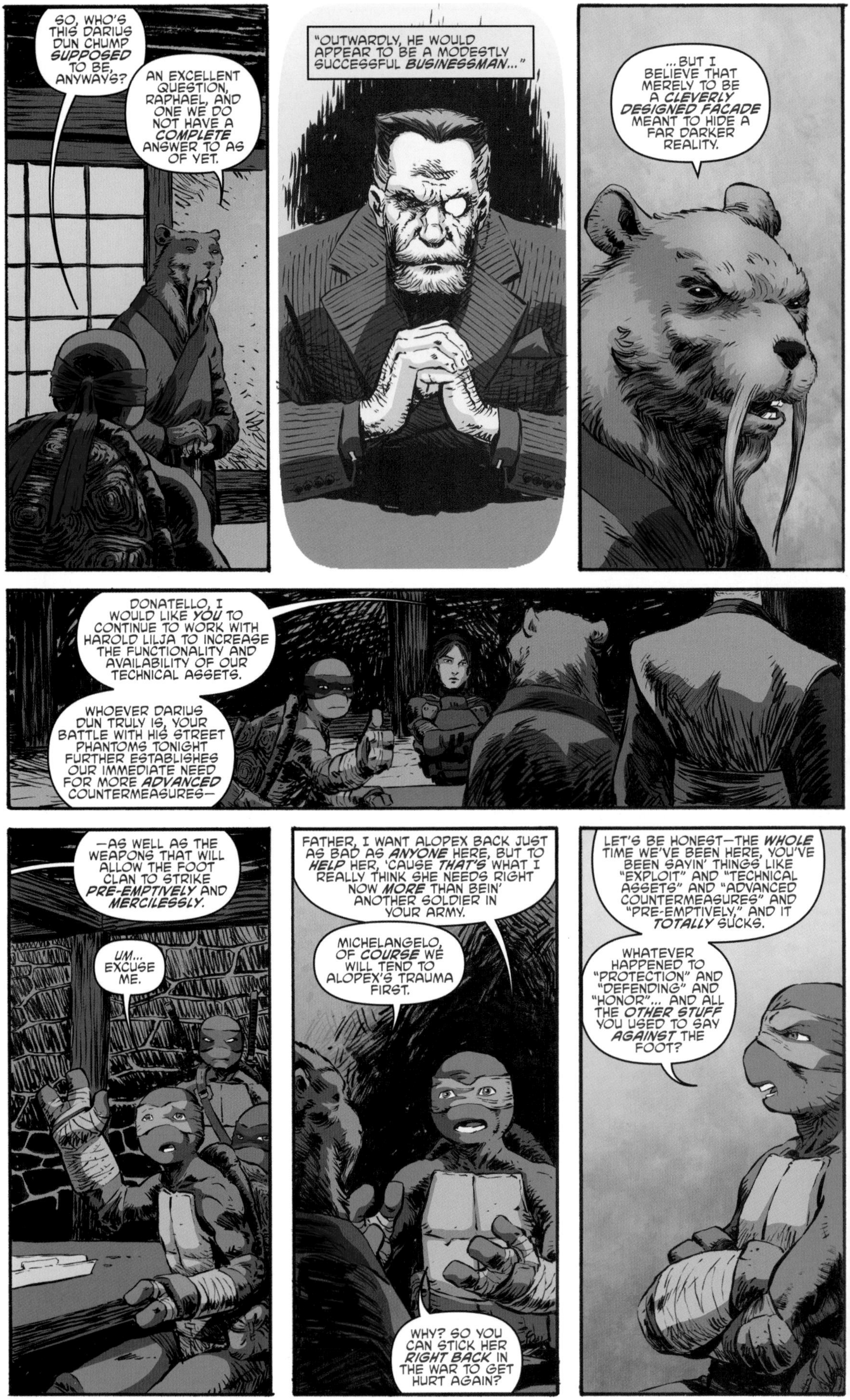
SO, WHO'S THIS DARIUS DUN CHUMP SUPPOSED TO BE, ANYWAYS?
AN EXCELLENT QUESTION, RAPHAEL, AND ONE WE DO NOT HAVE A COMPLETE ANSWER TO AS OF YET.
"OUTWARDLY, HE WOULD APPEAR TO BE A MODESTLY SUCCESSFUL BUSINESSMAN..."
...BUT I BELIEVE THAT MERELY TO BE A CLEVERLY DESIGNED FACADE MEANT TO HIDE A FAR DARKER REALITY.
DONATELLO, I WOULD LIKE YOU TO CONTINUE TO WORK WITH HAROLD LILJA TO INCREASE THE FUNCTIONALITY AND AVAILABILITY OF OUR TECHNICAL ASSETS.
WHOEVER DARIUS DUN TRULY IS, YOUR BATTLE WITH HIS STREET PHANTOMS TONIGHT FURTHER ESTABLISHES OUR IMMEDIATE NEED FOR MORE ADVANCED COUNTERMEASURES—
—AS WELL AS THE WEAPONS THAT WILL ALLOW THE FOOT CLAN TO STRIKE PRE-EMPTIVELY AND MERCILESSLY.
UM... EXCUSE ME.
FATHER, I WANT ALOPEX BACK JUST AS BAD AS ANYONE HERE, BUT TO HELP HER, 'CAUSE THAT'S WHAT I REALLY THINK SHE NEEDS RIGHT NOW MORE THAN BEIN' ANOTHER SOLDIER IN YOUR ARMY.
MICHELANGELO, OF COURSE WE WILL TEND TO ALOPEX'S TRAUMA FIRST.
WHY? SO YOU CAN STICK HER RIGHT BACK IN THE WAR TO GET HURT AGAIN?
LET'S BE HONEST—THE WHOLE TIME WE'VE BEEN HERE, YOU'VE BEEN SAYIN' THINGS LIKE "EXPLOIT" AND "TECHNICAL ASSETS" AND "ADVANCED COUNTERMEASURES" AND "PRE-EMPTIVELY," AND IT TOTALLY SUCKS.
WHATEVER HAPPENED TO "PROTECTION" AND "DEFENDING" AND "HONOR"... AND ALL THE OTHER STUFF YOU USED TO SAY AGAINST THE FOOT?

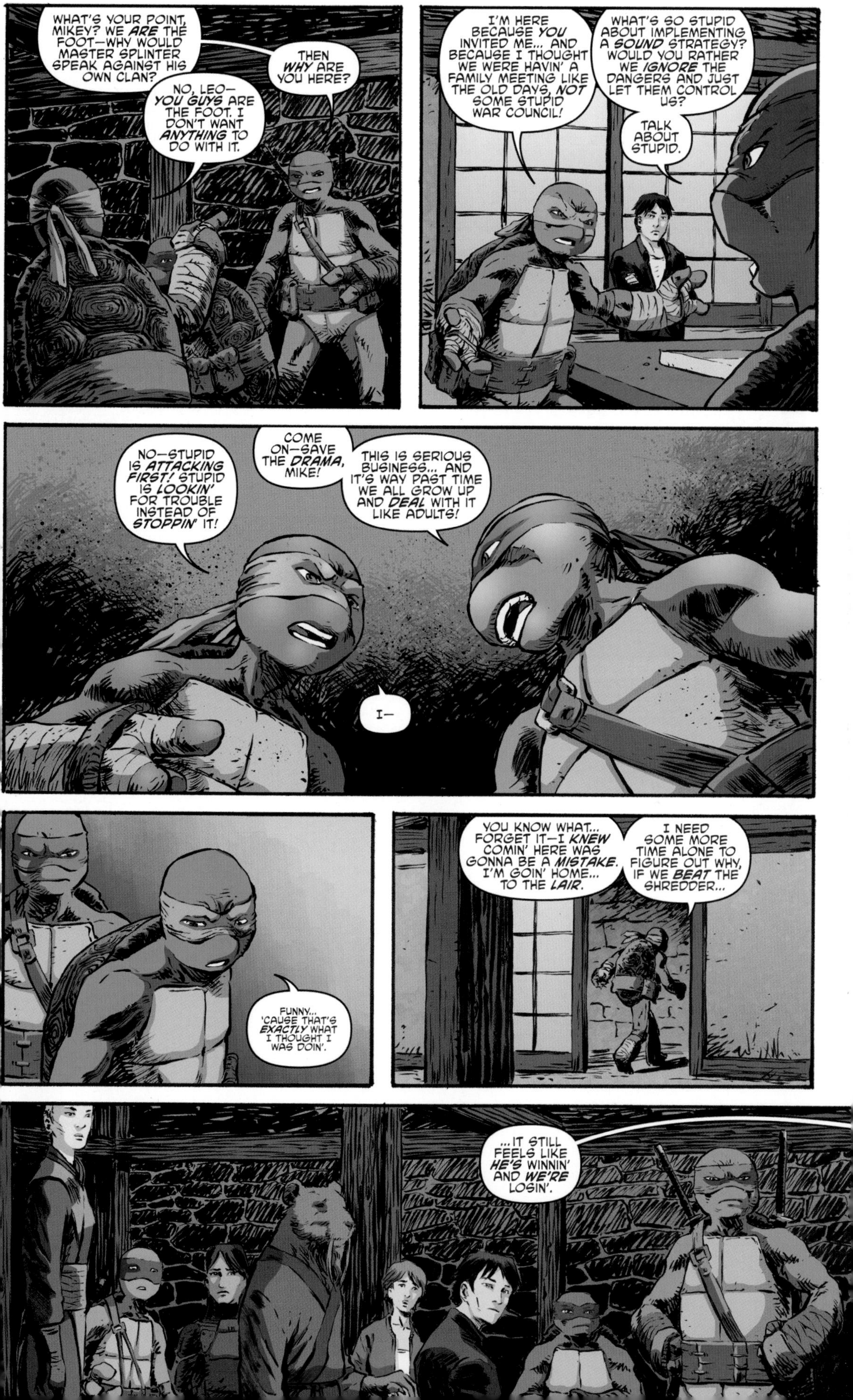
WHAT'S YOUR POINT, MIKEY? WE ARE THE FOOT—WHY WOULD MASTER SPLINTER SPEAK AGAINST HIS OWN CLAN?
THEN WHY ARE YOU HERE?
NO, LEO—YOU GUYS ARE THE FOOT. I DON'T WANT ANYTHING TO DO WITH IT.
I'M HERE BECAUSE YOU INVITED ME... AND BECAUSE I THOUGHT WE WERE HAVIN' A FAMILY MEETING LIKE THE OLD DAYS, NOT SOME STUPID WAR COUNCIL!
WHAT'S SO STUPID ABOUT IMPLEMENTING A SOUND STRATEGY? WOULD YOU RATHER WE IGNORE THE DANGERS AND JUST LET THEM CONTROL US?
TALK ABOUT STUPID.
NO—STUPID IS ATTACKING FIRST! STUPID IS LOOKIN' FOR TROUBLE INSTEAD OF STOPPIN' IT!
COME ON—SAVE THE DRAMA, MIKE!
THIS IS SERIOUS BUSINESS... AND IT'S WAY PAST TIME WE ALL GROW UP AND DEAL WITH IT LIKE ADULTS!
I—
FUNNY... 'CAUSE THAT'S EXACTLY WHAT I THOUGHT I WAS DOIN'.
YOU KNOW WHAT... FORGET IT—I KNEW COMIN' HERE WAS GONNA BE A MISTAKE. I'M GOIN' HOME... TO THE LAIR.
I NEED SOME MORE TIME ALONE TO FIGURE OUT WHY, IF WE BEAT THE SHREDDER...
...IT STILL FEELS LIKE HE'S WINNIN' AND WE'RE LOSIN'.

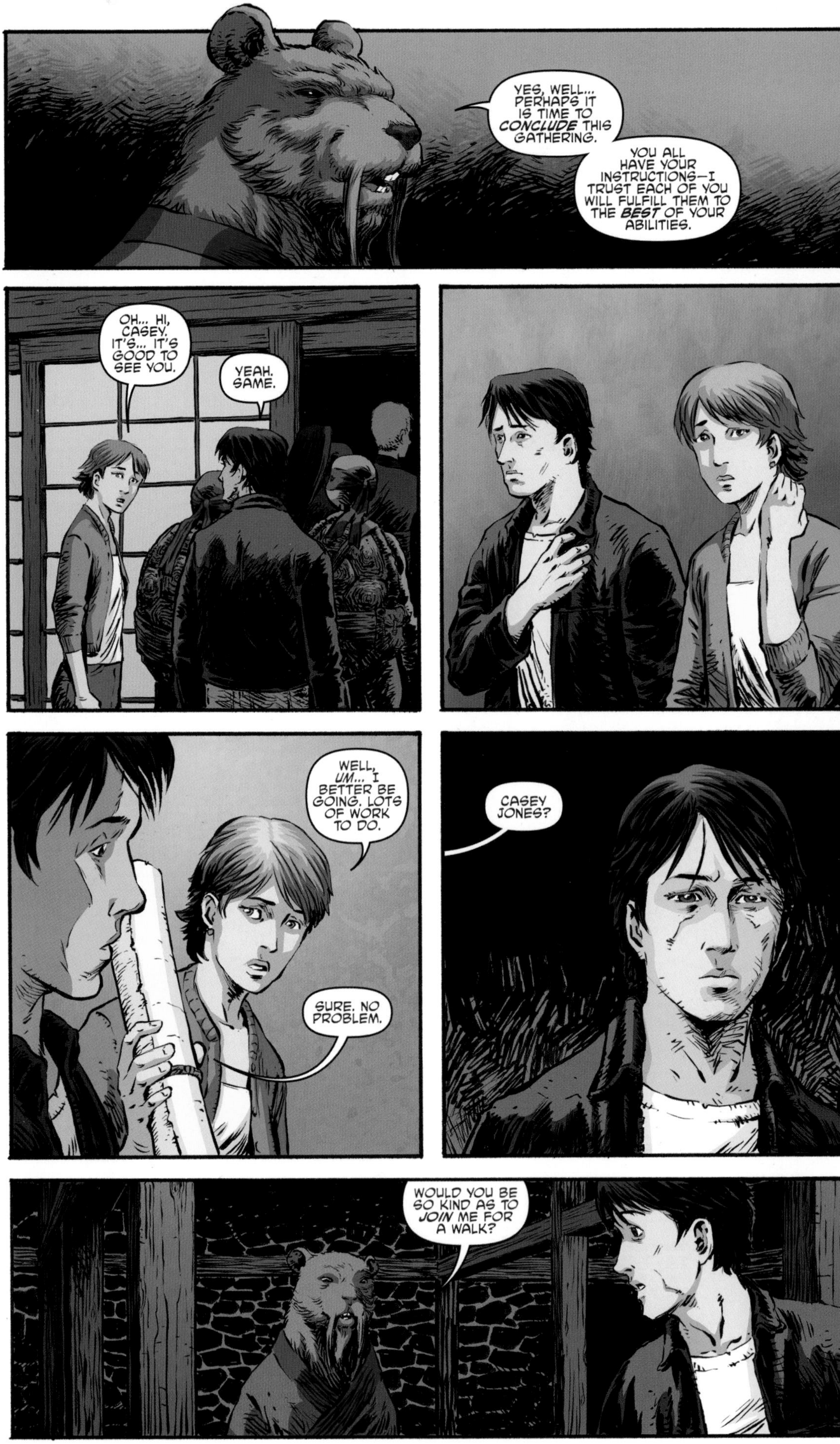
YES, WELL... PERHAPS IT IS TIME TO *CONCLUDE* THIS GATHERING.
YOU ALL HAVE YOUR INSTRUCTIONS—I TRUST EACH OF YOU WILL FULFILL THEM TO THE *BEST* OF YOUR ABILITIES.
OH... HI, CASEY. IT'S... IT'S GOOD TO SEE YOU.
YEAH. SAME.
WELL, *UM*... I BETTER BE GOING. LOTS OF WORK TO DO.
SURE. NO PROBLEM.
CASEY JONES?
WOULD YOU BE SO KIND AS TO *JOIN* ME FOR A WALK?

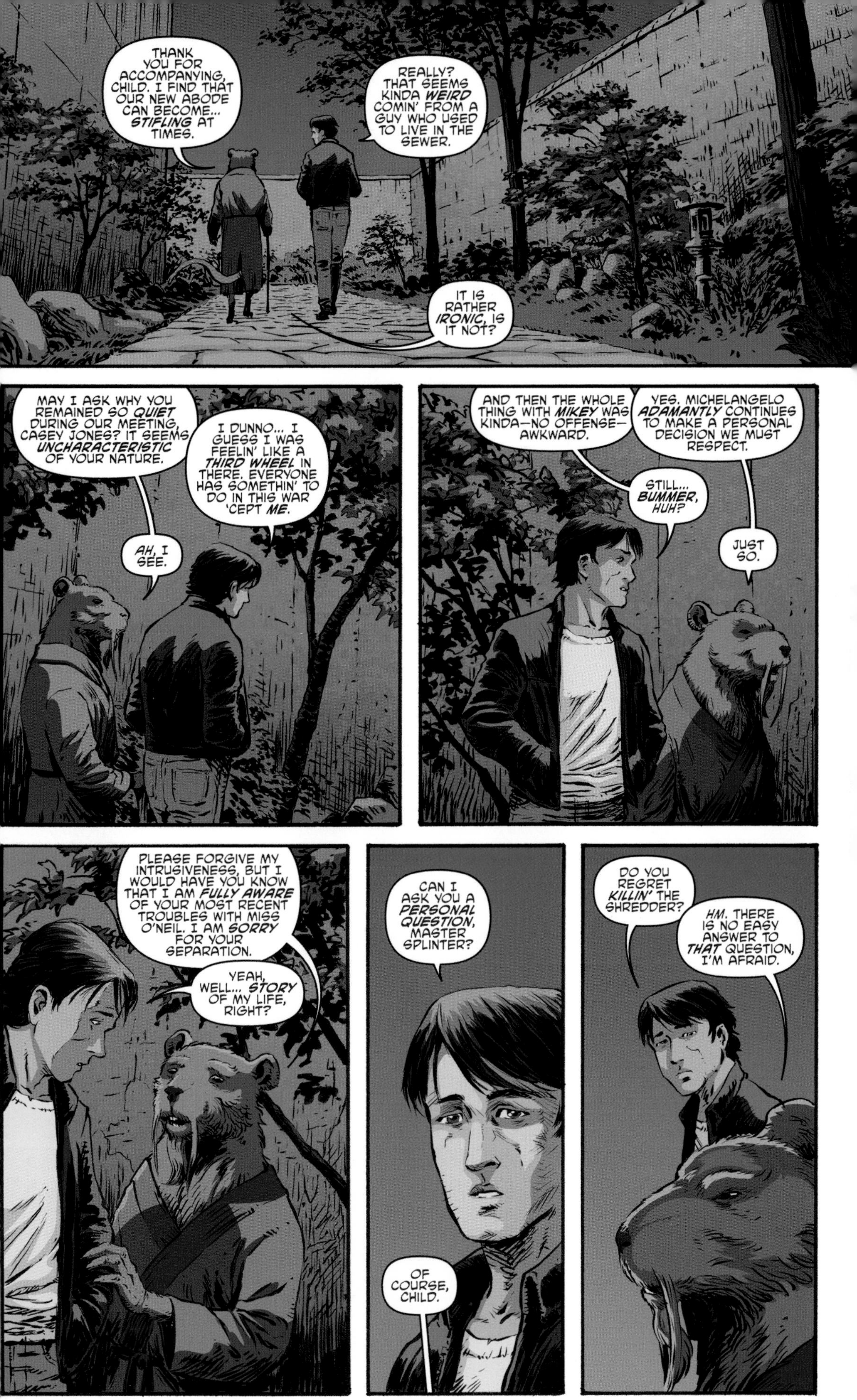
THANK YOU FOR ACCOMPANYING, CHILD. I FIND THAT OUR NEW ABODE CAN BECOME... STIFLING AT TIMES.
REALLY? THAT SEEMS KINDA WEIRD COMIN' FROM A GUY WHO USED TO LIVE IN THE SEWER.
IT IS RATHER IRONIC, IS IT NOT?
MAY I ASK WHY YOU REMAINED SO QUIET DURING OUR MEETING, CASEY JONES? IT SEEMS UNCHARACTERISTIC OF YOUR NATURE.
I DUNNO... I GUESS I WAS FEELIN' LIKE A THIRD WHEEL IN THERE. EVERYONE HAS SOMETHIN' TO DO IN THIS WAR 'CEPT ME.
AH, I SEE.
AND THEN THE WHOLE THING WITH MIKEY WAS KINDA—NO OFFENSE—AWKWARD.
YES. MICHELANGELO ADAMANTLY CONTINUES TO MAKE A PERSONAL DECISION WE MUST RESPECT.
STILL... BUMMER, HUH?
JUST SO.
PLEASE FORGIVE MY INTRUSIVENESS, BUT I WOULD HAVE YOU KNOW THAT I AM FULLY AWARE OF YOUR MOST RECENT TROUBLES WITH MISS O'NEIL. I AM SORRY FOR YOUR SEPARATION.
YEAH, WELL... STORY OF MY LIFE, RIGHT?
CAN I ASK YOU A PERSONAL QUESTION, MASTER SPLINTER?
OF COURSE, CHILD.
DO YOU REGRET KILLIN' THE SHREDDER?
HM. THERE IS NO EASY ANSWER TO THAT QUESTION, I'M AFRAID.

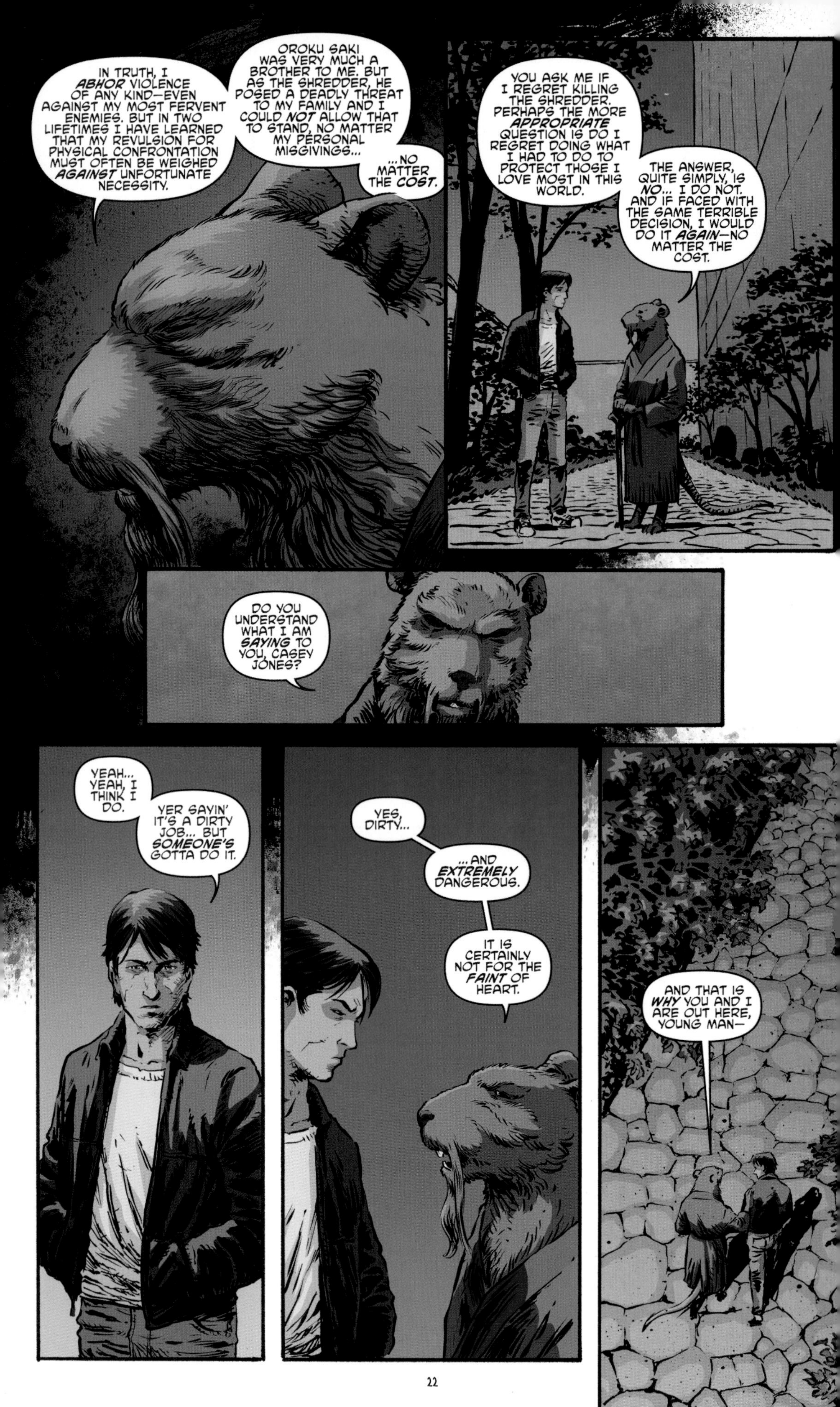
IN TRUTH, I ABHOR VIOLENCE OF ANY KIND—EVEN AGAINST MY MOST FERVENT ENEMIES. BUT IN TWO LIFETIMES I HAVE LEARNED THAT MY REVULSION FOR PHYSICAL CONFRONTATION MUST OFTEN BE WEIGHED AGAINST UNFORTUNATE NECESSITY.
OROKU SAKI WAS VERY MUCH A BROTHER TO ME. BUT AS THE SHREDDER, HE POSED A DEADLY THREAT TO MY FAMILY AND I COULD NOT ALLOW THAT TO STAND, NO MATTER MY PERSONAL MISGIVINGS...
...NO MATTER THE COST.
YOU ASK ME IF I REGRET KILLING THE SHREDDER. PERHAPS THE MORE APPROPRIATE QUESTION IS DO I REGRET DOING WHAT I HAD TO DO TO PROTECT THOSE I LOVE MOST IN THIS WORLD.
THE ANSWER, QUITE SIMPLY, IS NO... I DO NOT. AND IF FACED WITH THE SAME TERRIBLE DECISION, I WOULD DO IT AGAIN—NO MATTER THE COST.
DO YOU UNDERSTAND WHAT I AM SAYING TO YOU, CASEY JONES?
YEAH... YEAH, I THINK I DO.
YER SAYIN' IT'S A DIRTY JOB... BUT SOMEONE'S GOTTA DO IT.
YES, DIRTY...
...AND EXTREMELY DANGEROUS.
IT IS CERTAINLY NOT FOR THE FAINT OF HEART.
AND THAT IS WHY YOU AND I ARE OUT HERE, YOUNG MAN—

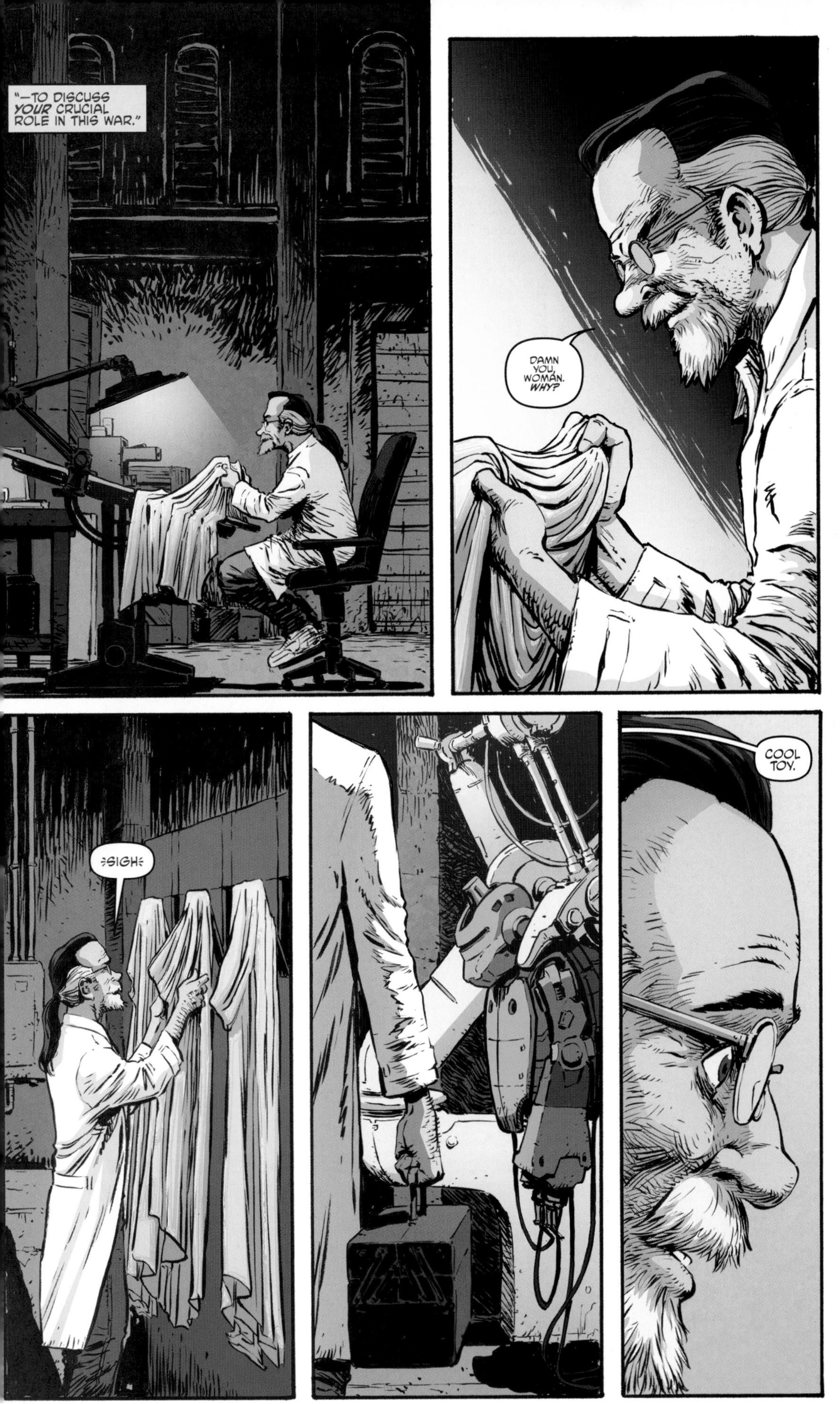
"—TO DISCUSS YOUR CRUCIAL ROLE IN THIS WAR."
DAMN YOU, WOMAN. WHY?
SIGH
COOL TOY.

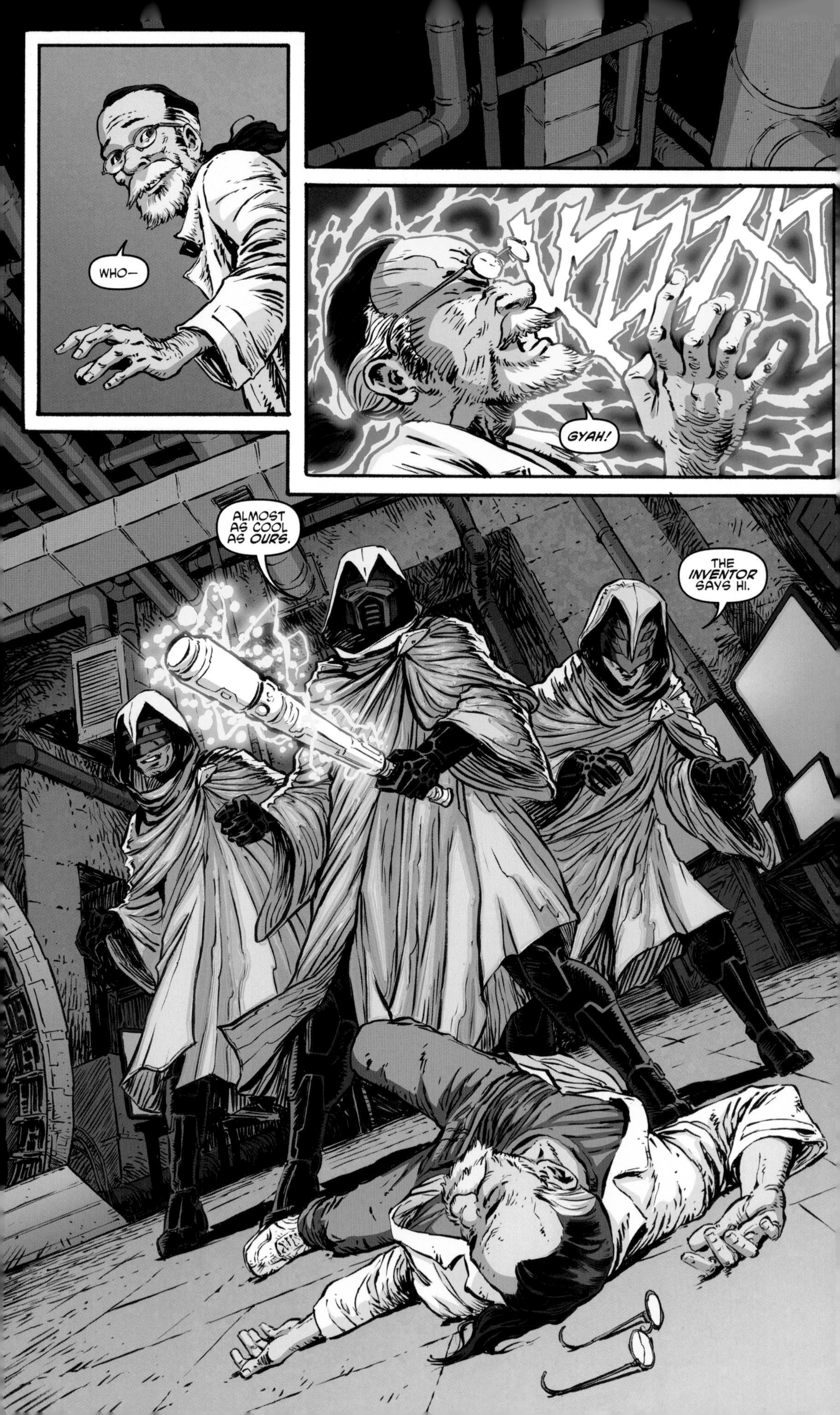
WHO—
GYAH!
ALMOST AS COOL AS OURS.
THE INVENTOR SAYS HI.

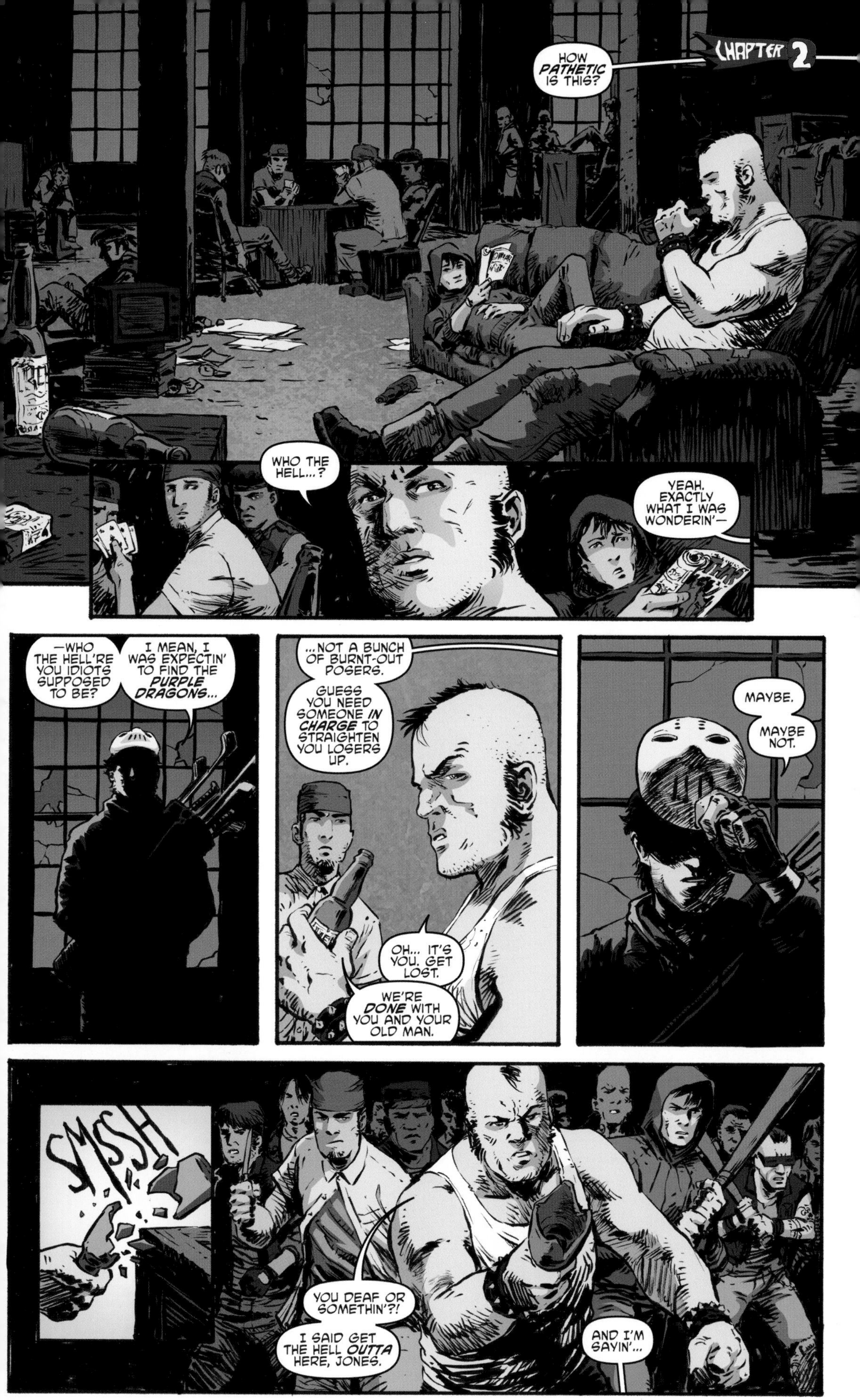
CHAPTER 2
HOW PATHETIC IS THIS?
WHO THE HELL...?
YEAH. EXACTLY WHAT I WAS WONDERIN'—
—WHO THE HELL'RE YOU IDIOTS SUPPOSED TO BE?
I MEAN, I WAS EXPECTIN' TO FIND THE PURPLE DRAGONS...
...NOT A BUNCH OF BURNT-OUT POSERS.
GUESS YOU NEED SOMEONE IN CHARGE TO STRAIGHTEN YOU LOSERS UP.
OH... IT'S YOU. GET LOST.
WE'RE DONE WITH YOU AND YOUR OLD MAN.
MAYBE.
MAYBE NOT.
SMSH
YOU DEAF OR SOMETHIN'?!
I SAID GET THE HELL OUTTA HERE, JONES.
AND I'M SAYIN'...

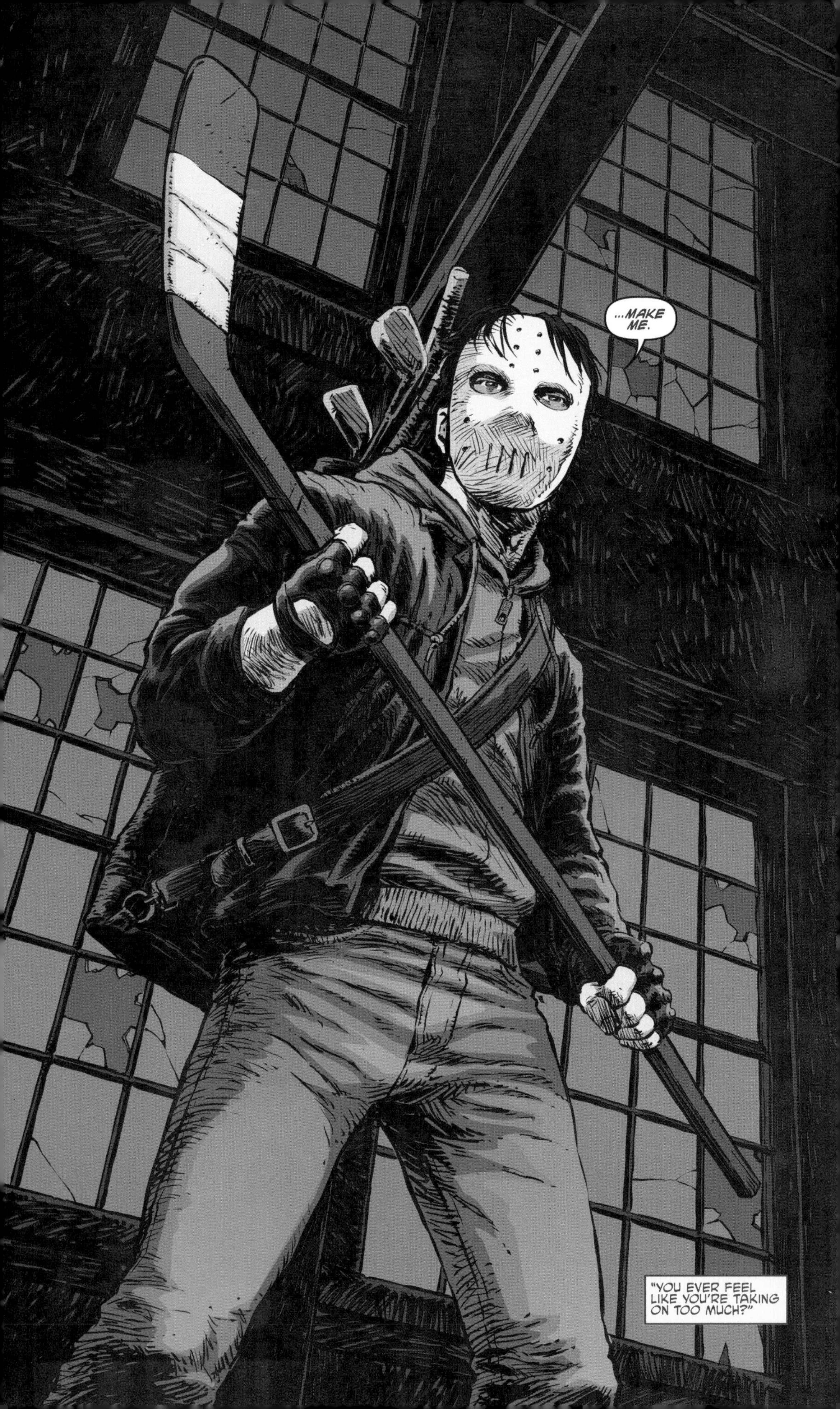
...MAKE ME.
"YOU EVER FEEL LIKE YOU'RE TAKING ON TOO MUCH?"

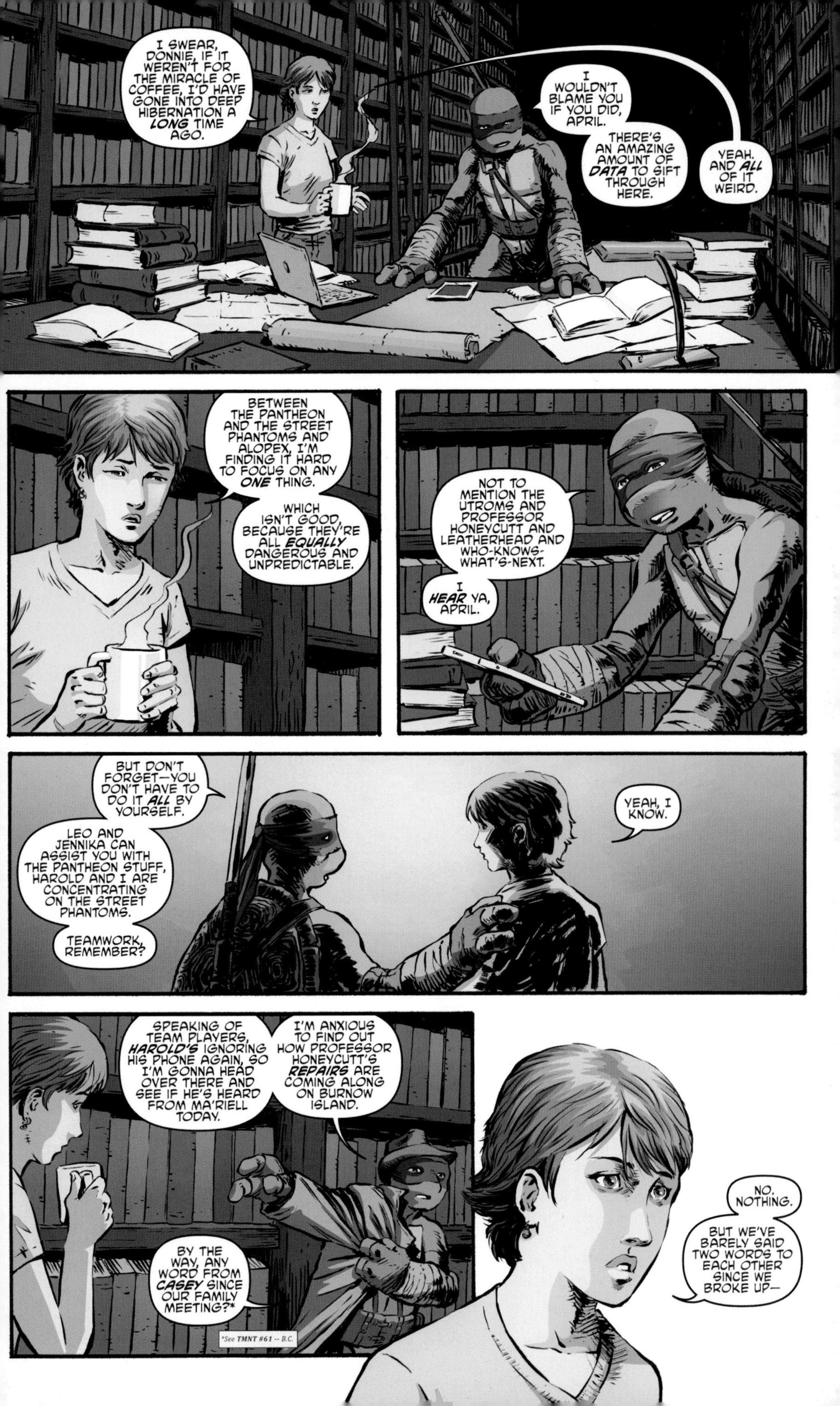
I SWEAR, DONNIE, IF IT WEREN'T FOR THE MIRACLE OF COFFEE, I'D HAVE GONE INTO DEEP HIBERNATION A LONG TIME AGO.
I WOULDN'T BLAME YOU IF YOU DID, APRIL.
THERE'S AN AMAZING AMOUNT OF DATA TO SIFT THROUGH HERE.
YEAH. AND ALL OF IT WEIRD.
BETWEEN THE PANTHEON AND THE STREET PHANTOMS AND ALOPEX, I'M FINDING IT HARD TO FOCUS ON ANY ONE THING.
WHICH ISN'T GOOD, BECAUSE THEY'RE ALL EQUALLY DANGEROUS AND UNPREDICTABLE.
NOT TO MENTION THE UTROMS AND PROFESSOR HONEYCUTT AND LEATHERHEAD AND WHO-KNOWS-WHAT'S-NEXT.
I HEAR YA, APRIL.
BUT DON'T FORGET—YOU DON'T HAVE TO DO IT ALL BY YOURSELF.
LEO AND JENNIKA CAN ASSIST YOU WITH THE PANTHEON STUFF, HAROLD AND I ARE CONCENTRATING ON THE STREET PHANTOMS.
TEAMWORK, REMEMBER?
YEAH, I KNOW.
SPEAKING OF TEAM PLAYERS, HAROLD'S IGNORING HIS PHONE AGAIN, SO I'M GONNA HEAD OVER THERE AND SEE IF HE'S HEARD FROM MA'RIELL TODAY.
I'M ANXIOUS TO FIND OUT HOW PROFESSOR HONEYCUTT'S REPAIRS ARE COMING ALONG ON BURNOW ISLAND.
BY THE WAY, ANY WORD FROM CASEY SINCE OUR FAMILY MEETING?*
*See TMNT #61 -- B.C.
NO. NOTHING.
BUT WE'VE BARELY SAID TWO WORDS TO EACH OTHER SINCE WE BROKE UP—

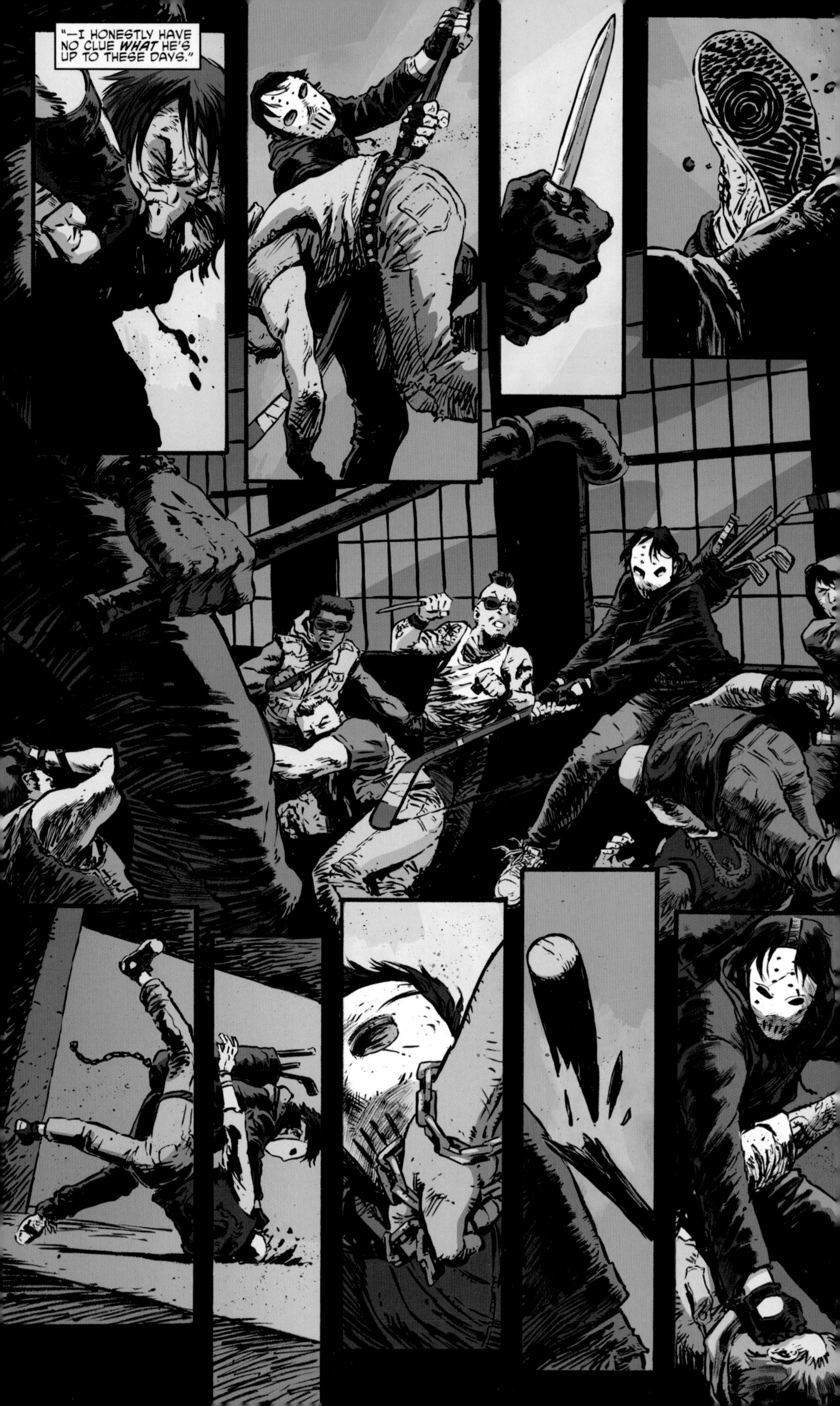
"—I HONESTLY HAVE NO CLUE WHAT HE'S UP TO THESE DAYS."

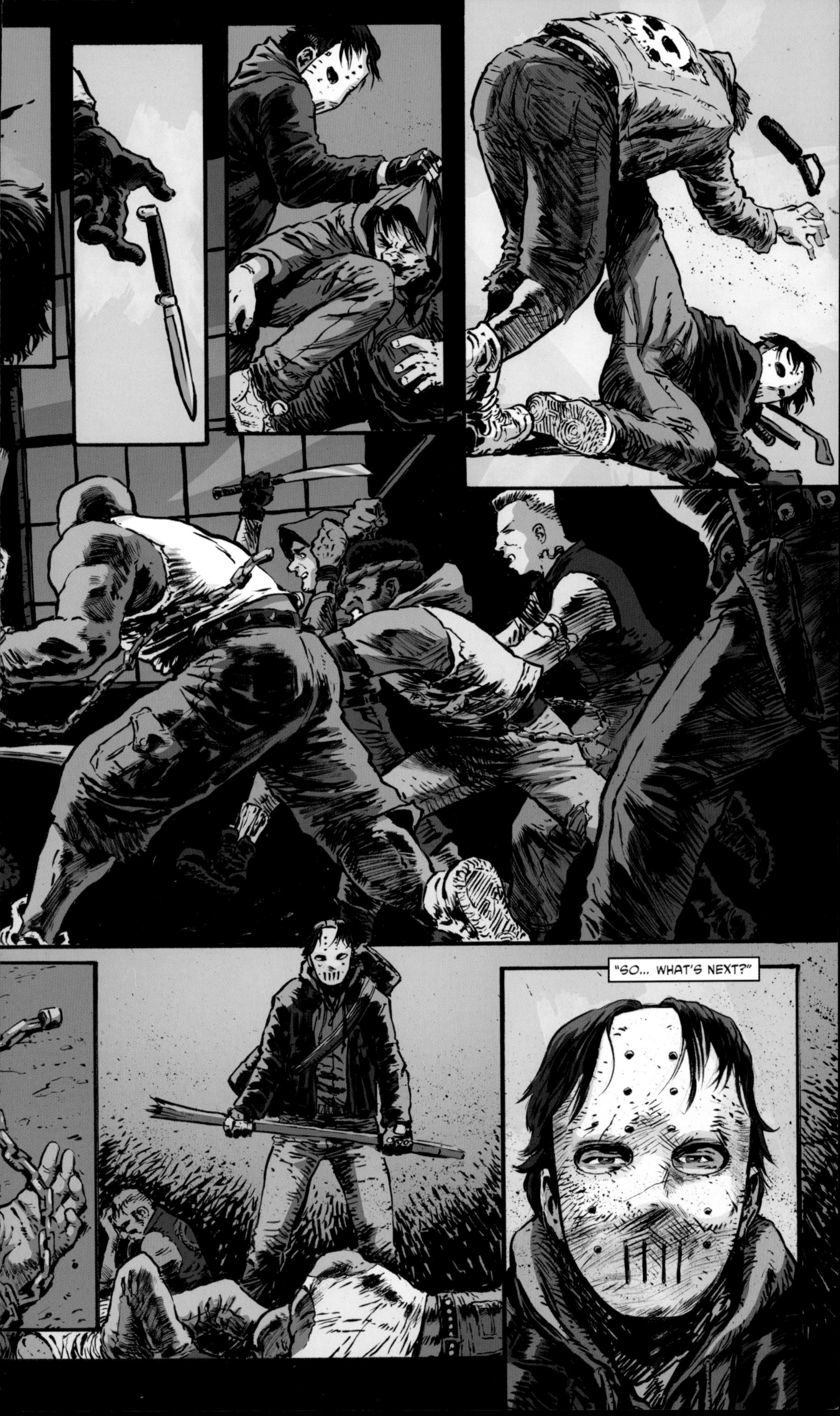
"SO... WHAT'S NEXT?"

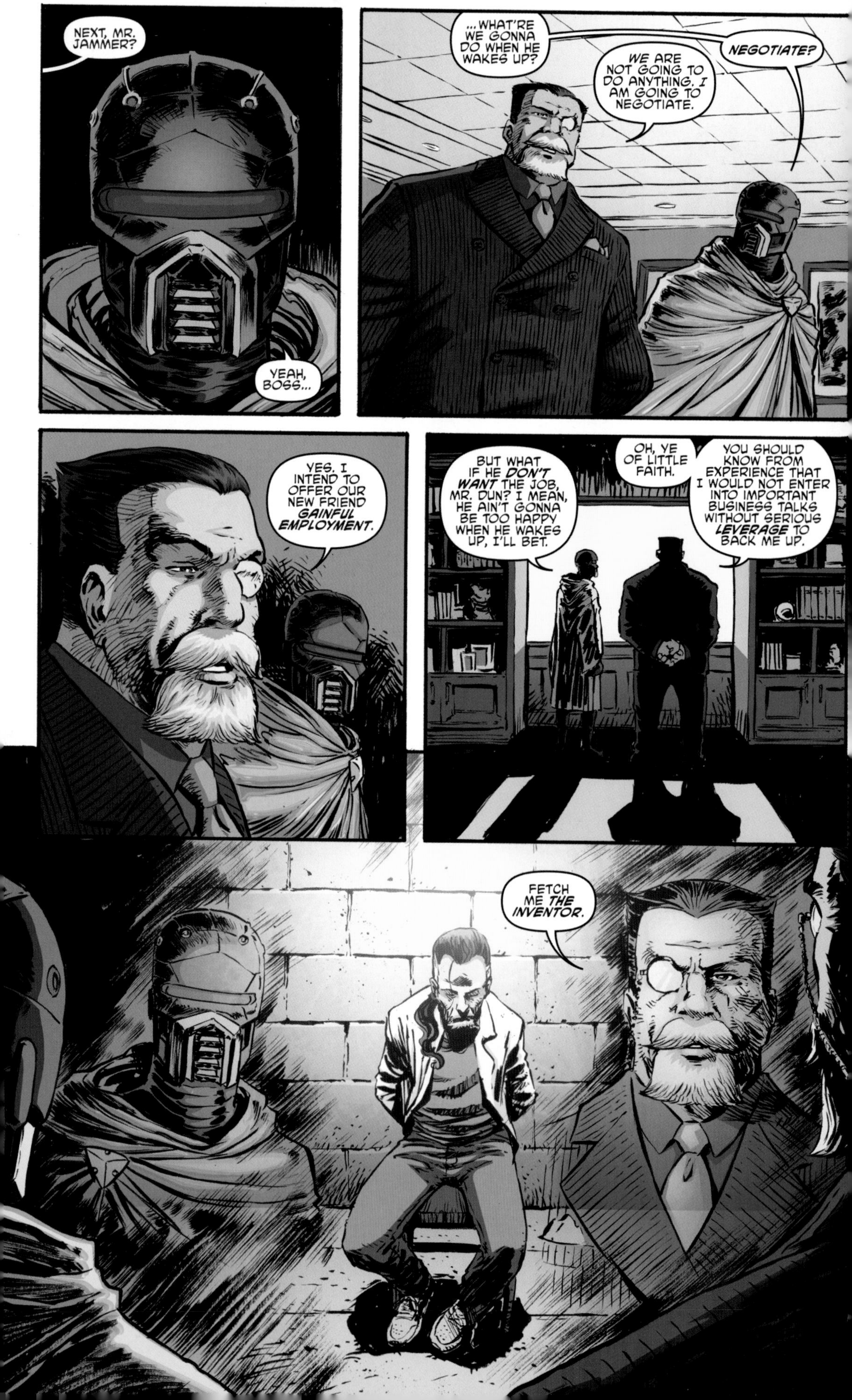
NEXT, MR. JAMMER?
YEAH, BOSS...
...WHAT'RE WE GONNA DO WHEN HE WAKES UP?
WE ARE NOT GOING TO DO ANYTHING. I AM GOING TO NEGOTIATE.
NEGOTIATE?
YES. I INTEND TO OFFER OUR NEW FRIEND GAINFUL EMPLOYMENT.
BUT WHAT IF HE DON'T WANT THE JOB, MR. DUN? I MEAN, HE AIN'T GONNA BE TOO HAPPY WHEN HE WAKES UP, I'LL BET.
OH, YE OF LITTLE FAITH.
YOU SHOULD KNOW FROM EXPERIENCE THAT I WOULD NOT ENTER INTO IMPORTANT BUSINESS TALKS WITHOUT SERIOUS LEVERAGE TO BACK ME UP.
FETCH ME THE INVENTOR.

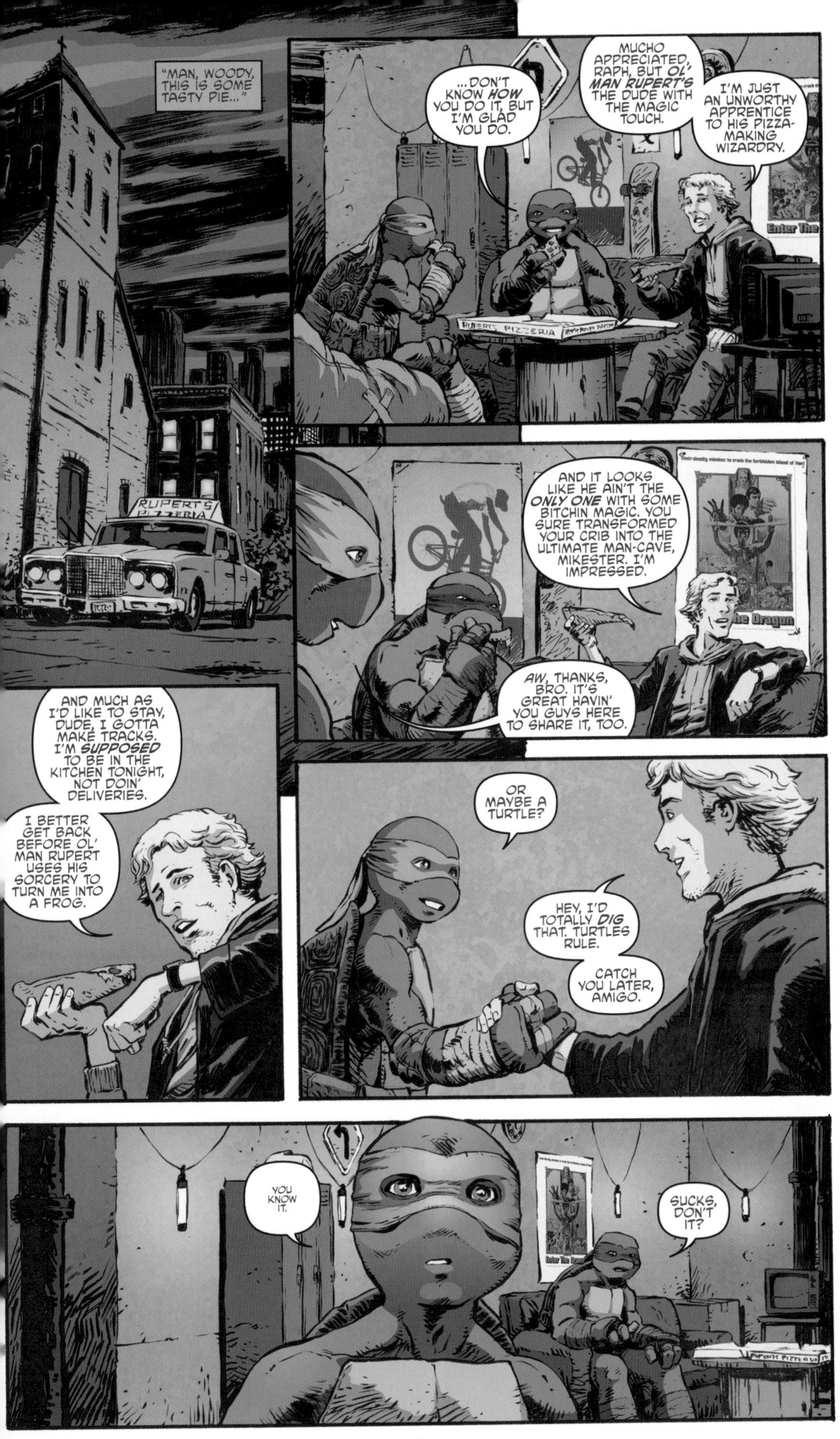
"MAN, WOODY, THIS IS SOME TASTY PIE..."
RUPERT'S PIZZERIA
...DON'T KNOW HOW YOU DO IT, BUT I'M GLAD YOU DO.
MUCHO APPRECIATED, RAPH, BUT OL' MAN RUPERT'S THE DUDE WITH THE MAGIC TOUCH.
I'M JUST AN UNWORTHY APPRENTICE TO HIS PIZZA-MAKING WIZARDRY.
RUPERT'S PIZZERIA
Enter The
Their deadly mission: to crack the forbidden island of Han!
AND IT LOOKS LIKE HE AIN'T THE ONLY ONE WITH SOME BITCHIN MAGIC. YOU SURE TRANSFORMED YOUR CRIB INTO THE ULTIMATE MAN-CAVE, MIKESTER. I'M IMPRESSED.
AW, THANKS, BRO. IT'S GREAT HAVIN' YOU GUYS HERE TO SHARE IT, TOO.
AND MUCH AS I'D LIKE TO STAY, DUDE, I GOTTA MAKE TRACKS. I'M SUPPOSED TO BE IN THE KITCHEN TONIGHT, NOT DOIN' DELIVERIES.
I BETTER GET BACK BEFORE OL' MAN RUPERT USES HIS SORCERY TO TURN ME INTO A FROG.
OR MAYBE A TURTLE?
HEY, I'D TOTALLY DIG THAT. TURTLES RULE.
CATCH YOU LATER, AMIGO.
YOU KNOW IT.
SUCKS, DON'T IT?

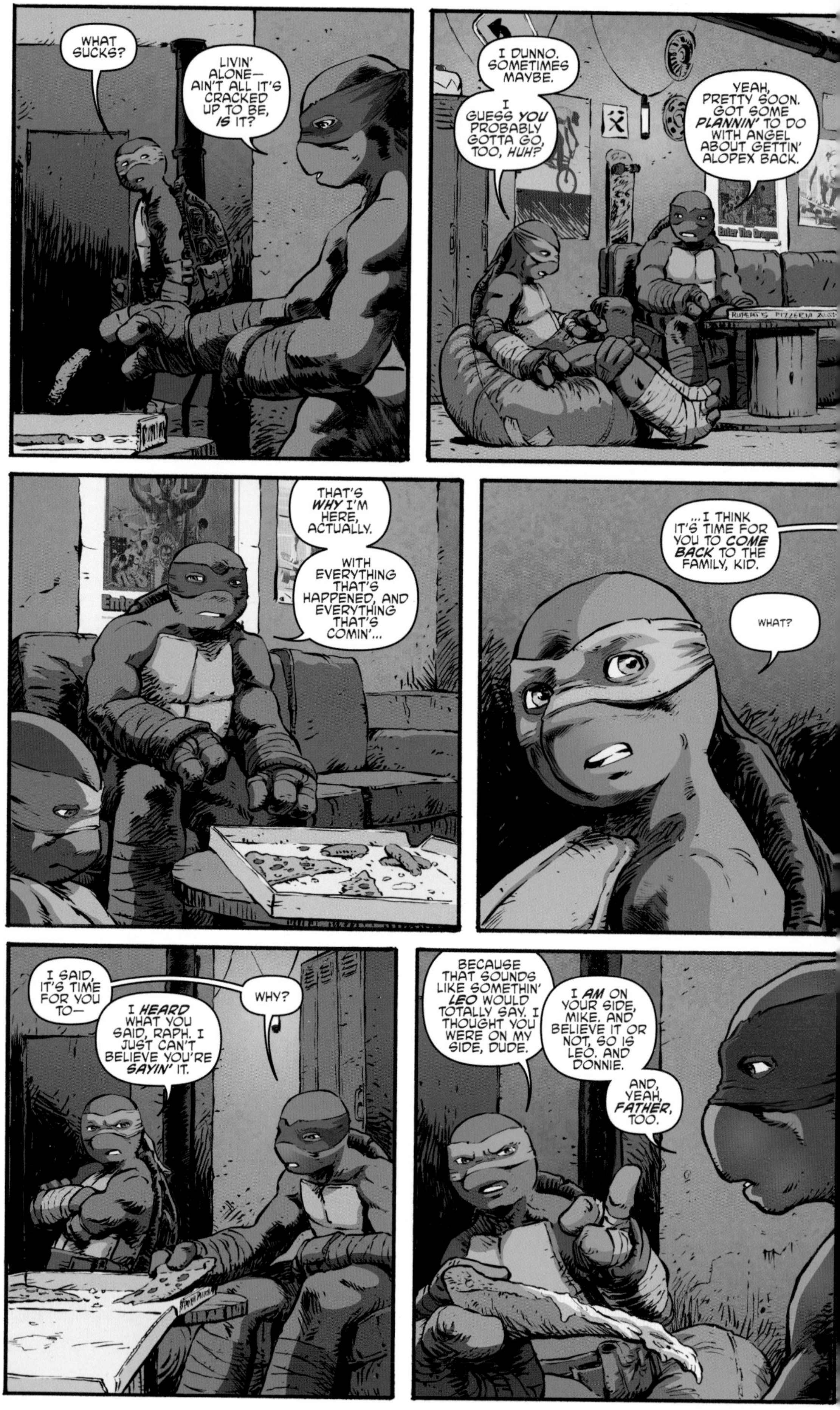
WHAT SUCKS?
LIVIN' ALONE— AIN'T ALL IT'S CRACKED UP TO BE, IS IT?
I DUNNO. SOMETIMES MAYBE.
I GUESS YOU PROBABLY GOTTA GO, TOO, HUH?
YEAH, PRETTY SOON. GOT SOME PLANNIN' TO DO WITH ANGEL ABOUT GETTIN' ALOPEX BACK.
Enter The Dragon
RUPERT'S PIZZERIA
THAT'S WHY I'M HERE, ACTUALLY.
WITH EVERYTHING THAT'S HAPPENED, AND EVERYTHING THAT'S COMIN'...
...I THINK IT'S TIME FOR YOU TO COME BACK TO THE FAMILY, KID.
WHAT?
I SAID, IT'S TIME FOR YOU TO—
WHY?
I HEARD WHAT YOU SAID, RAPH. I JUST CAN'T BELIEVE YOU'RE SAYIN' IT.
BECAUSE THAT SOUNDS LIKE SOMETHIN' LEO WOULD TOTALLY SAY. I THOUGHT YOU WERE ON MY SIDE, DUDE.
I AM ON YOUR SIDE, MIKE. AND BELIEVE IT OR NOT, SO IS LEO. AND DONNIE.
AND, YEAH, FATHER, TOO.

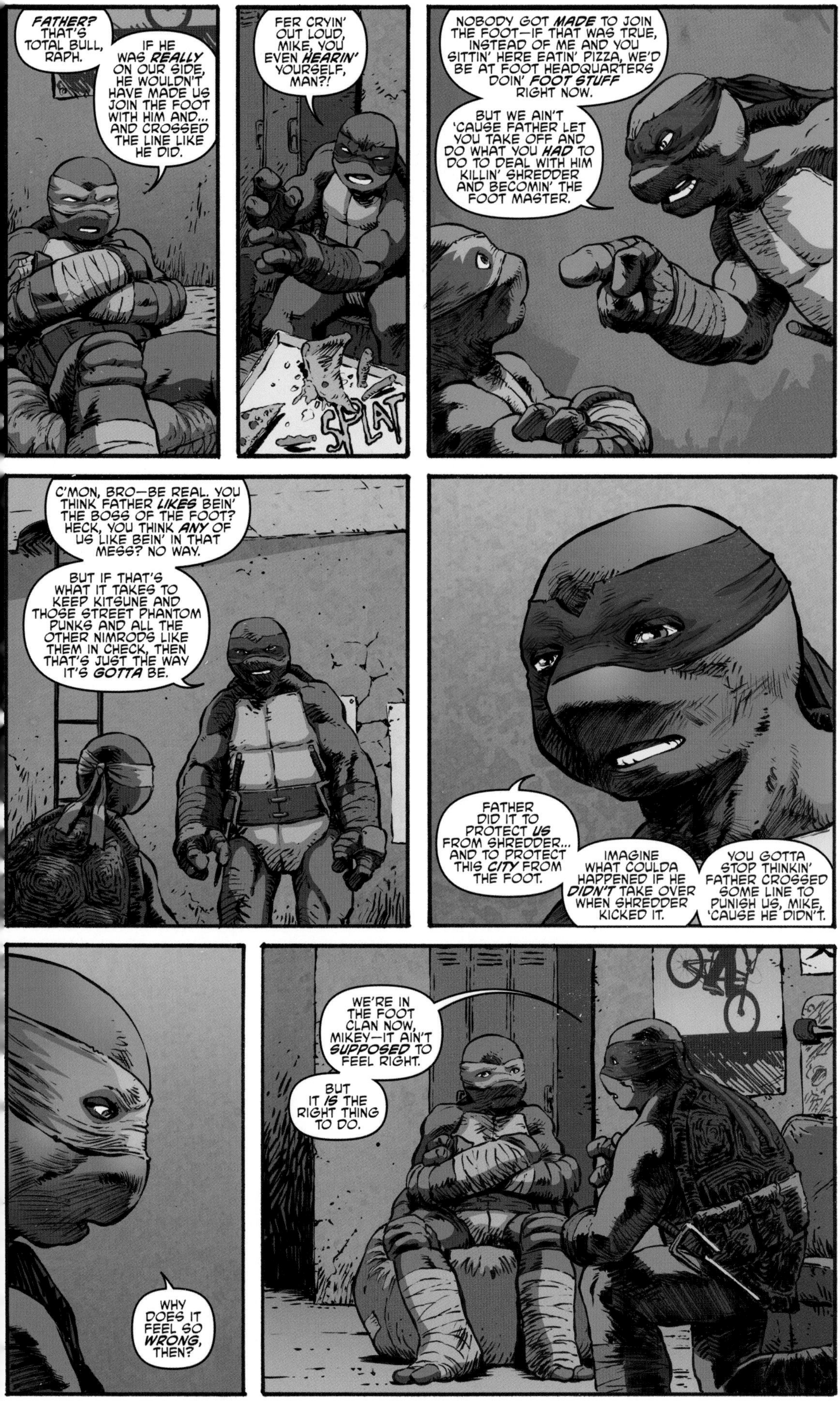
FATHER? THAT'S TOTAL BULL, RAPH.
IF HE WAS REALLY ON OUR SIDE, HE WOULDN'T HAVE MADE US JOIN THE FOOT WITH HIM AND... AND CROSSED THE LINE LIKE HE DID.
FER CRYIN' OUT LOUD, MIKE, YOU EVEN HEARIN' YOURSELF, MAN?!
SPLAT
NOBODY GOT MADE TO JOIN THE FOOT—IF THAT WAS TRUE, INSTEAD OF ME AND YOU SITTIN' HERE EATIN' PIZZA, WE'D BE AT FOOT HEADQUARTERS DOIN' FOOT STUFF RIGHT NOW.
BUT WE AIN'T 'CAUSE FATHER LET YOU TAKE OFF AND DO WHAT YOU HAD TO DO TO DEAL WITH HIM KILLIN' SHREDDER AND BECOMIN' THE FOOT MASTER.
C'MON, BRO—BE REAL. YOU THINK FATHER LIKES BEIN' THE BOSS OF THE FOOT? HECK, YOU THINK ANY OF US LIKE BEIN' IN THAT MESS? NO WAY.
BUT IF THAT'S WHAT IT TAKES TO KEEP KITSUNE AND THOSE STREET PHANTOM PUNKS AND ALL THE OTHER NIMRODS LIKE THEM IN CHECK, THEN THAT'S JUST THE WAY IT'S GOTTA BE.
FATHER DID IT TO PROTECT US FROM SHREDDER... AND TO PROTECT THIS CITY FROM THE FOOT.
IMAGINE WHAT COULDA HAPPENED IF HE DIDN'T TAKE OVER WHEN SHREDDER KICKED IT.
YOU GOTTA STOP THINKIN' FATHER CROSSED SOME LINE TO PUNISH US, MIKE, 'CAUSE HE DIDN'T.
WHY DOES IT FEEL SO WRONG, THEN?
WE'RE IN THE FOOT CLAN NOW, MIKEY—IT AIN'T SUPPOSED TO FEEL RIGHT.
BUT IT IS THE RIGHT THING TO DO.

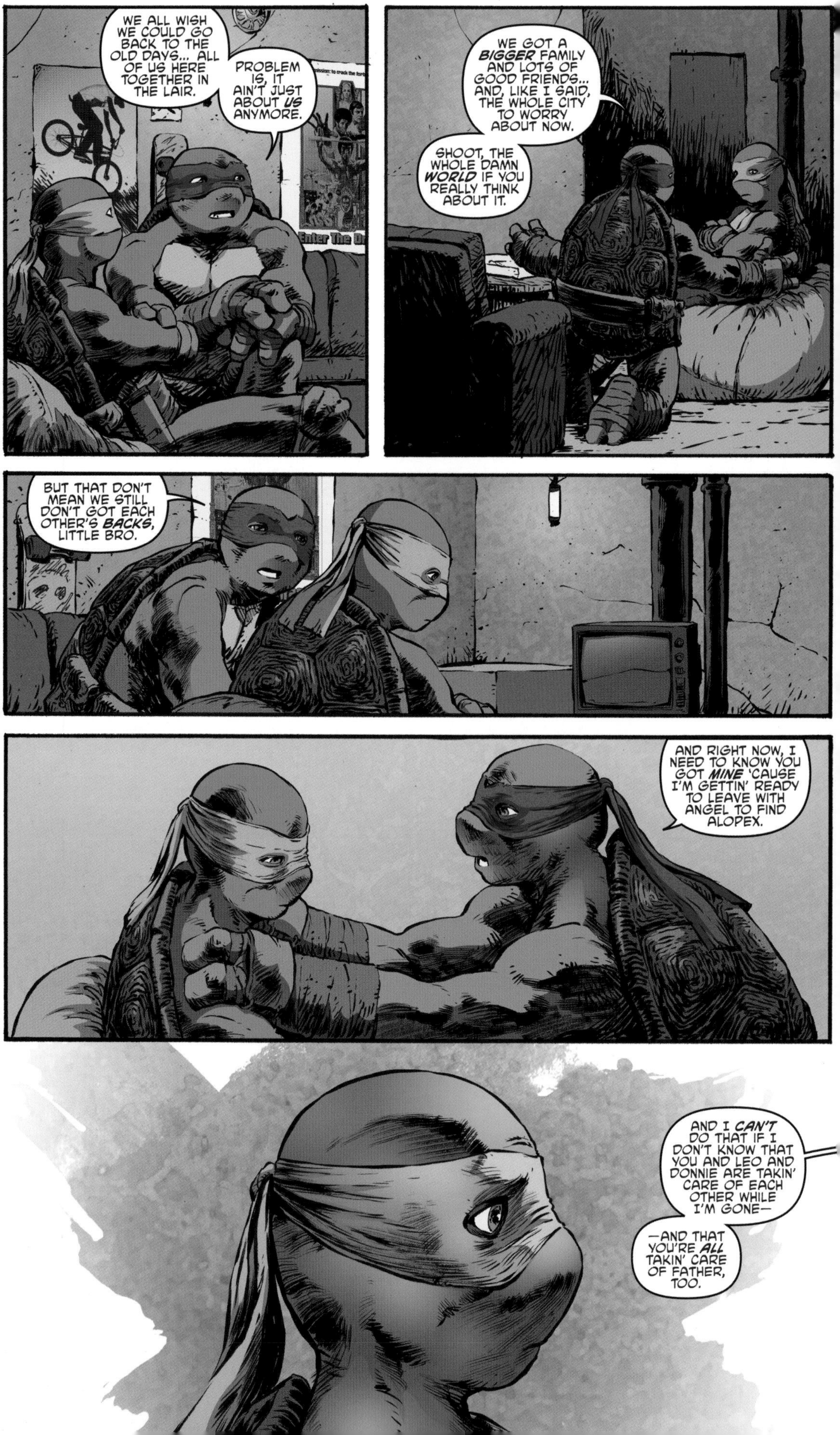
WE ALL WISH WE COULD GO BACK TO THE OLD DAYS... ALL OF US HERE TOGETHER IN THE LAIR.
PROBLEM IS, IT AIN'T JUST ABOUT *US* ANYMORE.
WE GOT A *BIGGER* FAMILY AND LOTS OF GOOD FRIENDS... AND, LIKE I SAID, THE WHOLE CITY TO WORRY ABOUT NOW.
SHOOT, THE WHOLE DAMN *WORLD* IF YOU REALLY THINK ABOUT IT.
BUT THAT DON'T MEAN WE STILL DON'T GOT EACH OTHER'S *BACKS*, LITTLE BRO.
AND RIGHT NOW, I NEED TO KNOW YOU GOT *MINE* 'CAUSE I'M GETTIN' READY TO LEAVE WITH ANGEL TO FIND ALOPEX.
AND I *CAN'T* DO THAT IF I DON'T KNOW THAT YOU AND LEO AND DONNIE ARE TAKIN' CARE OF EACH OTHER WHILE I'M GONE—
—AND THAT YOU'RE *ALL* TAKIN' CARE OF FATHER, TOO.

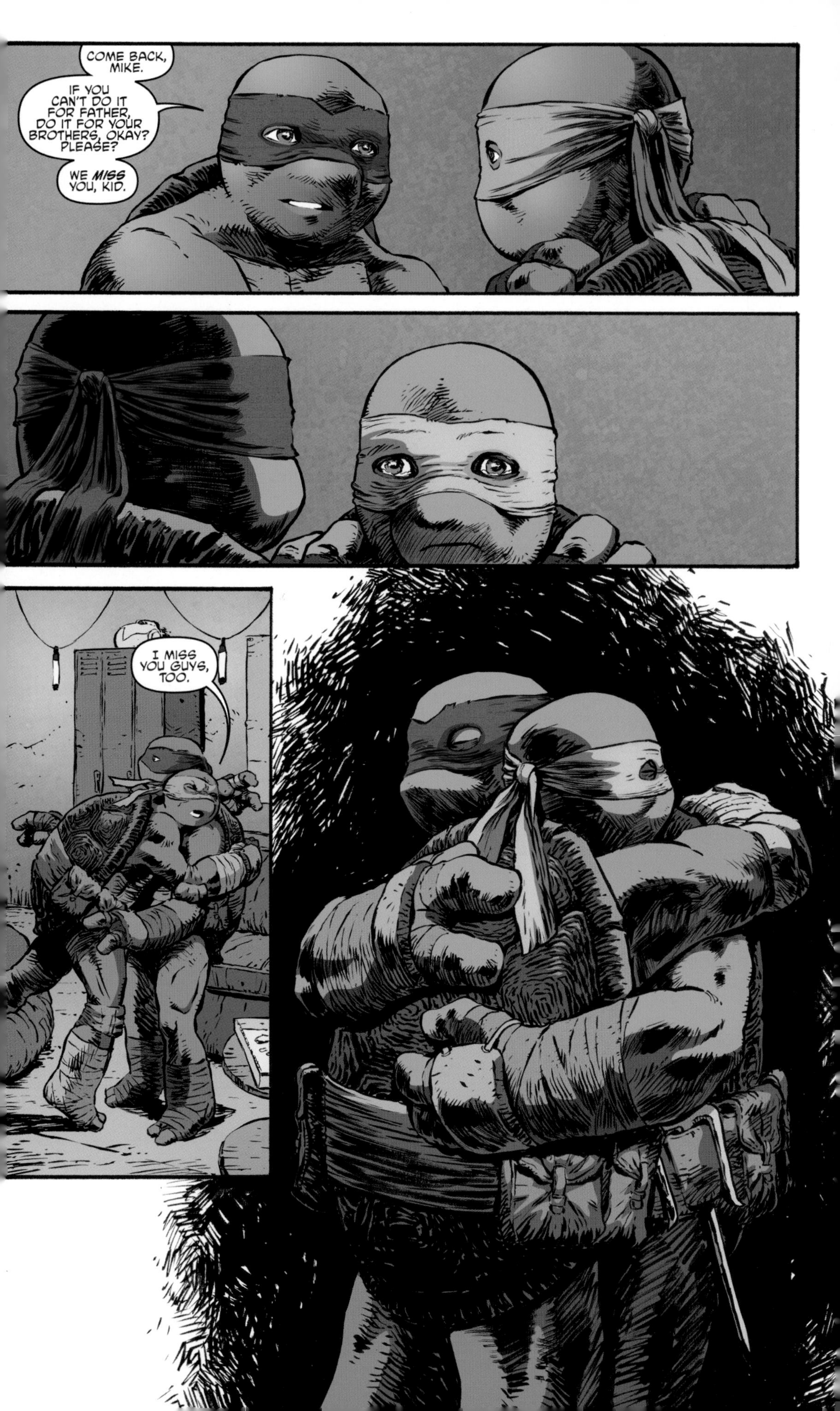
COME BACK, MIKE.
IF YOU CAN'T DO IT FOR FATHER, DO IT FOR YOUR BROTHERS, OKAY? PLEASE?
WE *MISS* YOU, KID.
I MISS YOU GUYS, TOO.

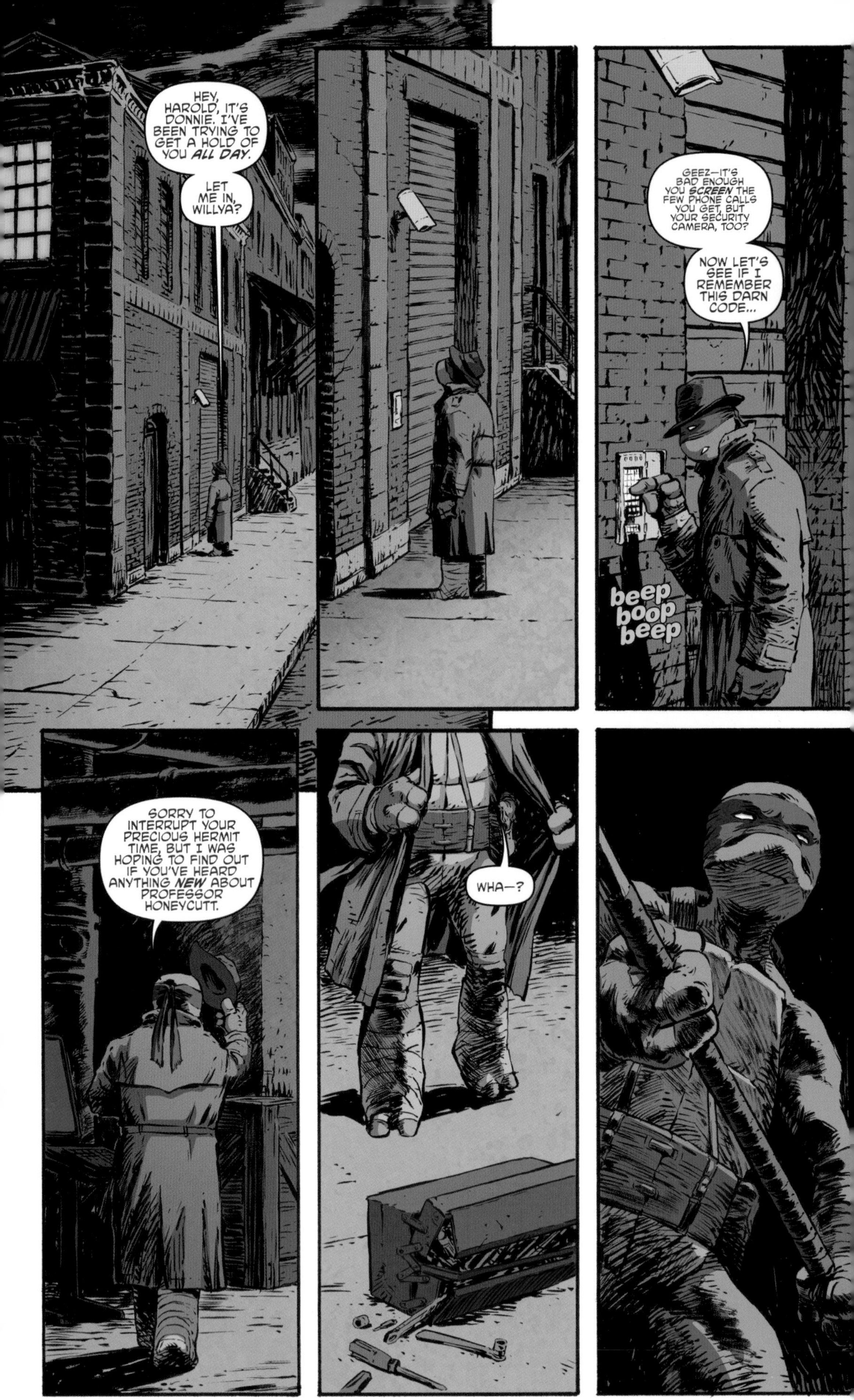
HEY, HAROLD, IT'S DONNIE. I'VE BEEN TRYING TO GET A HOLD OF YOU ALL DAY.
LET ME IN, WILLYA?
GEEZ—IT'S BAD ENOUGH YOU SCREEN THE FEW PHONE CALLS YOU GET, BUT YOUR SECURITY CAMERA, TOO?
NOW LET'S SEE IF I REMEMBER THIS DARN CODE...
beep boop beep
SORRY TO INTERRUPT YOUR PRECIOUS HERMIT TIME, BUT I WAS HOPING TO FIND OUT IF YOU'VE HEARD ANYTHING NEW ABOUT PROFESSOR HONEYCUTT.
WHA—?

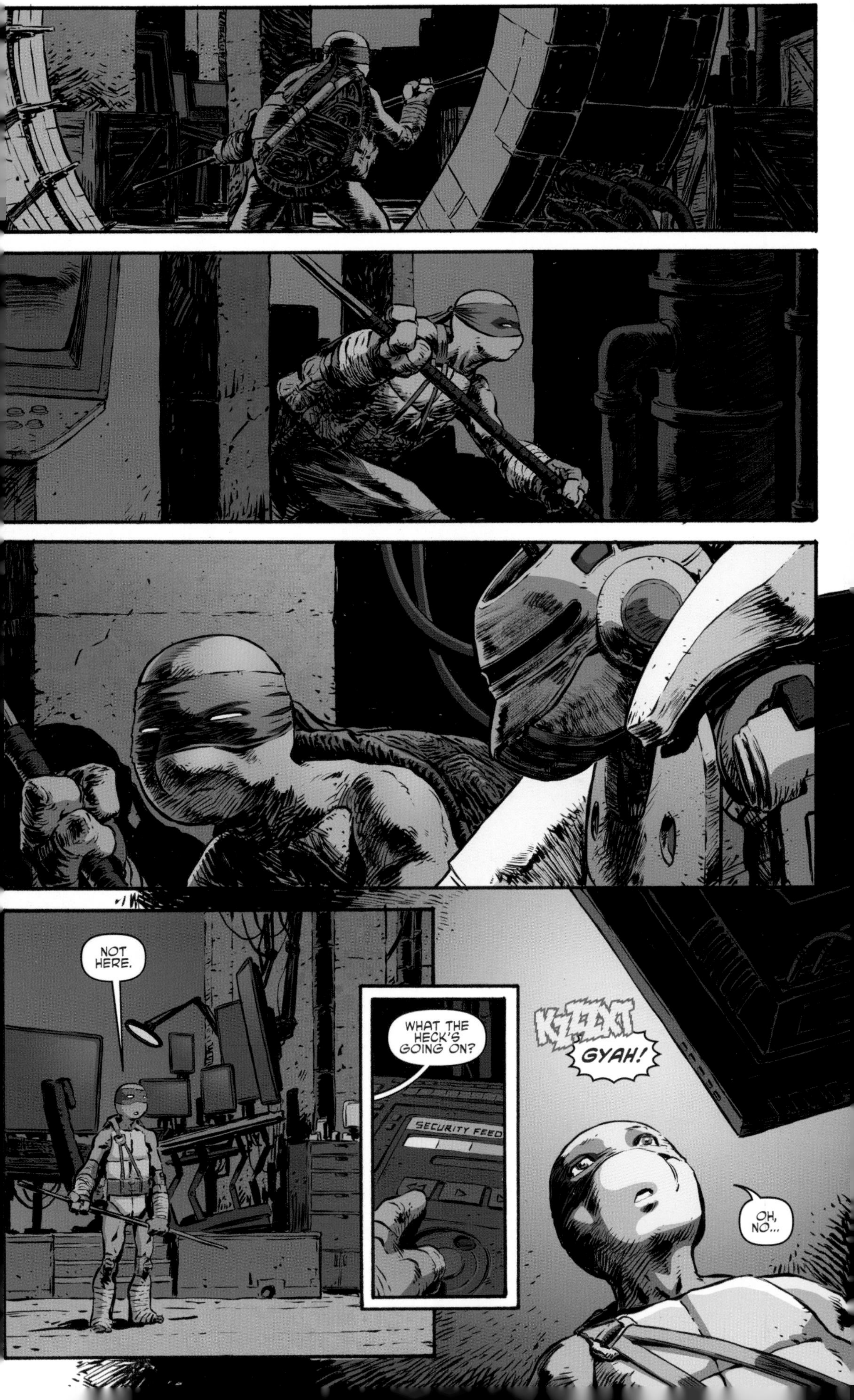
NOT HERE.
WHAT THE HECK'S GOING ON?
SECURITY FEED
KZZZXT
GYAH!
OH, NO...

"...THEY *TOOK* HIM."

TO START, PLEASE ALLOW ME TO THANK YOU FOR TAKING THIS MEETING...

...*INVENTOR.*

WELL, IT'S NOT LIKE I HAD MUCH OF A *CHOICE* IN THE MATTER—

—NOT WITH THESE DIMWITTED NEANDERTHALS *DRAGGING* ME IN HERE BY FORCE.

AND, FOR THE THOUSANDTH TIME, MY NAME IS *DOCTOR LIBBY MEITNER...* NOT "THE INVENTOR."

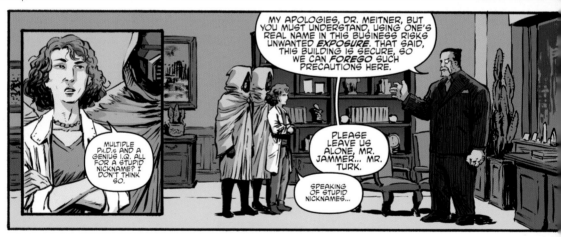

MY APOLOGIES, DR. MEITNER, BUT YOU MUST UNDERSTAND, USING ONE'S REAL NAME IN THIS BUSINESS RISKS UNWANTED *EXPOSURE.* THAT SAID, THIS BUILDING IS SECURE, SO WE CAN *FOREGO* SUCH PRECAUTIONS HERE.

MULTIPLE PH.D.S AND A GENIUS I.Q. ALL FOR A STUPID NICKNAME? I DON'T THINK SO.

PLEASE LEAVE US ALONE, MR. JAMMER... MR. TURK.

SPEAKING OF STUPID NICKNAMES...

YOU HEARD THE MAN, TURK. LET'S ROLL.

YO.

I SEE MY *CLOAKS* ARE STILL WORKING AS ADVERTISED. PLUG AND PLAY.

SO SIMPLE, EVEN THOSE DULLARD'S CAN *OPERATE* THEM.

YES... AND NO.

PLEASE TAKE A SEAT, DOCTOR. WE HAVE *MUCH* TO DISCUSS.

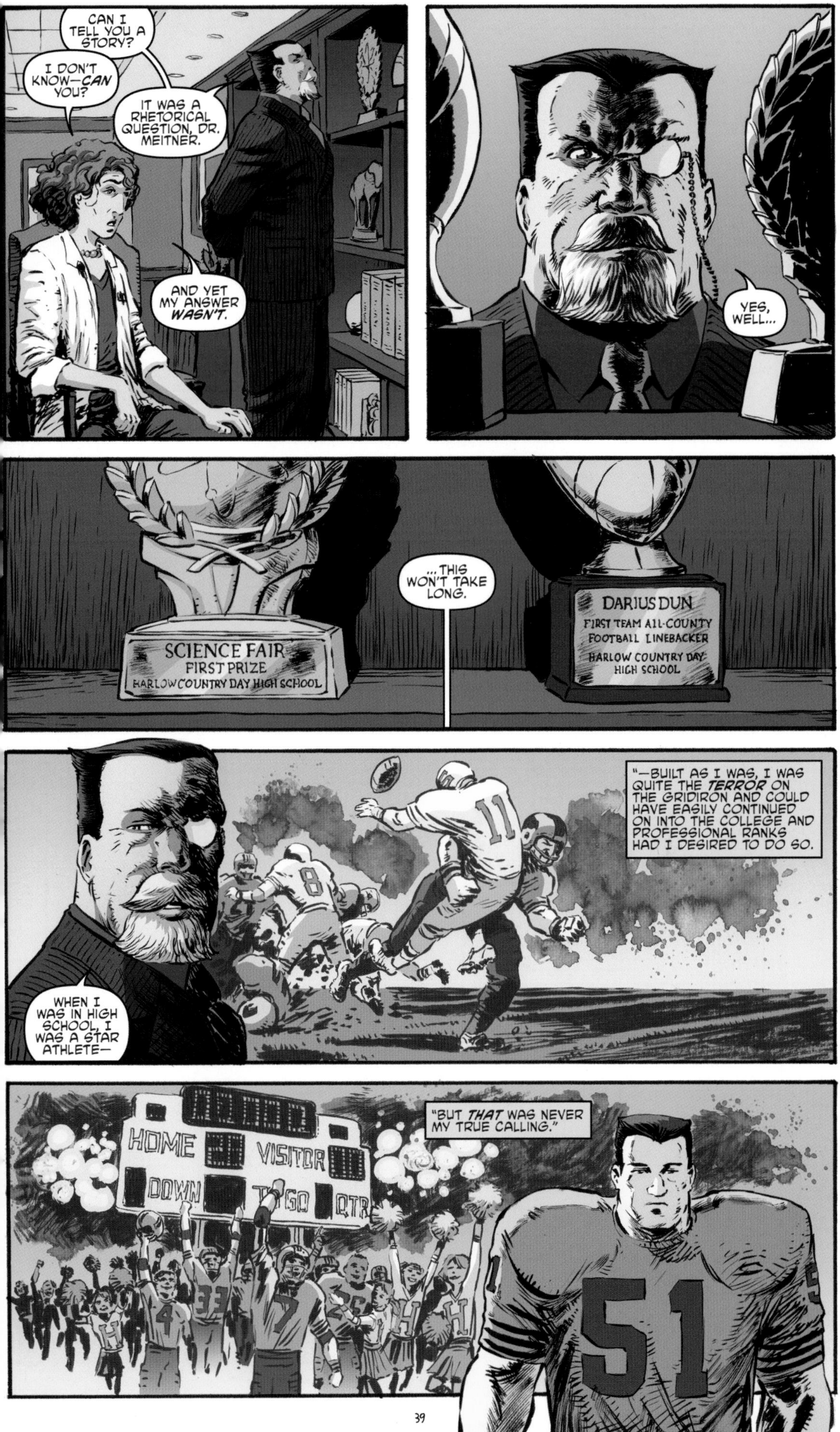
CAN I TELL YOU A STORY?
I DON'T KNOW—*CAN* YOU?
IT WAS A RHETORICAL QUESTION, DR. MEITNER.
AND YET MY ANSWER ***WASN'T***.
YES, WELL...
...THIS WON'T TAKE LONG.
SCIENCE FAIR
FIRST PRIZE
HARLOW COUNTRY DAY HIGH SCHOOL
DARIUS DUN
FIRST TEAM ALL-COUNTY
FOOTBALL LINEBACKER
HARLOW COUNTRY DAY HIGH SCHOOL
WHEN I WAS IN HIGH SCHOOL, I WAS A STAR ATHLETE—
"—BUILT AS I WAS, I WAS QUITE THE ***TERROR*** ON THE GRIDIRON AND COULD HAVE EASILY CONTINUED ON INTO THE COLLEGE AND PROFESSIONAL RANKS HAD I DESIRED TO DO SO.
HOME
VISITOR
DOWN
TO GO
QTR
"BUT *THAT* WAS NEVER MY TRUE CALLING."

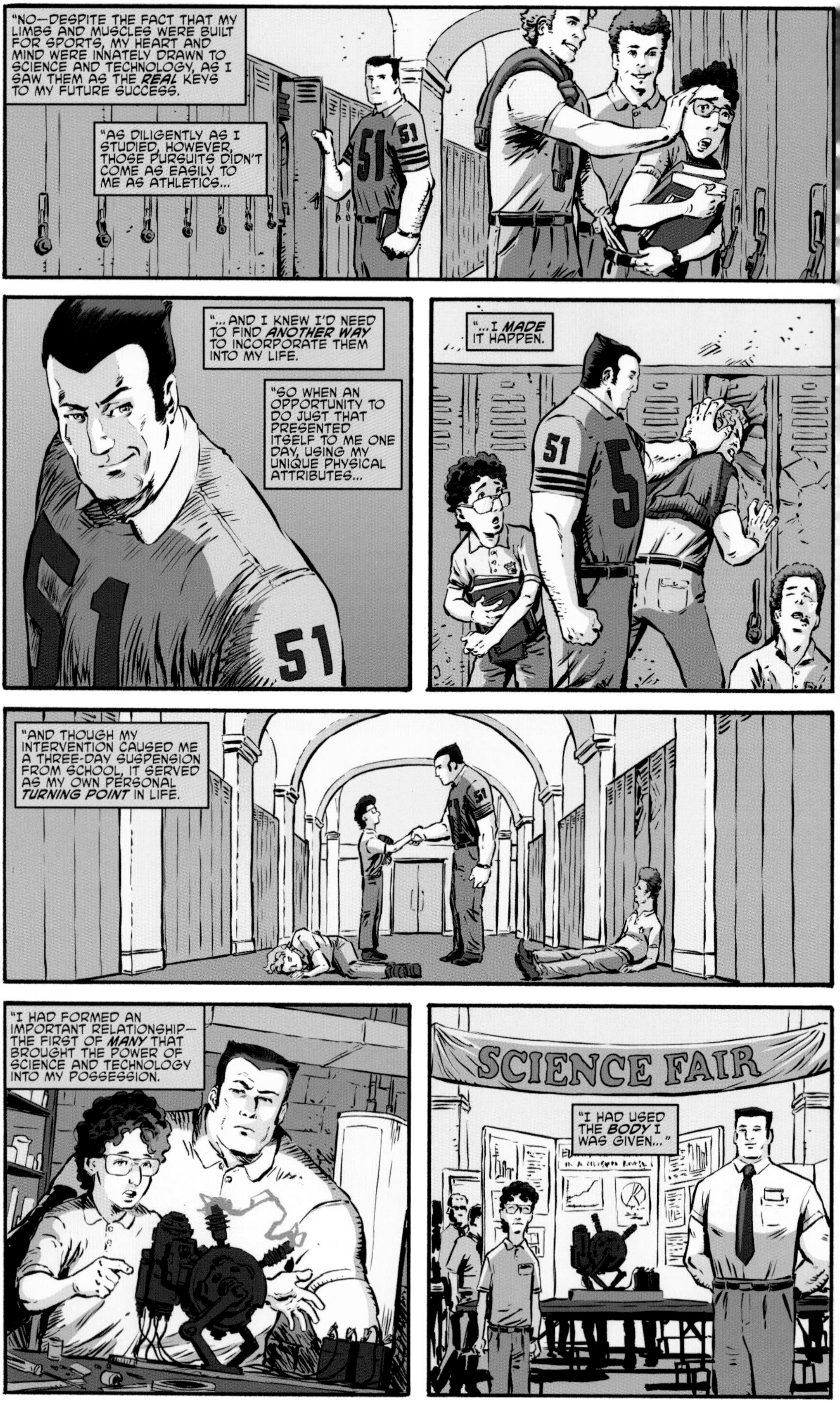
"NO—DESPITE THE FACT THAT MY LIMBS AND MUSCLES WERE BUILT FOR SPORTS, MY HEART AND MIND WERE INNATELY DRAWN TO SCIENCE AND TECHNOLOGY, AS I SAW THEM AS THE *REAL* KEYS TO MY FUTURE SUCCESS.
"AS DILIGENTLY AS I STUDIED, HOWEVER, THOSE PURSUITS DIDN'T COME AS EASILY TO ME AS ATHLETICS...
"...AND I KNEW I'D NEED TO FIND ***ANOTHER WAY*** TO INCORPORATE THEM INTO MY LIFE.
"SO WHEN AN OPPORTUNITY TO DO JUST THAT PRESENTED ITSELF TO ME ONE DAY, USING MY UNIQUE PHYSICAL ATTRIBUTES...
"...I *MADE* IT HAPPEN.
"AND THOUGH MY INTERVENTION CAUSED ME A THREE-DAY SUSPENSION FROM SCHOOL, IT SERVED AS MY OWN PERSONAL ***TURNING POINT*** IN LIFE.
"I HAD FORMED AN IMPORTANT RELATIONSHIP—THE FIRST OF *MANY* THAT BROUGHT THE POWER OF SCIENCE AND TECHNOLOGY INTO MY POSSESSION.
SCIENCE FAIR
"I HAD USED THE *BODY* I WAS GIVEN..."

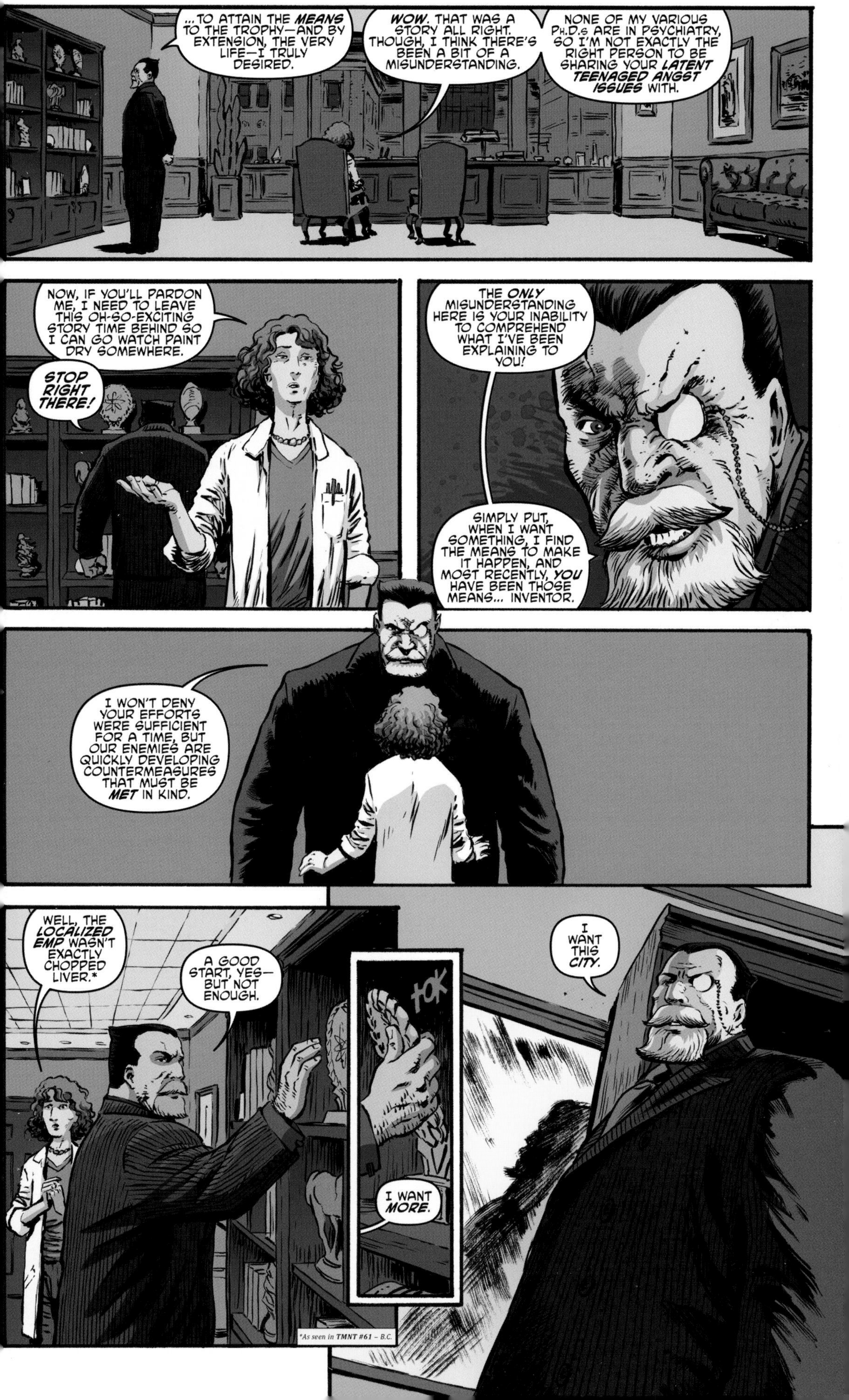
...TO ATTAIN THE MEANS TO THE TROPHY—AND BY EXTENSION, THE VERY LIFE—I TRULY DESIRED.
WOW. THAT WAS A STORY ALL RIGHT. THOUGH, I THINK THERE'S BEEN A BIT OF A MISUNDERSTANDING.
NONE OF MY VARIOUS PH.D.S ARE IN PSYCHIATRY, SO I'M NOT EXACTLY THE RIGHT PERSON TO BE SHARING YOUR LATENT TEENAGED ANGST ISSUES WITH.
NOW, IF YOU'LL PARDON ME, I NEED TO LEAVE THIS OH-SO-EXCITING STORY TIME BEHIND SO I CAN GO WATCH PAINT DRY SOMEWHERE.
STOP RIGHT THERE!
THE ONLY MISUNDERSTANDING HERE IS YOUR INABILITY TO COMPREHEND WHAT I'VE BEEN EXPLAINING TO YOU!
SIMPLY PUT, WHEN I WANT SOMETHING, I FIND THE MEANS TO MAKE IT HAPPEN, AND MOST RECENTLY, YOU HAVE BEEN THOSE MEANS... INVENTOR.
I WON'T DENY YOUR EFFORTS WERE SUFFICIENT FOR A TIME, BUT OUR ENEMIES ARE QUICKLY DEVELOPING COUNTERMEASURES THAT MUST BE MET IN KIND.
WELL, THE LOCALIZED EMP WASN'T EXACTLY CHOPPED LIVER.*
A GOOD START, YES—BUT NOT ENOUGH.
TOK
I WANT MORE.
I WANT THIS CITY.
*As seen in TMNT #61 – B.C.

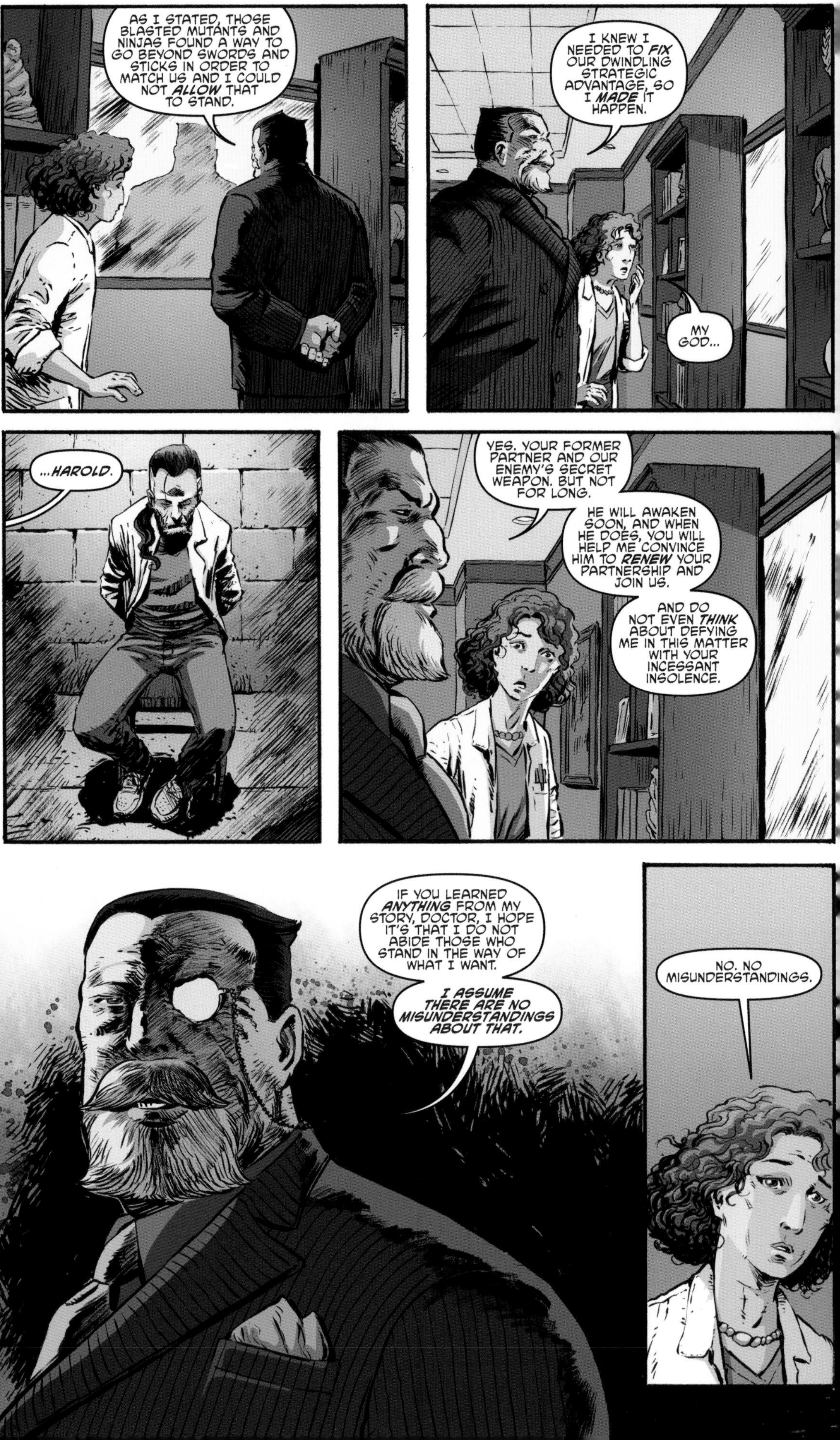

AS I STATED, THOSE BLASTED MUTANTS AND NINJAS FOUND A WAY TO GO BEYOND SWORDS AND STICKS IN ORDER TO MATCH US AND I COULD NOT *ALLOW* THAT TO STAND.
I KNEW I NEEDED TO *FIX* OUR DWINDLING STRATEGIC ADVANTAGE, SO I *MADE* IT HAPPEN.
MY GOD...
...*HAROLD*.
YES. YOUR FORMER PARTNER AND OUR ENEMY'S SECRET WEAPON. BUT NOT FOR LONG.
HE WILL AWAKEN SOON, AND WHEN HE DOES, YOU WILL HELP ME CONVINCE HIM TO *RENEW* YOUR PARTNERSHIP AND JOIN US.
AND DO NOT EVEN *THINK* ABOUT DEFYING ME IN THIS MATTER WITH YOUR INCESSANT INSOLENCE.
IF YOU LEARNED *ANYTHING* FROM MY STORY, DOCTOR, I HOPE IT'S THAT I DO NOT ABIDE THOSE WHO STAND IN THE WAY OF WHAT I WANT.
I ASSUME THERE ARE NO MISUNDERSTANDINGS ABOUT THAT.
NO. NO MISUNDERSTANDINGS.

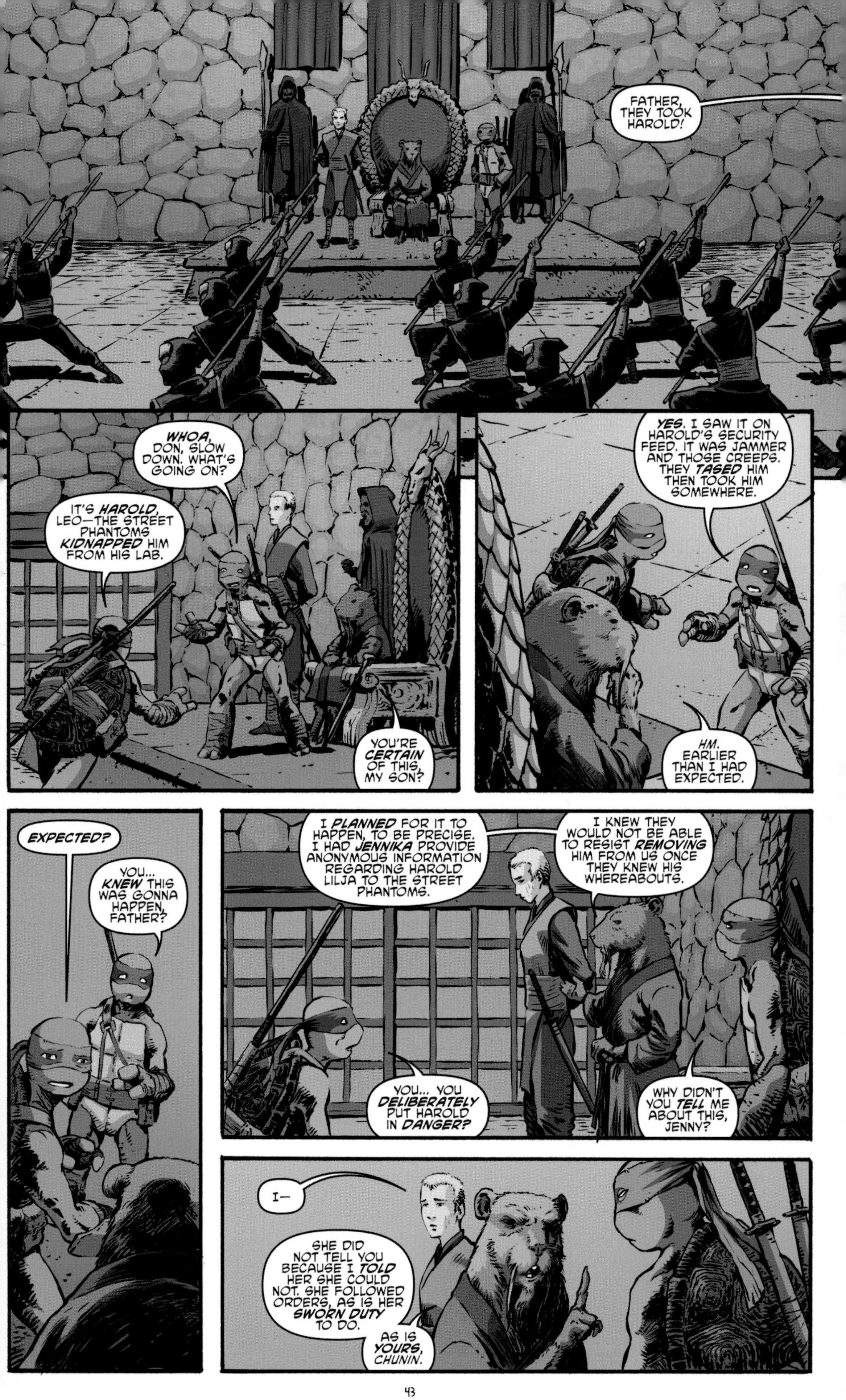
FATHER, THEY TOOK HAROLD!
WHOA, DON, SLOW DOWN. WHAT'S GOING ON?
IT'S HAROLD, LEO—THE STREET PHANTOMS KIDNAPPED HIM FROM HIS LAB.
YOU'RE CERTAIN OF THIS, MY SON?
YES. I SAW IT ON HAROLD'S SECURITY FEED. IT WAS JAMMER AND THOSE CREEPS. THEY TASED HIM THEN TOOK HIM SOMEWHERE.
HM. EARLIER THAN I HAD EXPECTED.
EXPECTED?
YOU... KNEW THIS WAS GONNA HAPPEN, FATHER?
I PLANNED FOR IT TO HAPPEN, TO BE PRECISE. I HAD JENNIKA PROVIDE ANONYMOUS INFORMATION REGARDING HAROLD LILJA TO THE STREET PHANTOMS.
I KNEW THEY WOULD NOT BE ABLE TO RESIST REMOVING HIM FROM US ONCE THEY KNEW HIS WHEREABOUTS.
YOU... YOU DELIBERATELY PUT HAROLD IN DANGER?
WHY DIDN'T YOU TELL ME ABOUT THIS, JENNY?
I—
SHE DID NOT TELL YOU BECAUSE I TOLD HER SHE COULD NOT. SHE FOLLOWED ORDERS, AS IS HER SWORN DUTY TO DO.
AS IS YOURS, CHUNIN.

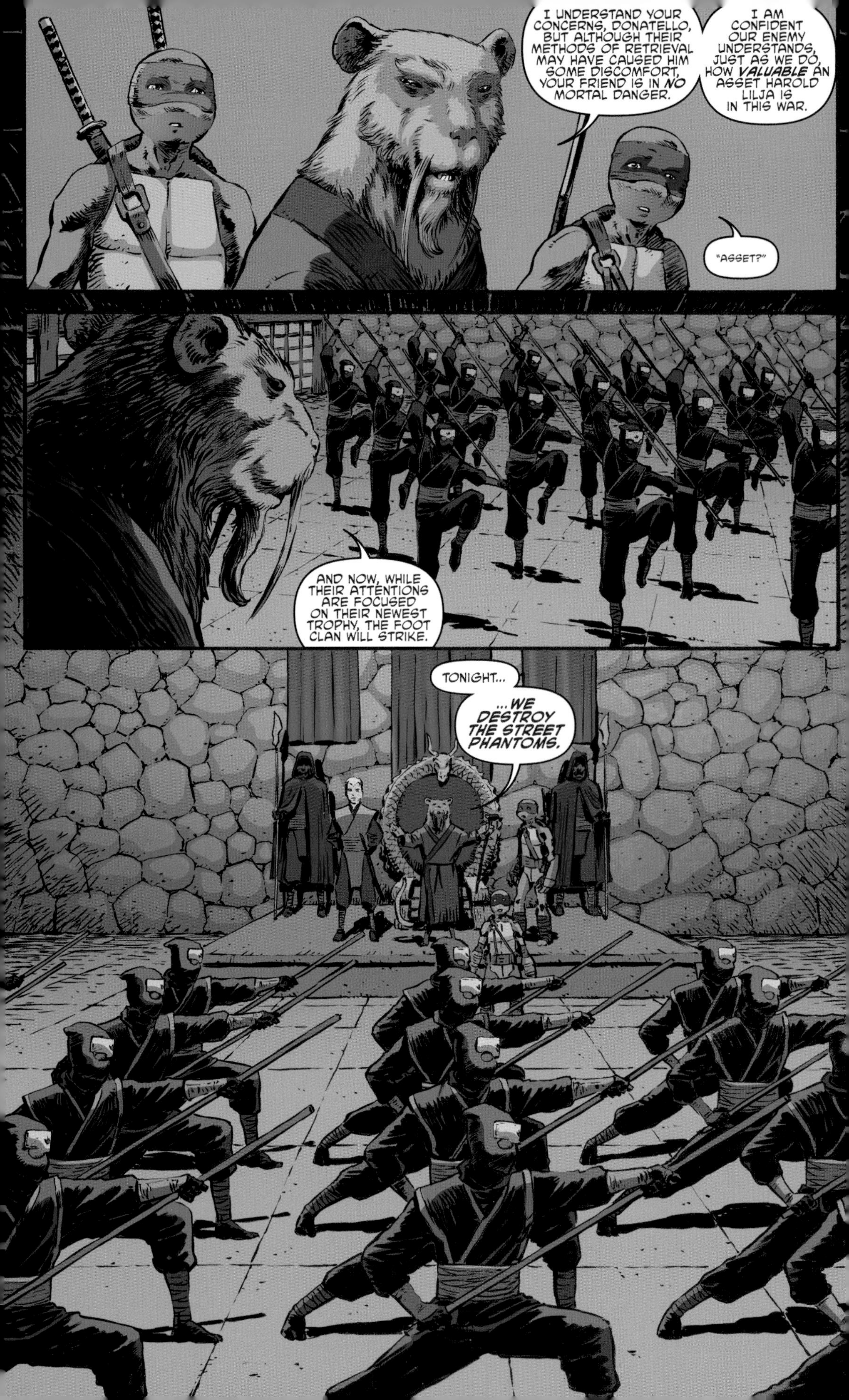
I UNDERSTAND YOUR CONCERNS, DONATELLO, BUT ALTHOUGH THEIR METHODS OF RETRIEVAL MAY HAVE CAUSED HIM SOME DISCOMFORT, YOUR FRIEND IS IN NO MORTAL DANGER.
I AM CONFIDENT OUR ENEMY UNDERSTANDS, JUST AS WE DO, HOW VALUABLE AN ASSET HAROLD LILJA IS IN THIS WAR.
"ASSET?"
AND NOW, WHILE THEIR ATTENTIONS ARE FOCUSED ON THEIR NEWEST TROPHY, THE FOOT CLAN WILL STRIKE.
TONIGHT...
...WE DESTROY THE STREET PHANTOMS.

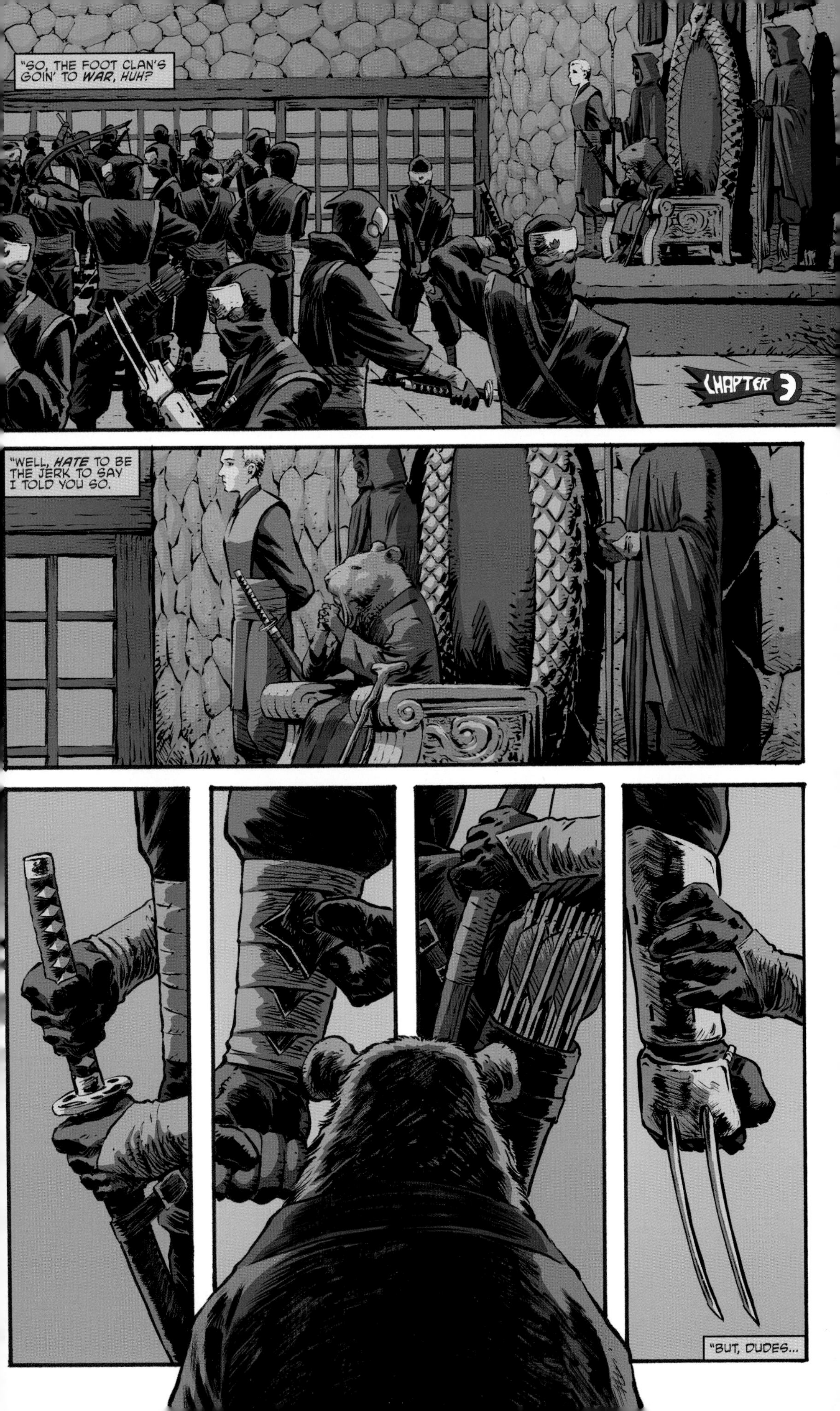

"SO, THE FOOT CLAN'S GOIN' TO WAR, HUH?
CHAPTER 3
"WELL, HATE TO BE THE JERK TO SAY I TOLD YOU SO.
"BUT, DUDES...

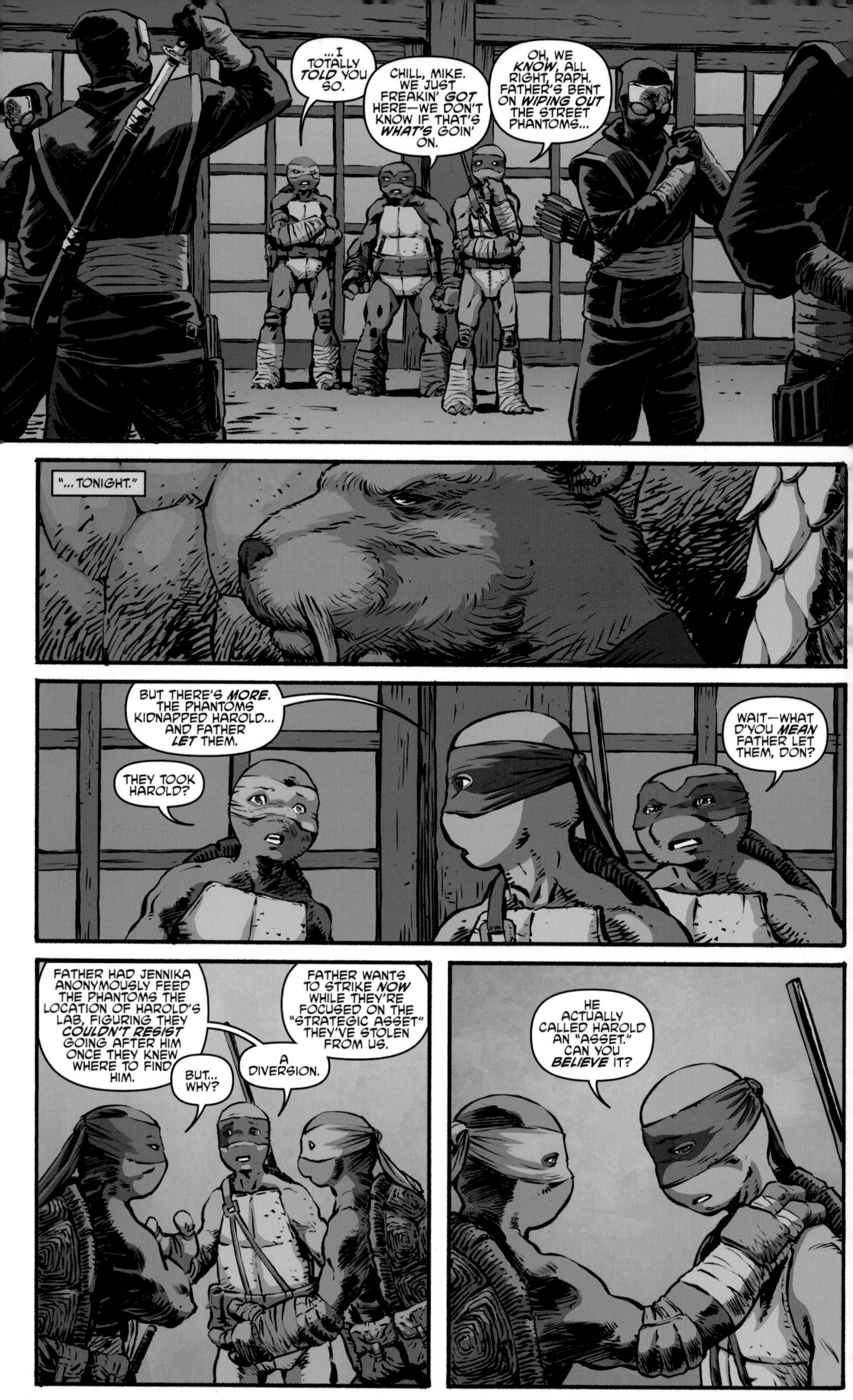
...I TOTALLY *TOLD* YOU SO.
CHILL, MIKE. WE JUST FREAKIN' *GOT* HERE—WE DON'T KNOW IF THAT'S *WHAT'S* GOIN' ON.
OH, WE *KNOW*, ALL RIGHT, RAPH. FATHER'S BENT ON *WIPING OUT* THE STREET PHANTOMS...
"... TONIGHT."
BUT THERE'S *MORE*. THE PHANTOMS KIDNAPPED HAROLD... AND FATHER *LET* THEM.
THEY TOOK HAROLD?
WAIT—WHAT D'YOU *MEAN* FATHER LET THEM, DON?
FATHER HAD JENNIKA ANONYMOUSLY FEED THE PHANTOMS THE LOCATION OF HAROLD'S LAB, FIGURING THEY *COULDN'T RESIST* GOING AFTER HIM ONCE THEY KNEW WHERE TO FIND HIM.
BUT... WHY?
A DIVERSION.
FATHER WANTS TO STRIKE *NOW* WHILE THEY'RE FOCUSED ON THE "STRATEGIC ASSET" THEY'VE STOLEN FROM US.
HE ACTUALLY CALLED HAROLD AN "ASSET." CAN YOU *BELIEVE* IT?

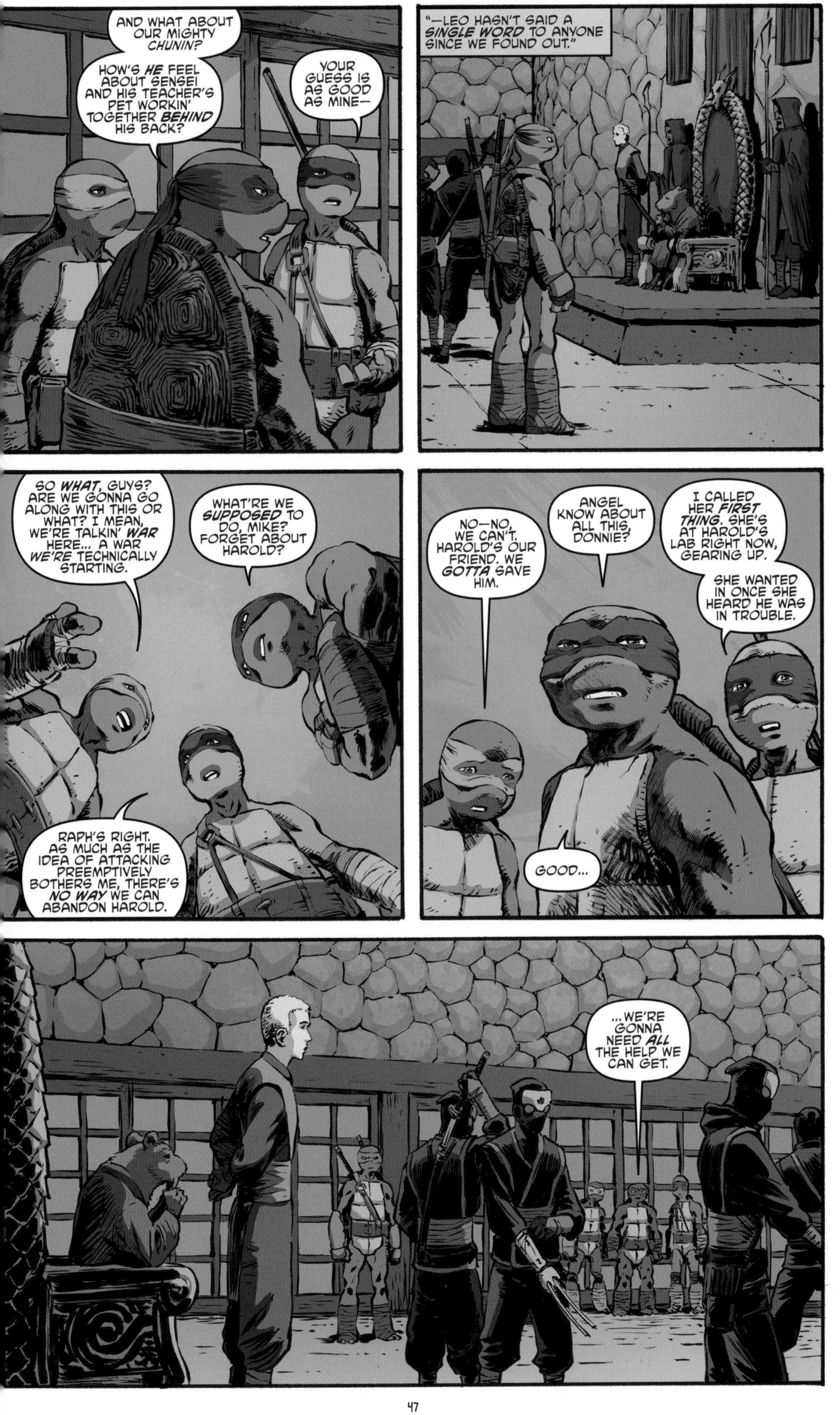
AND WHAT ABOUT OUR MIGHTY CHUNIN?
HOW'S HE FEEL ABOUT SENSEI AND HIS TEACHER'S PET WORKIN' TOGETHER BEHIND HIS BACK?
YOUR GUESS IS AS GOOD AS MINE—
"—LEO HASN'T SAID A SINGLE WORD TO ANYONE SINCE WE FOUND OUT."
SO WHAT, GUYS? ARE WE GONNA GO ALONG WITH THIS OR WHAT? I MEAN, WE'RE TALKIN' WAR HERE... A WAR WE'RE TECHNICALLY STARTING.
WHAT'RE WE SUPPOSED TO DO, MIKE? FORGET ABOUT HAROLD?
RAPH'S RIGHT. AS MUCH AS THE IDEA OF ATTACKING PREEMPTIVELY BOTHERS ME, THERE'S NO WAY WE CAN ABANDON HAROLD.
NO—NO, WE CAN'T. HAROLD'S OUR FRIEND. WE GOTTA SAVE HIM.
ANGEL KNOW ABOUT ALL THIS, DONNIE?
I CALLED HER FIRST THING. SHE'S AT HAROLD'S LAB RIGHT NOW, GEARING UP.
SHE WANTED IN ONCE SHE HEARD HE WAS IN TROUBLE.
GOOD...
...WE'RE GONNA NEED ALL THE HELP WE CAN GET.

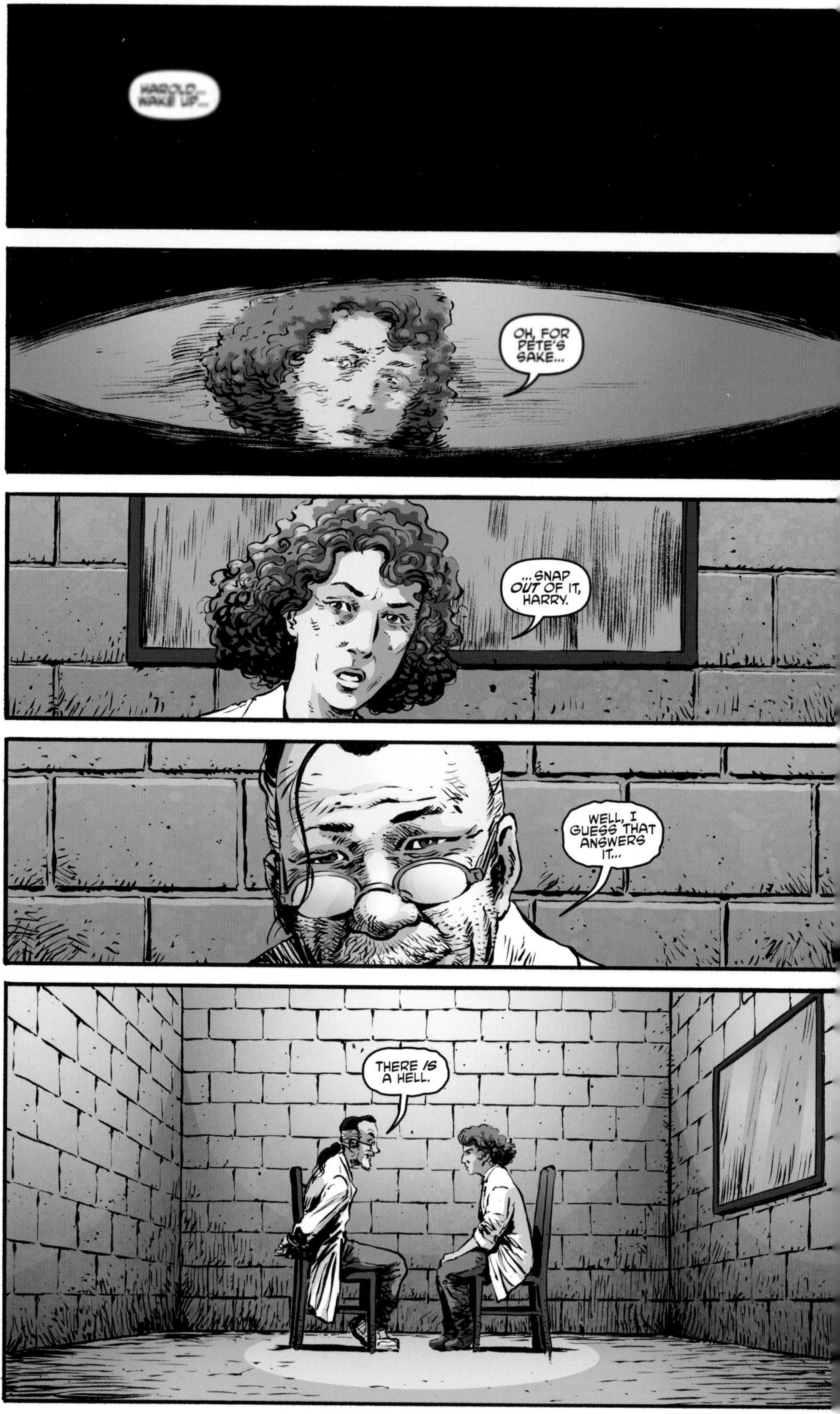
HAROLD... WAKE UP...
OH, FOR PETE'S SAKE...
...SNAP OUT OF IT, HARRY.
WELL, I GUESS THAT ANSWERS IT...
THERE IS A HELL.

GIVE IT A REST, HARRY. YOU KNOW *FULL WELL* YOU'RE NOT DEAD.

YOU MIGHT BE RIGHT.

LET'S SEE... MY HANDS ARE *LASHED* TO A CHAIR, I HAVE THE WORLD'S *WORST* MIGRAINE, AND I'M OBVIOUSLY BEING *MONITORED* THROUGH A POORLY DISGUISED TWO-WAY MIRROR.

CLUB MED, MAYBE?

NO, WAIT— *YOU'RE* STILL HERE.

DEFINITELY HELL.

SAME OLD SARDONIC JACKASS AS EVER, I SEE.

DO YOU EVEN *REALIZE* THE TROUBLE YOU'RE IN?

I'M THINKING THAT'S A BETTER QUESTION FOR *YOU*, LIBBY. KIDNAPPING? REALLY?

TELL ME—WAS THE MONEY GRAB *WORTH* IT?

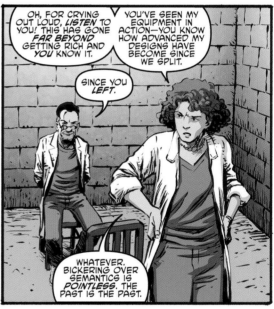

OH, FOR CRYING OUT LOUD, *LISTEN* TO YOU! THIS HAS GONE *FAR BEYOND* GETTING RICH AND *YOU* KNOW IT.

YOU'VE SEEN MY EQUIPMENT IN ACTION—YOU KNOW HOW ADVANCED MY DESIGNS HAVE BECOME SINCE WE SPLIT.

SINCE YOU *LEFT*.

WHATEVER. BICKERING OVER SEMANTICS IS *POINTLESS*. THE PAST IS THE PAST.

BUT THE *FUTURE*?

I KNOW WHAT YOU'VE BEEN UP TO IN YOUR LAB, HARRY... WHAT YOU'VE *ACCOMPLISHED* ON A SHOESTRING BUDGET DURING THE YEARS WE'VE BEEN APART.

JUST IMAGINE THE AMAZING THINGS WE COULD DO NOW, TOGETHER, WITH THE AMPLE RESOURCES I HAVE AVAILABLE TO ME—RESOURCES THAT COULD EASILY BE *YOURS*, TOO.

SHE'S *RIGHT*, MR. LILJA...

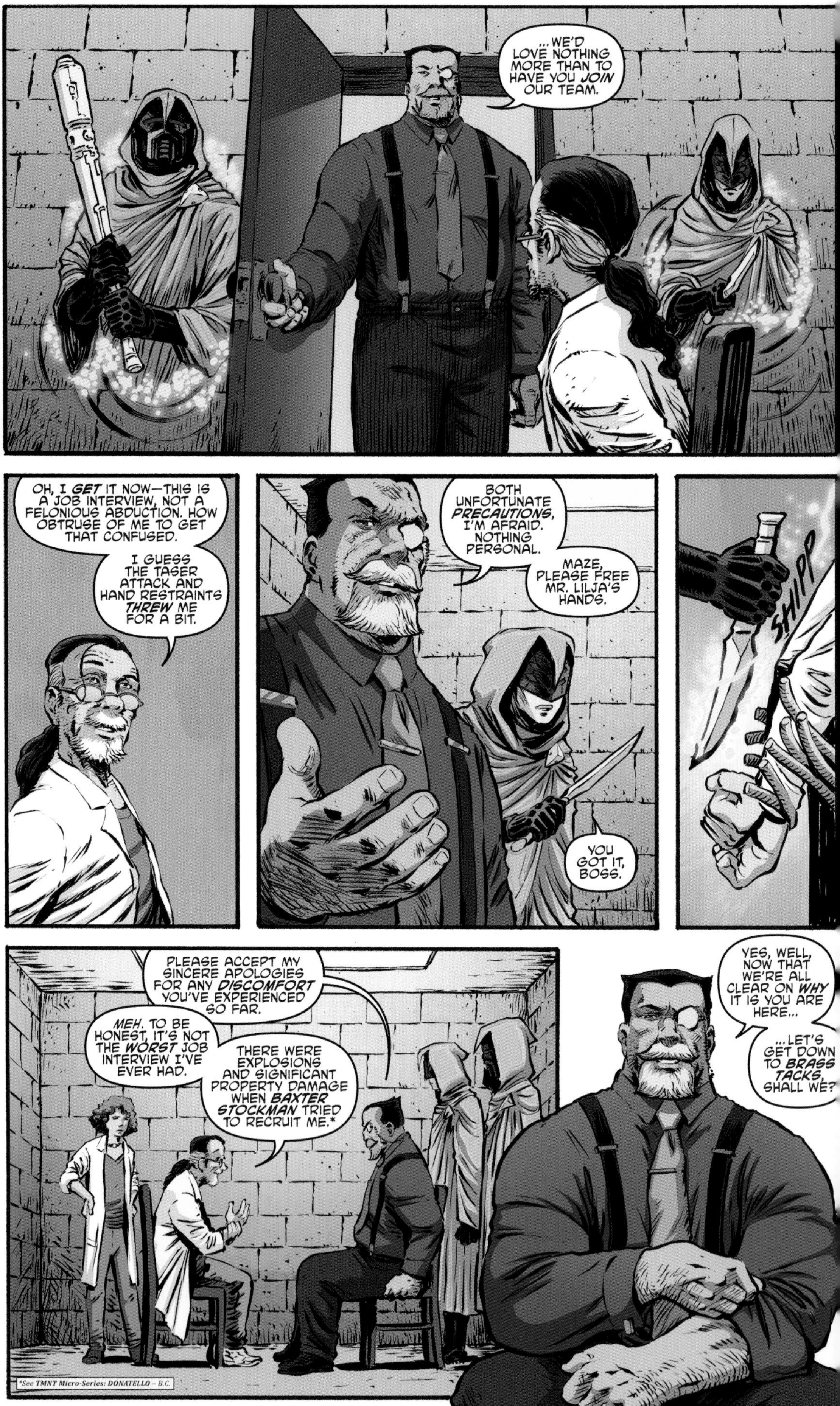
...WE'D LOVE NOTHING MORE THAN TO HAVE YOU JOIN OUR TEAM.
OH, I GET IT NOW—THIS IS A JOB INTERVIEW, NOT A FELONIOUS ABDUCTION. HOW OBTRUSE OF ME TO GET THAT CONFUSED.
I GUESS THE TASER ATTACK AND HAND RESTRAINTS THREW ME FOR A BIT.
BOTH UNFORTUNATE PRECAUTIONS, I'M AFRAID. NOTHING PERSONAL.
MAZE, PLEASE FREE MR. LILJA'S HANDS.
YOU GOT IT, BOSS.
SHIPP
PLEASE ACCEPT MY SINCERE APOLOGIES FOR ANY DISCOMFORT YOU'VE EXPERIENCED SO FAR.
MEH. TO BE HONEST, IT'S NOT THE WORST JOB INTERVIEW I'VE EVER HAD.
THERE WERE EXPLOSIONS AND SIGNIFICANT PROPERTY DAMAGE WHEN BAXTER STOCKMAN TRIED TO RECRUIT ME.*
YES, WELL, NOW THAT WE'RE ALL CLEAR ON WHY IT IS YOU ARE HERE...
...LET'S GET DOWN TO BRASS TACKS, SHALL WE?
*See TMNT Micro-Series: DONATELLO – B.C.

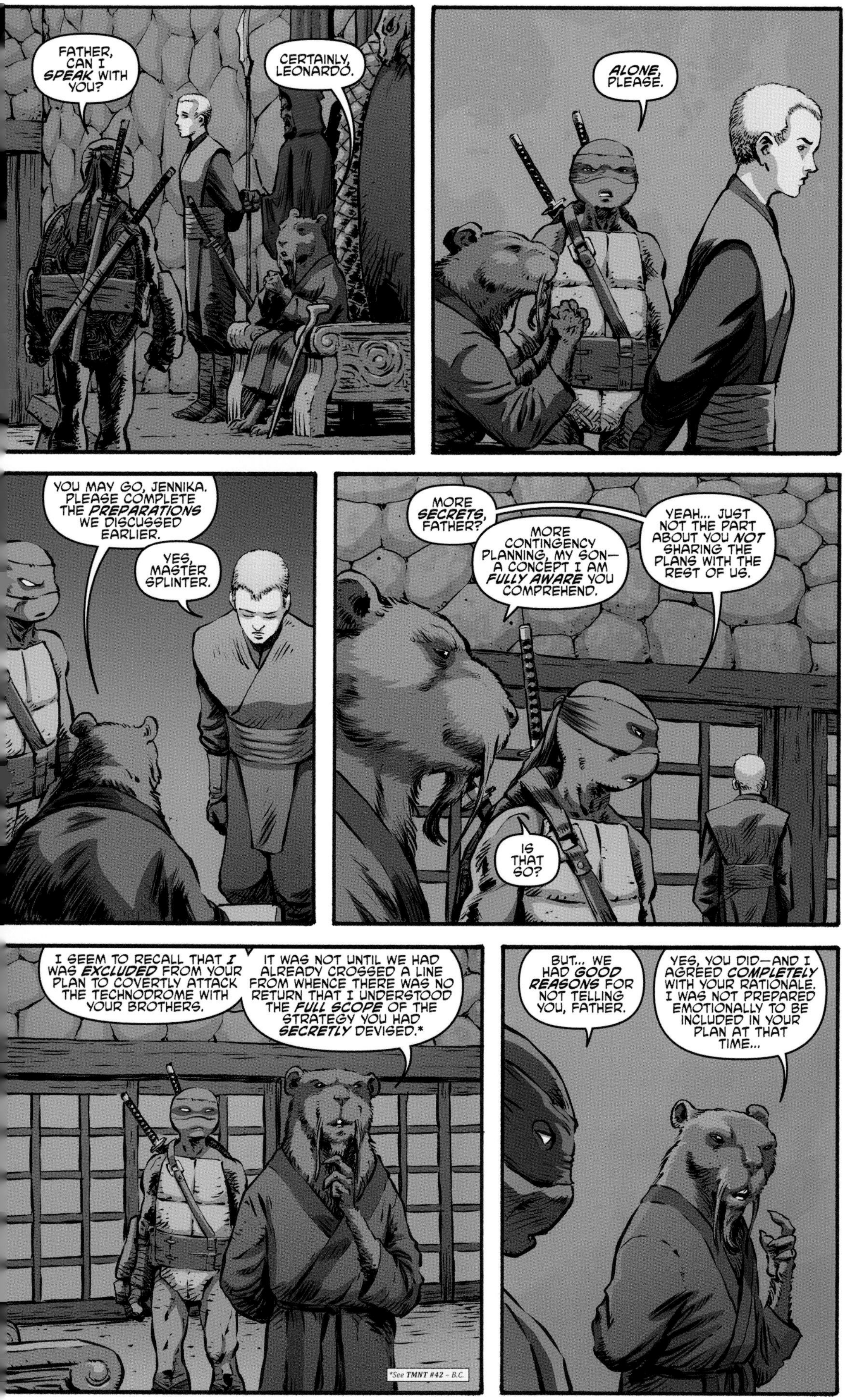

FATHER, CAN I SPEAK WITH YOU?
CERTAINLY, LEONARDO.
ALONE, PLEASE.
YOU MAY GO, JENNIKA. PLEASE COMPLETE THE PREPARATIONS WE DISCUSSED EARLIER.
YES, MASTER SPLINTER.
MORE SECRETS, FATHER?
MORE CONTINGENCY PLANNING, MY SON— A CONCEPT I AM FULLY AWARE YOU COMPREHEND.
YEAH... JUST NOT THE PART ABOUT YOU NOT SHARING THE PLANS WITH THE REST OF US.
IS THAT SO?
I SEEM TO RECALL THAT I WAS EXCLUDED FROM YOUR PLAN TO COVERTLY ATTACK THE TECHNODROME WITH YOUR BROTHERS.
IT WAS NOT UNTIL WE HAD ALREADY CROSSED A LINE FROM WHENCE THERE WAS NO RETURN THAT I UNDERSTOOD THE FULL SCOPE OF THE STRATEGY YOU HAD SECRETLY DEVISED.*
*See TMNT #42 – B.C.
BUT... WE HAD GOOD REASONS FOR NOT TELLING YOU, FATHER.
YES, YOU DID—AND I AGREED COMPLETELY WITH YOUR RATIONALE. I WAS NOT PREPARED EMOTIONALLY TO BE INCLUDED IN YOUR PLAN AT THAT TIME...

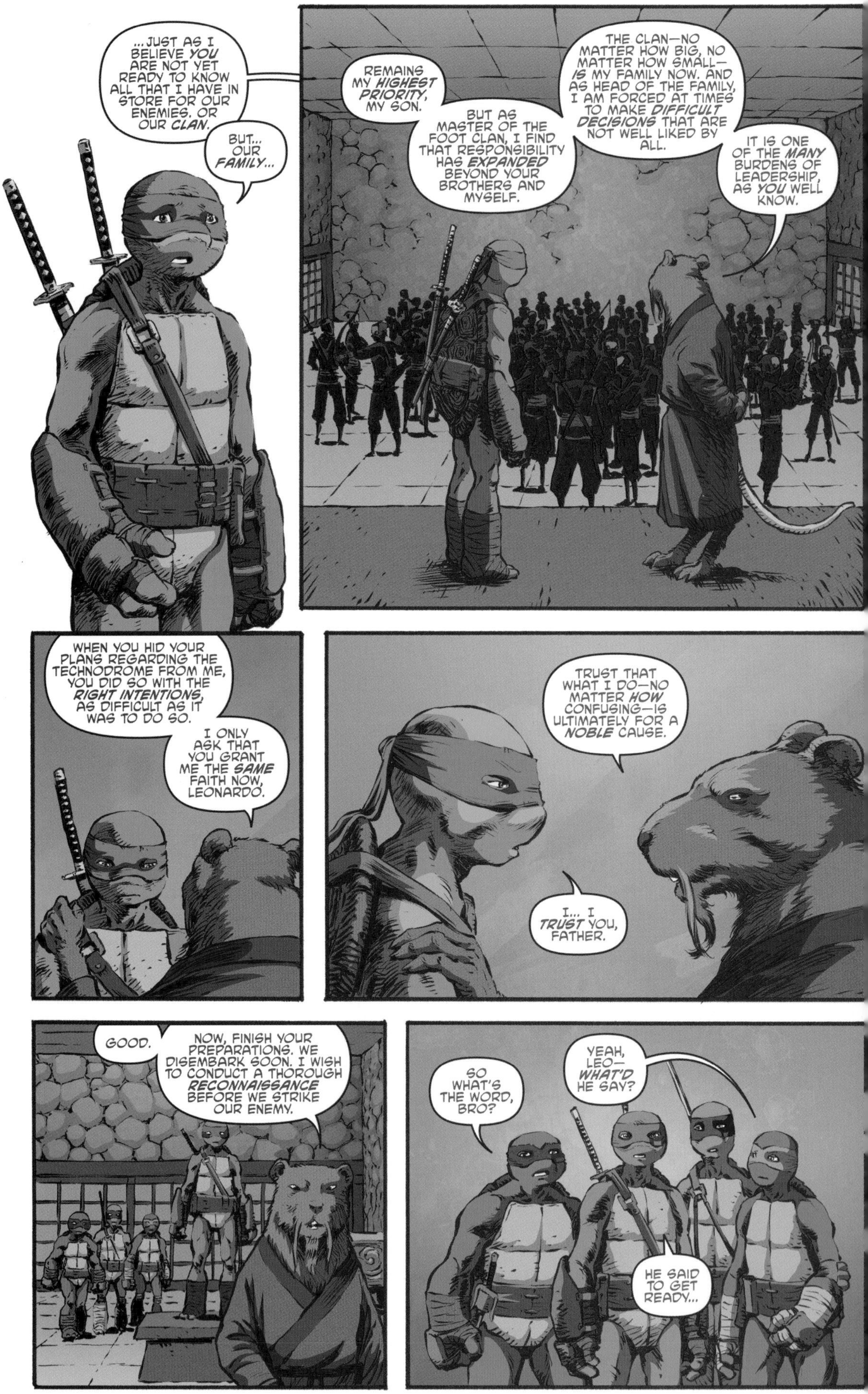
...JUST AS I BELIEVE YOU ARE NOT YET READY TO KNOW ALL THAT I HAVE IN STORE FOR OUR ENEMIES. OR OUR CLAN.
BUT... OUR FAMILY...
REMAINS MY HIGHEST PRIORITY, MY SON.
BUT AS MASTER OF THE FOOT CLAN, I FIND THAT RESPONSIBILITY HAS EXPANDED BEYOND YOUR BROTHERS AND MYSELF.
THE CLAN—NO MATTER HOW BIG, NO MATTER HOW SMALL—IS MY FAMILY NOW. AND AS HEAD OF THE FAMILY, I AM FORCED AT TIMES TO MAKE DIFFICULT DECISIONS THAT ARE NOT WELL LIKED BY ALL.
IT IS ONE OF THE MANY BURDENS OF LEADERSHIP, AS YOU WELL KNOW.
WHEN YOU HID YOUR PLANS REGARDING THE TECHNODROME FROM ME, YOU DID SO WITH THE RIGHT INTENTIONS, AS DIFFICULT AS IT WAS TO DO SO.
I ONLY ASK THAT YOU GRANT ME THE SAME FAITH NOW, LEONARDO.
TRUST THAT WHAT I DO—NO MATTER HOW CONFUSING—IS ULTIMATELY FOR A NOBLE CAUSE.
I... I TRUST YOU, FATHER.
GOOD.
NOW, FINISH YOUR PREPARATIONS. WE DISEMBARK SOON. I WISH TO CONDUCT A THOROUGH RECONNAISSANCE BEFORE WE STRIKE OUR ENEMY.
SO WHAT'S THE WORD, BRO?
YEAH, LEO—WHAT'D HE SAY?
HE SAID TO GET READY...

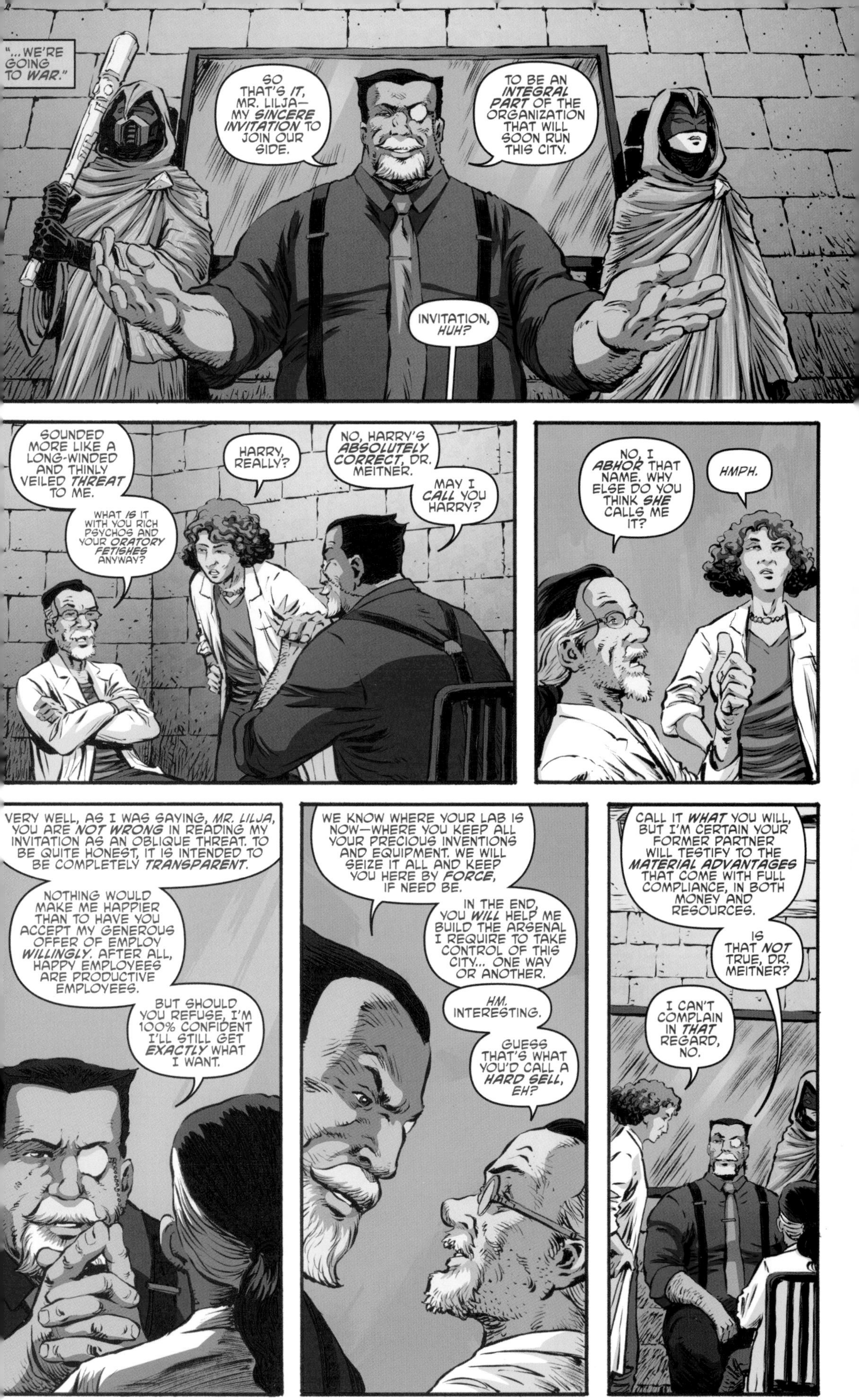
"...WE'RE GOING TO WAR."
SO THAT'S IT, MR. LILJA— MY SINCERE INVITATION TO JOIN OUR SIDE.
TO BE AN INTEGRAL PART OF THE ORGANIZATION THAT WILL SOON RUN THIS CITY.
INVITATION, HUH?
SOUNDED MORE LIKE A LONG-WINDED AND THINLY VEILED THREAT TO ME.
WHAT IS IT WITH YOU RICH PSYCHOS AND YOUR ORATORY FETISHES ANYWAY?
HARRY, REALLY?
NO, HARRY'S ABSOLUTELY CORRECT, DR. MEITNER.
MAY I CALL YOU HARRY?
NO, I ABHOR THAT NAME. WHY ELSE DO YOU THINK SHE CALLS ME IT?
HMPH.
VERY WELL, AS I WAS SAYING, MR. LILJA, YOU ARE NOT WRONG IN READING MY INVITATION AS AN OBLIQUE THREAT. TO BE QUITE HONEST, IT IS INTENDED TO BE COMPLETELY TRANSPARENT.
NOTHING WOULD MAKE ME HAPPIER THAN TO HAVE YOU ACCEPT MY GENEROUS OFFER OF EMPLOY WILLINGLY. AFTER ALL, HAPPY EMPLOYEES ARE PRODUCTIVE EMPLOYEES.
BUT SHOULD YOU REFUSE, I'M 100% CONFIDENT I'LL STILL GET EXACTLY WHAT I WANT.
WE KNOW WHERE YOUR LAB IS NOW—WHERE YOU KEEP ALL YOUR PRECIOUS INVENTIONS AND EQUIPMENT. WE WILL SEIZE IT ALL AND KEEP YOU HERE BY FORCE, IF NEED BE.
IN THE END, YOU WILL HELP ME BUILD THE ARSENAL I REQUIRE TO TAKE CONTROL OF THIS CITY... ONE WAY OR ANOTHER.
HM. INTERESTING.
GUESS THAT'S WHAT YOU'D CALL A HARD SELL, EH?
CALL IT WHAT YOU WILL, BUT I'M CERTAIN YOUR FORMER PARTNER WILL TESTIFY TO THE MATERIAL ADVANTAGES THAT COME WITH FULL COMPLIANCE, IN BOTH MONEY AND RESOURCES.
IS THAT NOT TRUE, DR. MEITNER?
I CAN'T COMPLAIN IN THAT REGARD, NO.

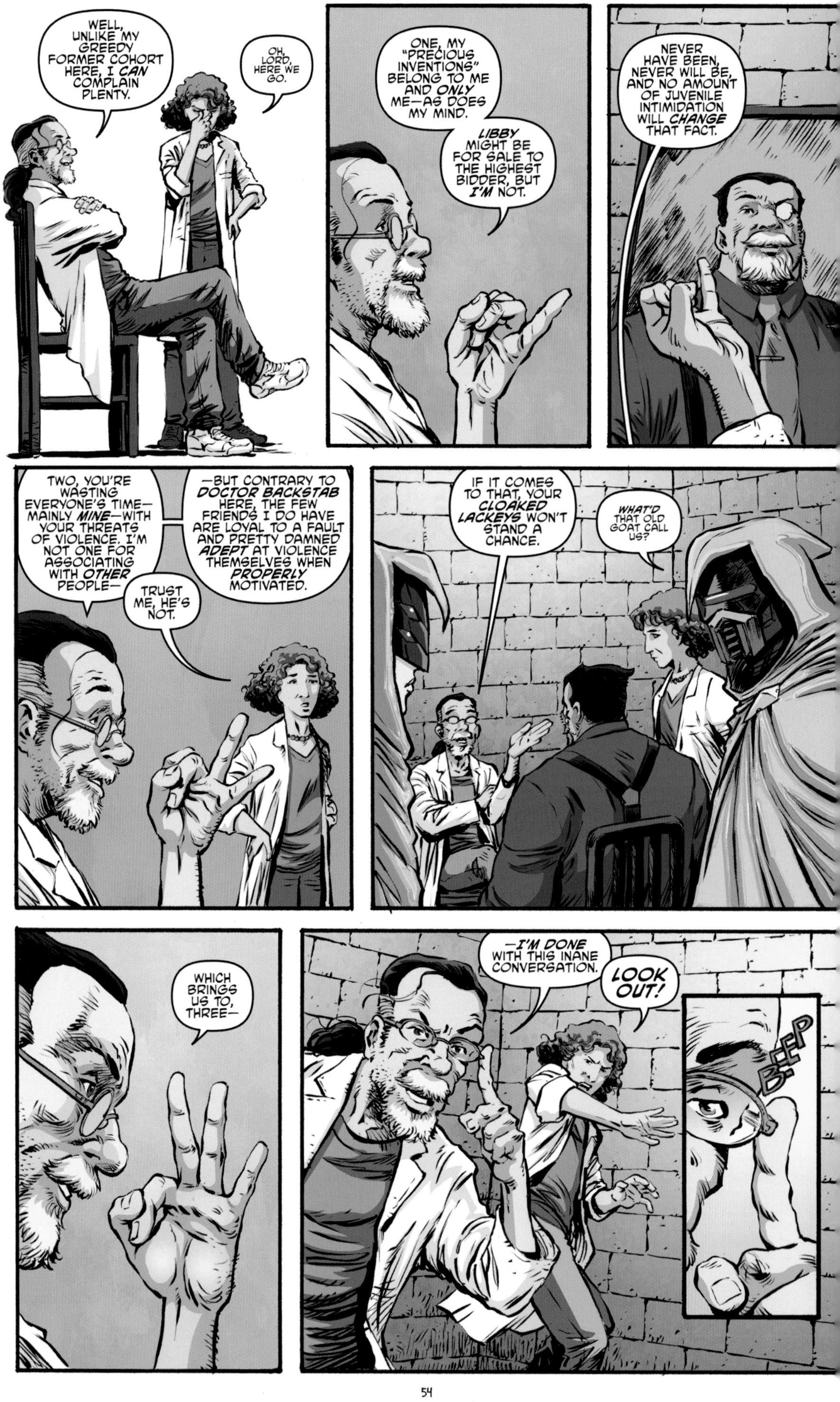
WELL, UNLIKE MY GREEDY FORMER COHORT HERE, I *CAN* COMPLAIN PLENTY.
OH, LORD, HERE WE GO.
ONE, MY "PRECIOUS INVENTIONS" BELONG TO ME AND *ONLY* ME—AS DOES MY MIND.
LIBBY MIGHT BE FOR SALE TO THE HIGHEST BIDDER, BUT *I'M* NOT.
NEVER HAVE BEEN, NEVER WILL BE, AND NO AMOUNT OF JUVENILE INTIMIDATION WILL *CHANGE* THAT FACT.
TWO, YOU'RE WASTING EVERYONE'S TIME—MAINLY *MINE*—WITH YOUR THREATS OF VIOLENCE. I'M NOT ONE FOR ASSOCIATING WITH *OTHER* PEOPLE—
TRUST ME, HE'S NOT.
—BUT CONTRARY TO *DOCTOR BACKSTAB* HERE, THE FEW FRIENDS I DO HAVE ARE LOYAL TO A FAULT AND PRETTY DAMNED *ADEPT* AT VIOLENCE THEMSELVES WHEN *PROPERLY* MOTIVATED.
IF IT COMES TO THAT, YOUR *CLOAKED LACKEYS* WON'T STAND A CHANCE.
WHAT'D THAT OLD GOAT CALL US?
WHICH BRINGS US TO, THREE—
—*I'M DONE* WITH THIS INANE CONVERSATION.
LOOK OUT!
BEEP

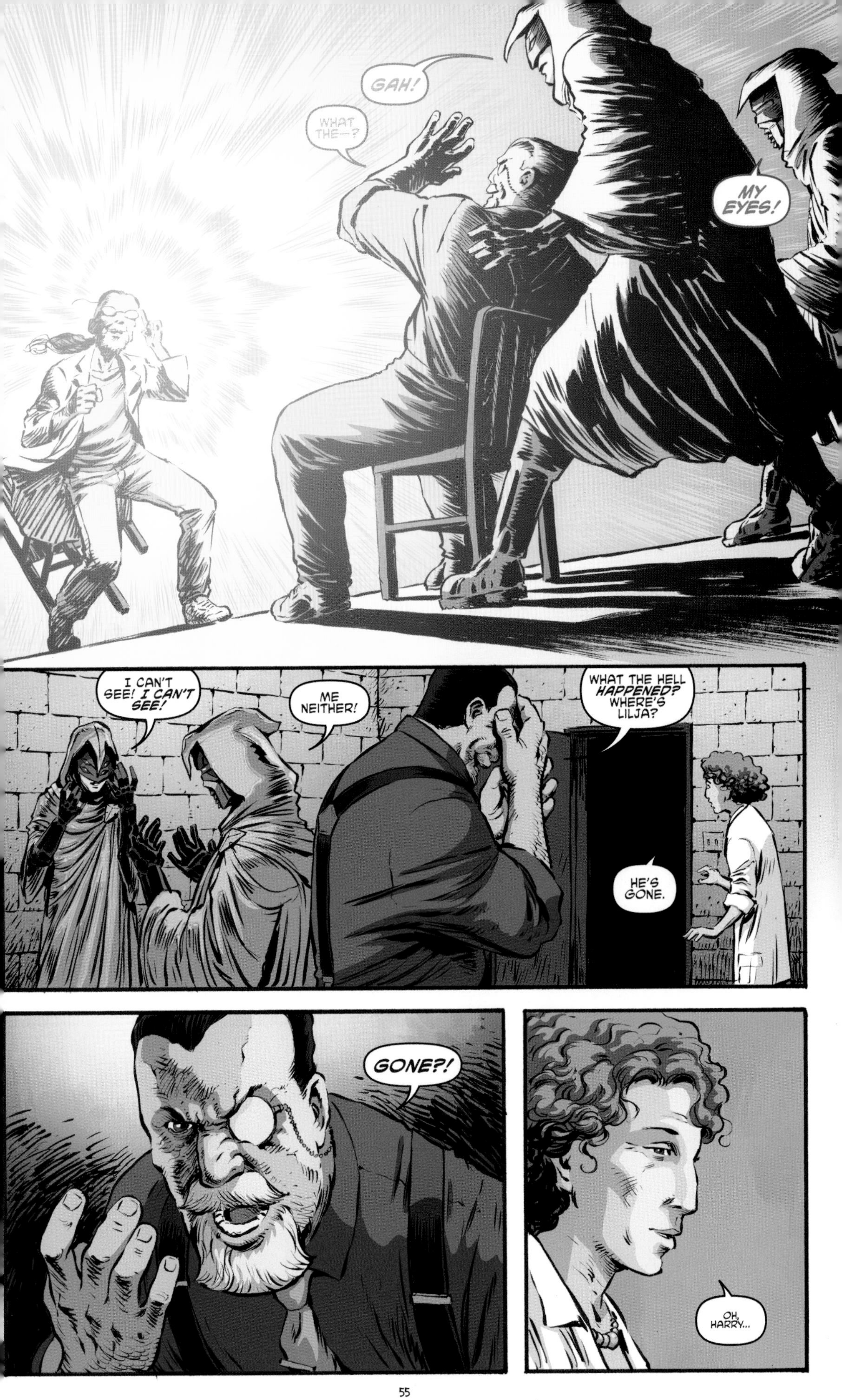
GAH!
WHAT THE--?
MY EYES!
I CAN'T SEE! I CAN'T SEE!
ME NEITHER!
WHAT THE HELL HAPPENED? WHERE'S LILJA?
HE'S GONE.
GONE?!
OH, HARRY...

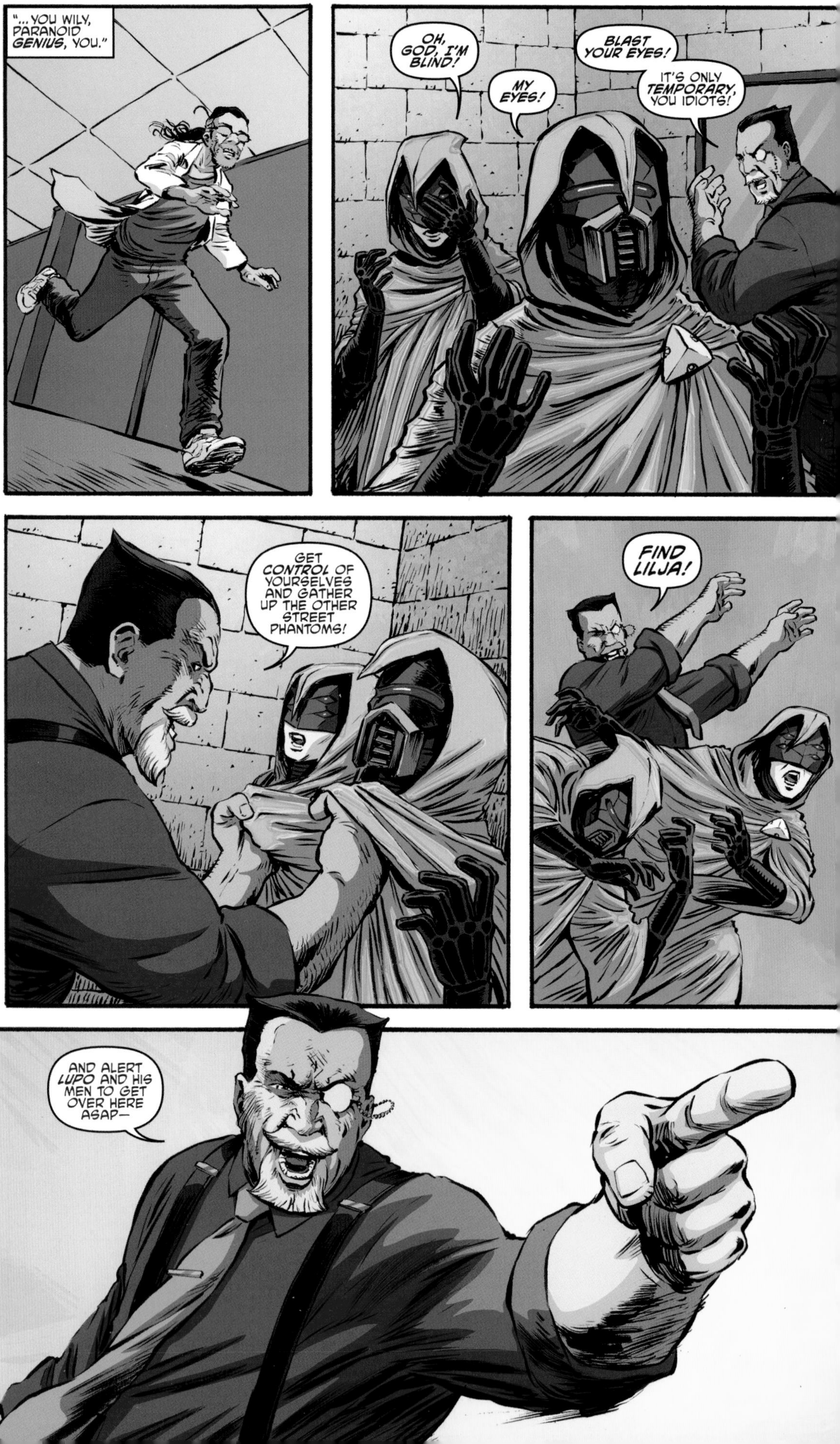
"...YOU WILY, PARANOID GENIUS, YOU."
OH, GOD, I'M BLIND!
MY EYES!
BLAST YOUR EYES!
IT'S ONLY TEMPORARY, YOU IDIOTS!
GET CONTROL OF YOURSELVES AND GATHER UP THE OTHER STREET PHANTOMS!
FIND LILJA!
AND ALERT LUPO AND HIS MEN TO GET OVER HERE ASAP—

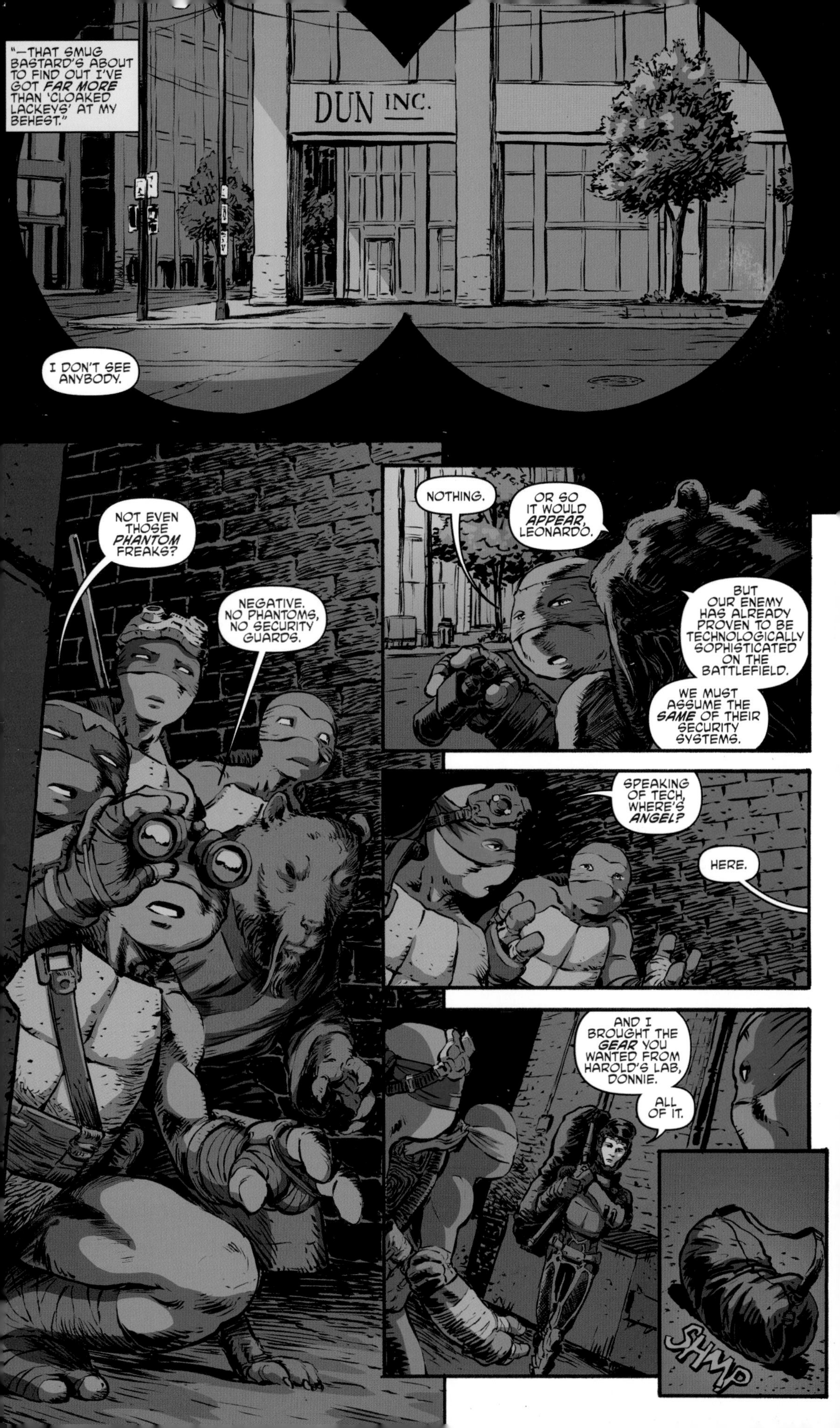
"—THAT SMUG BASTARD'S ABOUT TO FIND OUT I'VE GOT FAR MORE THAN 'CLOAKED LACKEYS' AT MY BEHEST."
DUN INC.
I DON'T SEE ANYBODY.
NOT EVEN THOSE PHANTOM FREAKS?
NEGATIVE. NO PHANTOMS, NO SECURITY GUARDS.
NOTHING.
OR SO IT WOULD APPEAR, LEONARDO.
BUT OUR ENEMY HAS ALREADY PROVEN TO BE TECHNOLOGICALLY SOPHISTICATED ON THE BATTLEFIELD.
WE MUST ASSUME THE SAME OF THEIR SECURITY SYSTEMS.
SPEAKING OF TECH, WHERE'S ANGEL?
HERE.
AND I BROUGHT THE GEAR YOU WANTED FROM HAROLD'S LAB, DONNIE.
ALL OF IT.
SHMP

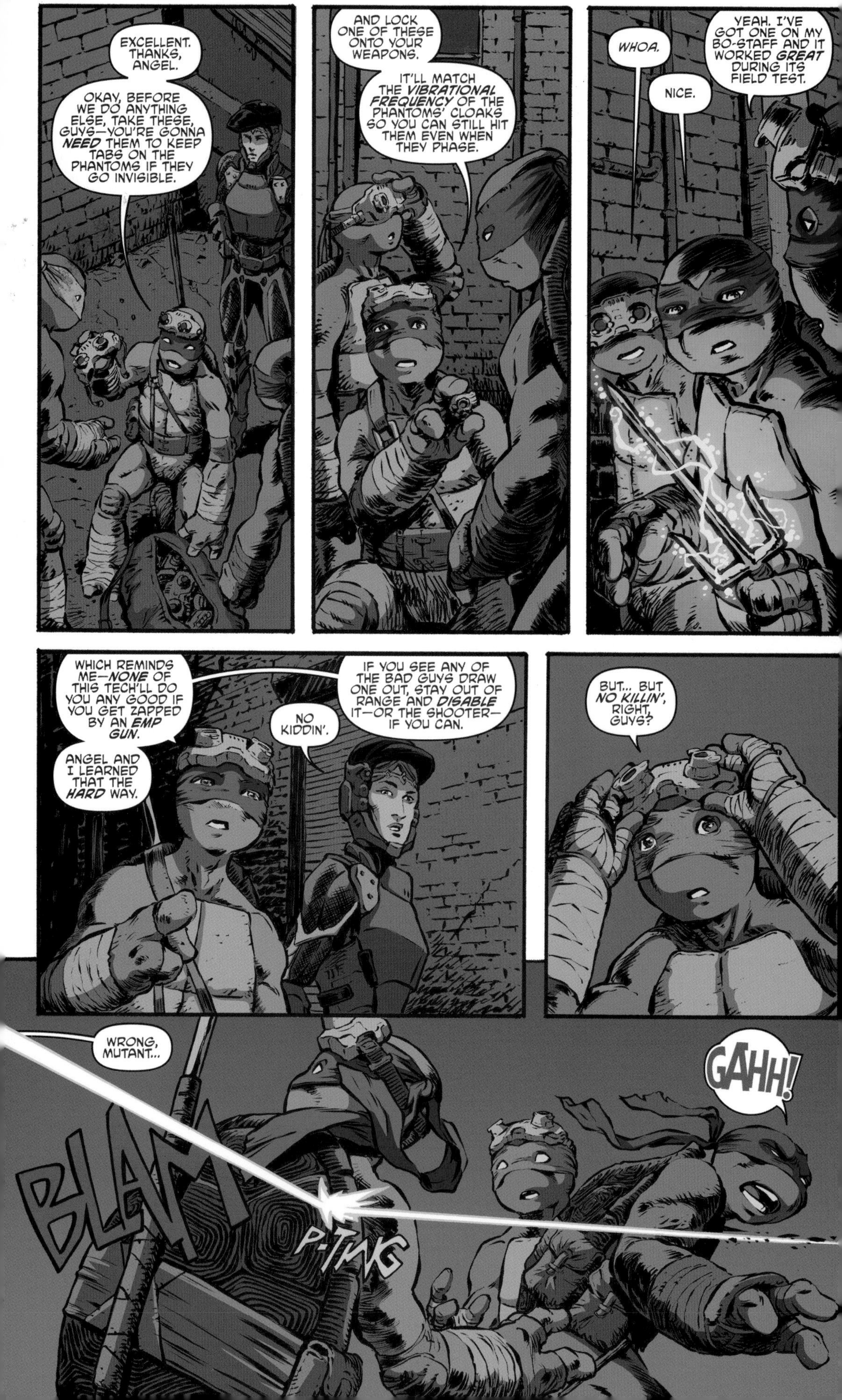
EXCELLENT. THANKS, ANGEL.
OKAY, BEFORE WE DO ANYTHING ELSE, TAKE THESE, GUYS—YOU'RE GONNA NEED THEM TO KEEP TABS ON THE PHANTOMS IF THEY GO INVISIBLE.
AND LOCK ONE OF THESE ONTO YOUR WEAPONS.
IT'LL MATCH THE VIBRATIONAL FREQUENCY OF THE PHANTOMS' CLOAKS SO YOU CAN STILL HIT THEM EVEN WHEN THEY PHASE.
WHOA.
NICE.
YEAH. I'VE GOT ONE ON MY BO-STAFF AND IT WORKED GREAT DURING ITS FIELD TEST.
WHICH REMINDS ME—NONE OF THIS TECH'LL DO YOU ANY GOOD IF YOU GET ZAPPED BY AN EMP GUN.
IF YOU SEE ANY OF THE BAD GUYS DRAW ONE OUT, STAY OUT OF RANGE AND DISABLE IT—OR THE SHOOTER—IF YOU CAN.
ANGEL AND I LEARNED THAT THE HARD WAY.
NO KIDDIN'.
BUT... BUT NO KILLIN', RIGHT, GUYS?
WRONG, MUTANT...
BLAM
P-TNNG
GAHH!

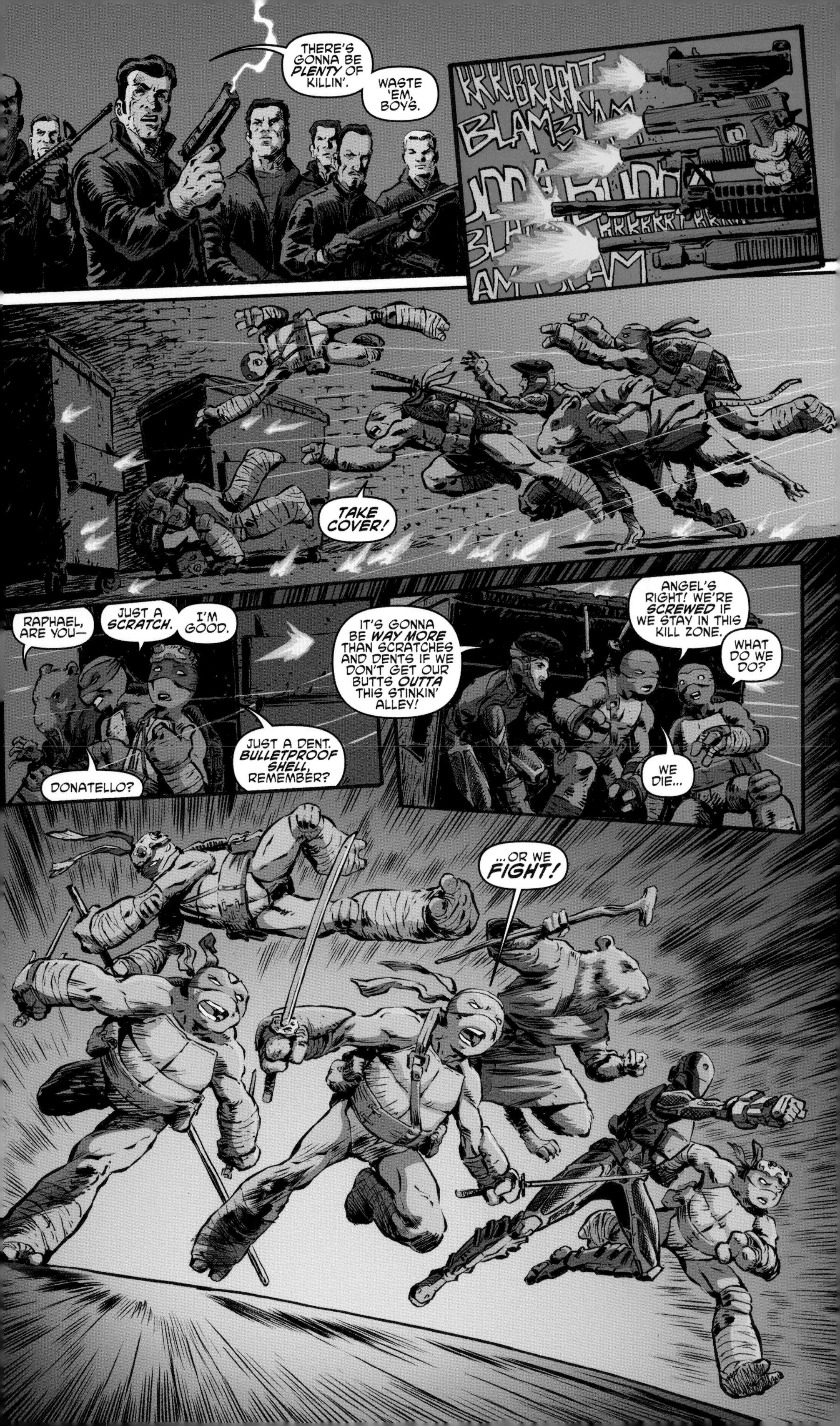

THERE'S GONNA BE PLENTY OF KILLIN'.
WASTE 'EM, BOYS.
TAKE COVER!
RAPHAEL, ARE YOU—
JUST A SCRATCH.
I'M GOOD.
DONATELLO?
JUST A DENT. BULLETPROOF SHELL, REMEMBER?
IT'S GONNA BE WAY MORE THAN SCRATCHES AND DENTS IF WE DON'T GET OUR BUTTS OUTTA THIS STINKIN' ALLEY!
ANGEL'S RIGHT! WE'RE SCREWED IF WE STAY IN THIS KILL ZONE.
WHAT DO WE DO?
WE DIE...
...OR WE FIGHT!

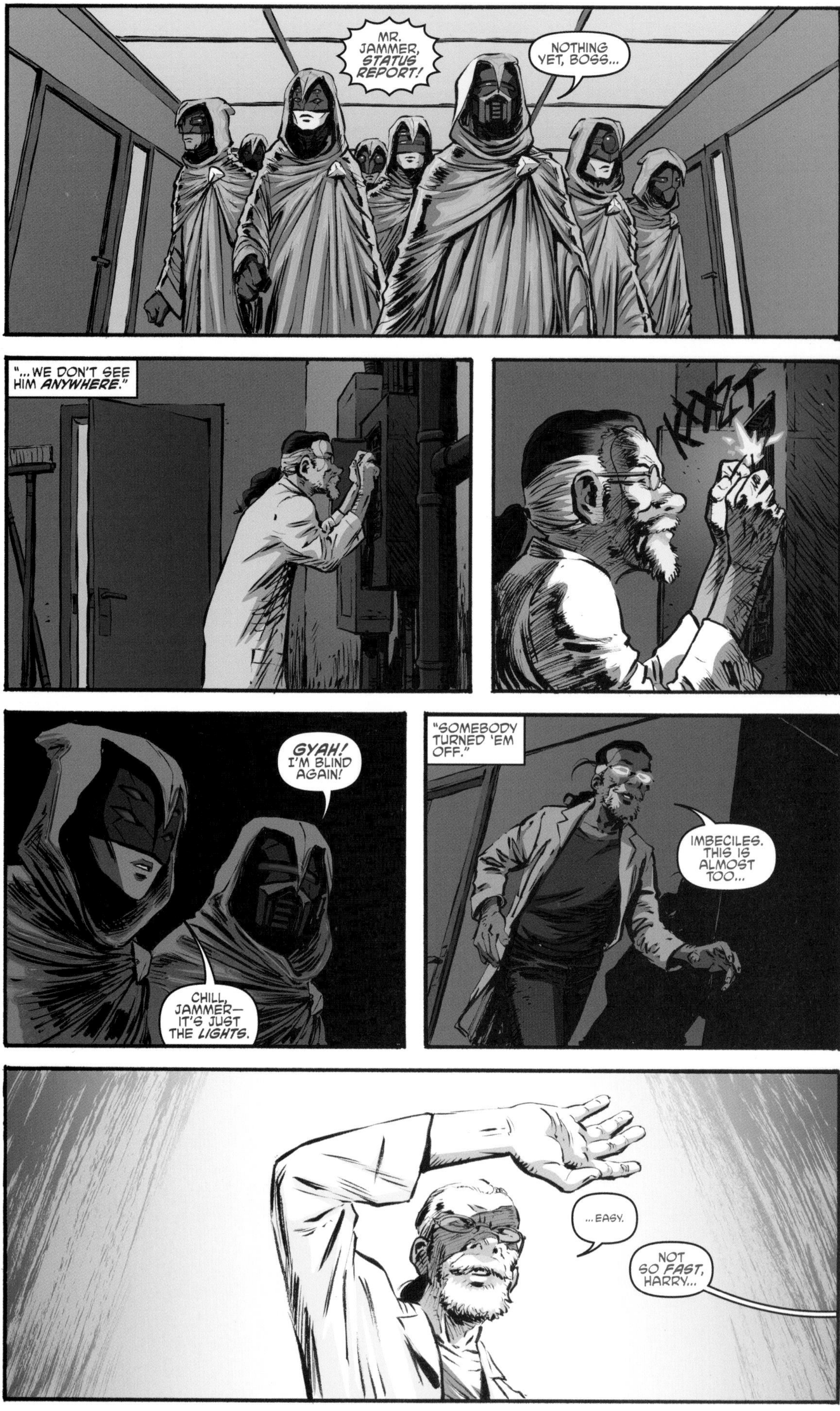
MR. JAMMER, STATUS REPORT!
NOTHING YET, BOSS...
"...WE DON'T SEE HIM ANYWHERE."
KKKZZT
GYAH! I'M BLIND AGAIN!
CHILL, JAMMER— IT'S JUST THE LIGHTS.
"SOMEBODY TURNED 'EM OFF."
IMBECILES. THIS IS ALMOST TOO...
...EASY.
NOT SO FAST, HARRY...

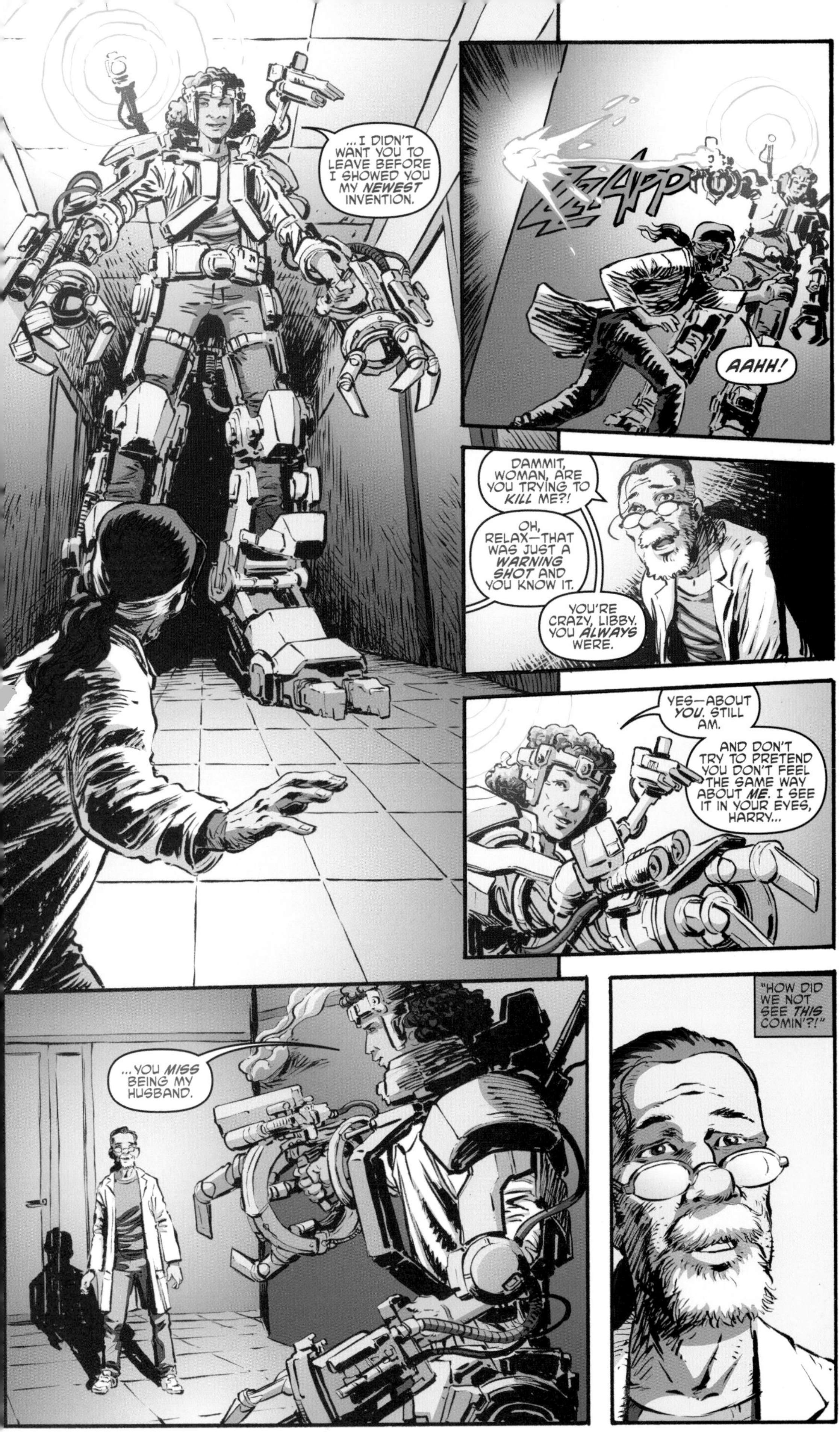
...I DIDN'T WANT YOU TO LEAVE BEFORE I SHOWED YOU MY *NEWEST* INVENTION.
ZZZAPP
AAHH!
DAMMIT, WOMAN, ARE YOU TRYING TO *KILL* ME?!
OH, RELAX—THAT WAS JUST A *WARNING SHOT* AND YOU KNOW IT.
YOU'RE CRAZY, LIBBY. YOU *ALWAYS* WERE.
YES—ABOUT *YOU*. STILL AM.
AND DON'T TRY TO PRETEND YOU DON'T FEEL THE SAME WAY ABOUT *ME*. I SEE IT IN YOUR EYES, HARRY...
...YOU *MISS* BEING MY HUSBAND.
"HOW DID WE NOT SEE *THIS* COMIN'?!"

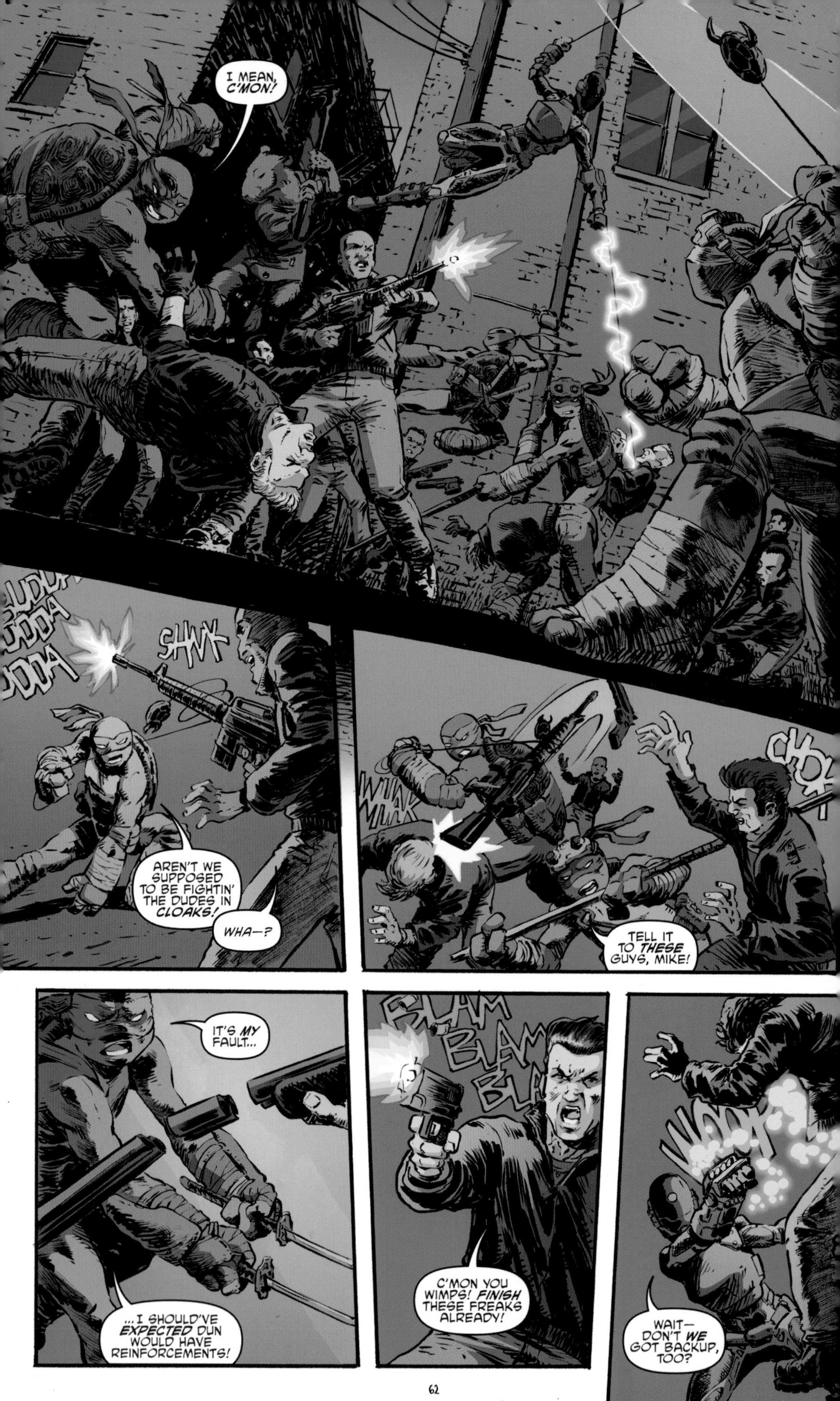

I MEAN, C'MON!
SHNK
ARE'NT WE SUPPOSED TO BE FIGHTIN' THE DUDES IN CLOAKS!
WHA—?
CHOK
TELL IT TO THESE GUYS, MIKE!
IT'S MY FAULT...
...I SHOULD'VE EXPECTED DUN WOULD HAVE REINFORCEMENTS!
BLAM BLAM
C'MON YOU WIMPS! FINISH THESE FREAKS ALREADY!
WAIT— DON'T WE GOT BACKUP, TOO?

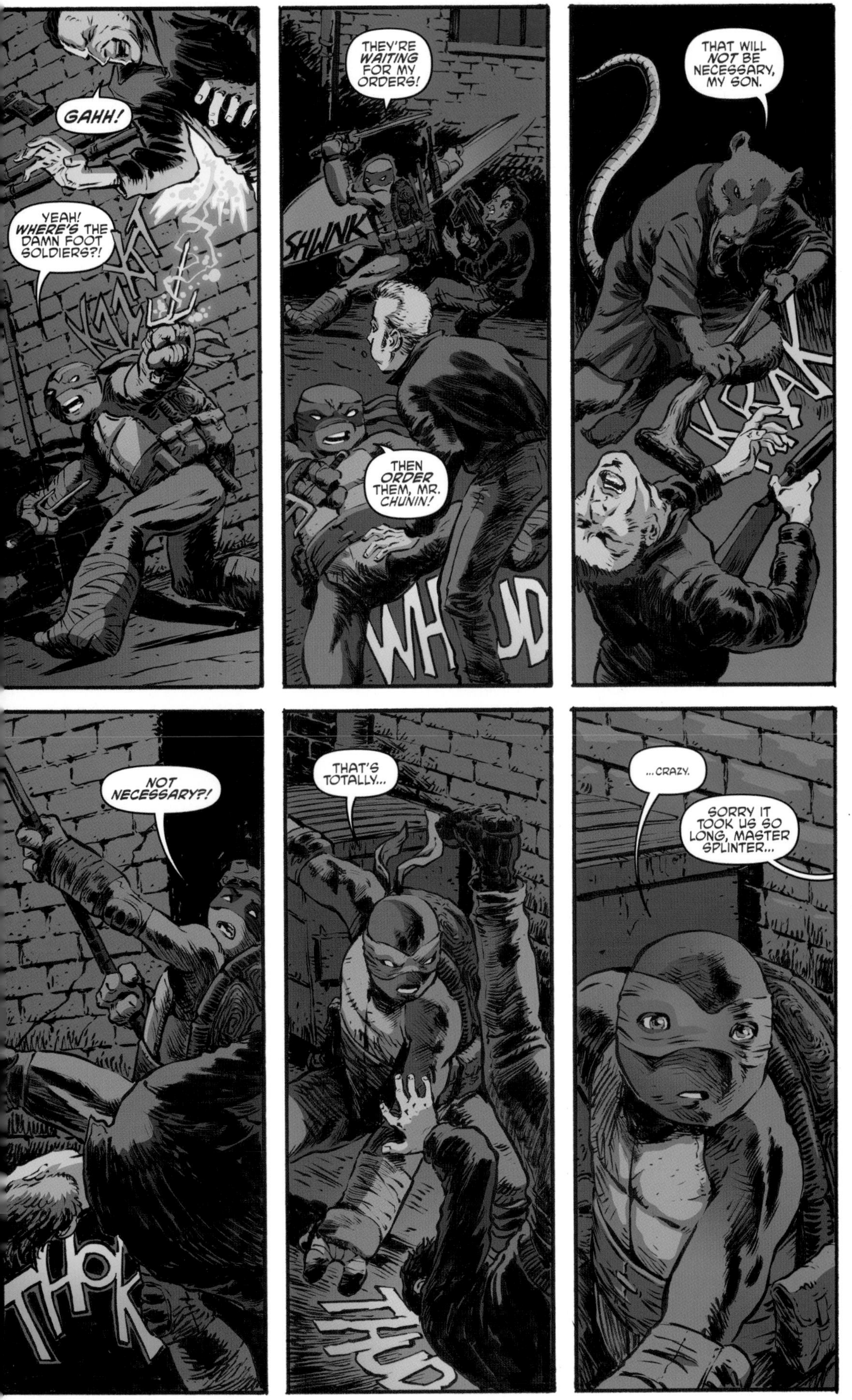
GAHH!
YEAH! WHERE'S THE DAMN FOOT SOLDIERS?!
THEY'RE WAITING FOR MY ORDERS!
SHWNK
THEN ORDER THEM, MR. CHUNIN!
WHUD
THAT WILL NOT BE NECESSARY, MY SON.
KRAK
NOT NECESSARY?!
THOK
THAT'S TOTALLY...
THUD
...CRAZY.
SORRY IT TOOK US SO LONG, MASTER SPLINTER...

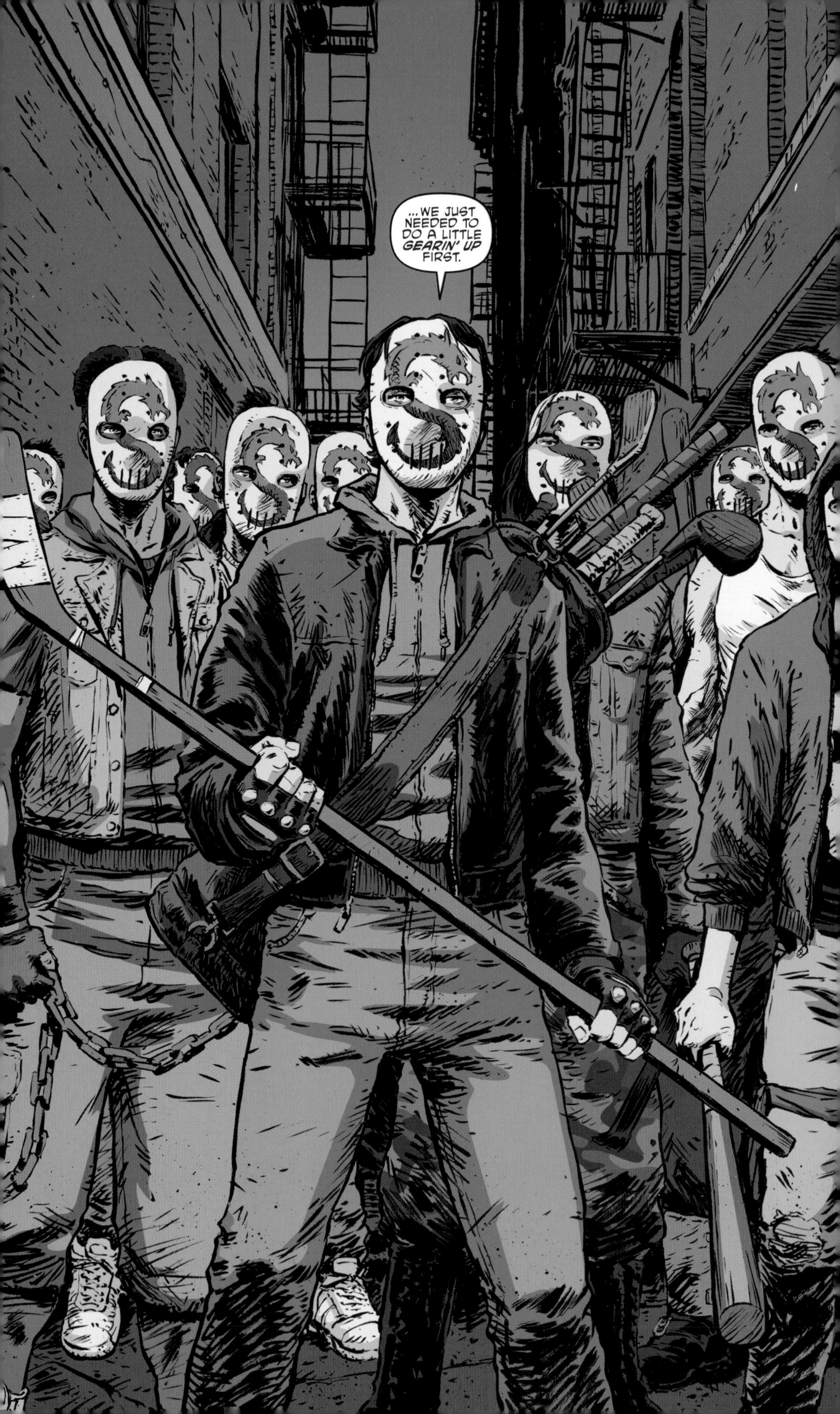
...WE JUST NEEDED TO DO A LITTLE GEARIN' UP FIRST.

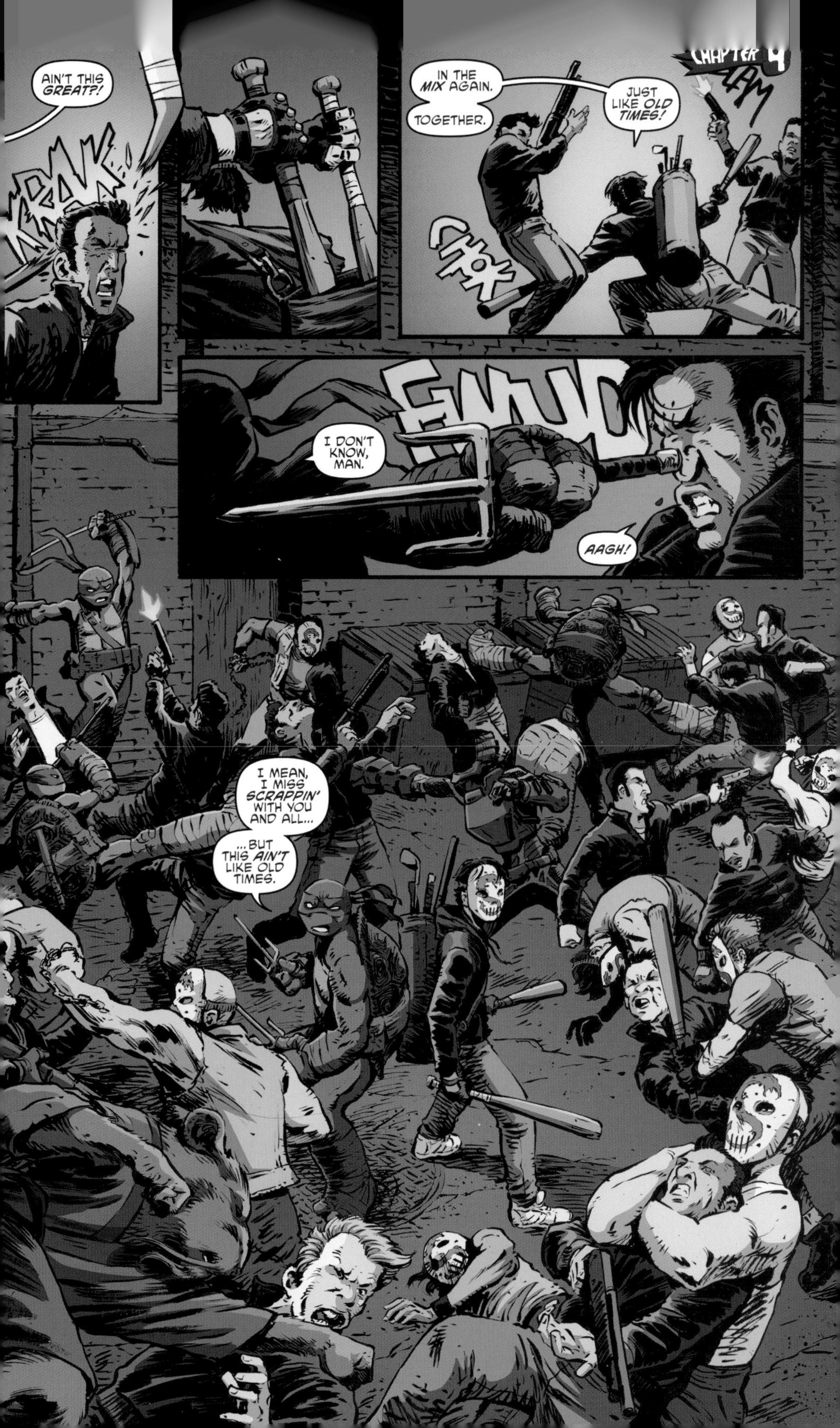
AIN'T THIS GREAT?!
KRAK
IN THE MIX AGAIN.
TOGETHER.
JUST LIKE OLD TIMES!
CHOK
I DON'T KNOW, MAN.
AAGH!
I MEAN, I MISS SCRAPPIN' WITH YOU AND ALL...
...BUT THIS AIN'T LIKE OLD TIMES.

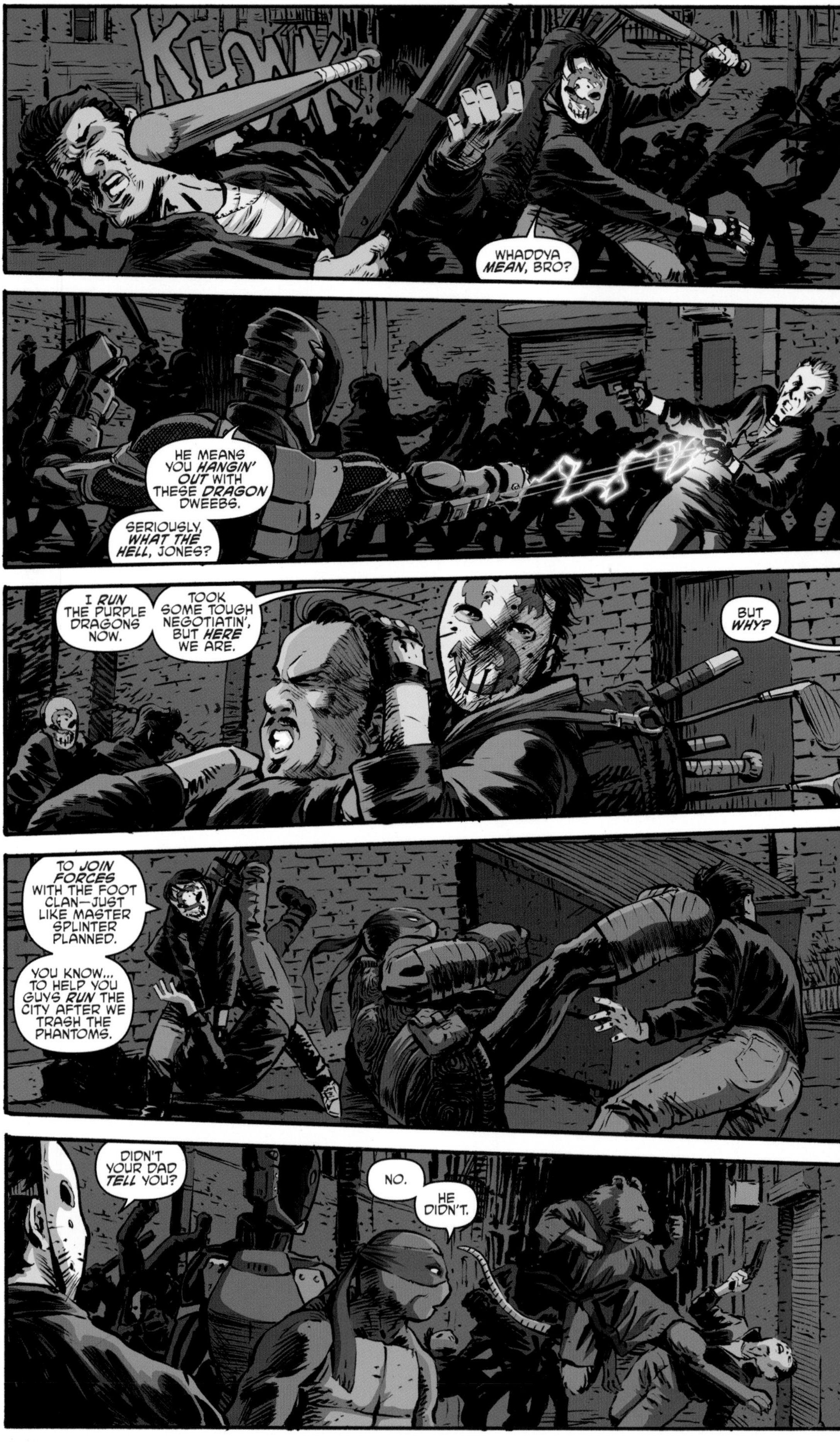
KLUNK
WHADDYA MEAN, BRO?
HE MEANS YOU HANGIN' OUT WITH THESE DRAGON DWEEBS.
SERIOUSLY, WHAT THE HELL, JONES?
I RUN THE PURPLE DRAGONS NOW.
TOOK SOME TOUGH NEGOTIATIN', BUT HERE WE ARE.
BUT WHY?
TO JOIN FORCES WITH THE FOOT CLAN—JUST LIKE MASTER SPLINTER PLANNED.
YOU KNOW... TO HELP YOU GUYS RUN THE CITY AFTER WE TRASH THE PHANTOMS.
DIDN'T YOUR DAD TELL YOU?
NO.
HE DIDN'T.

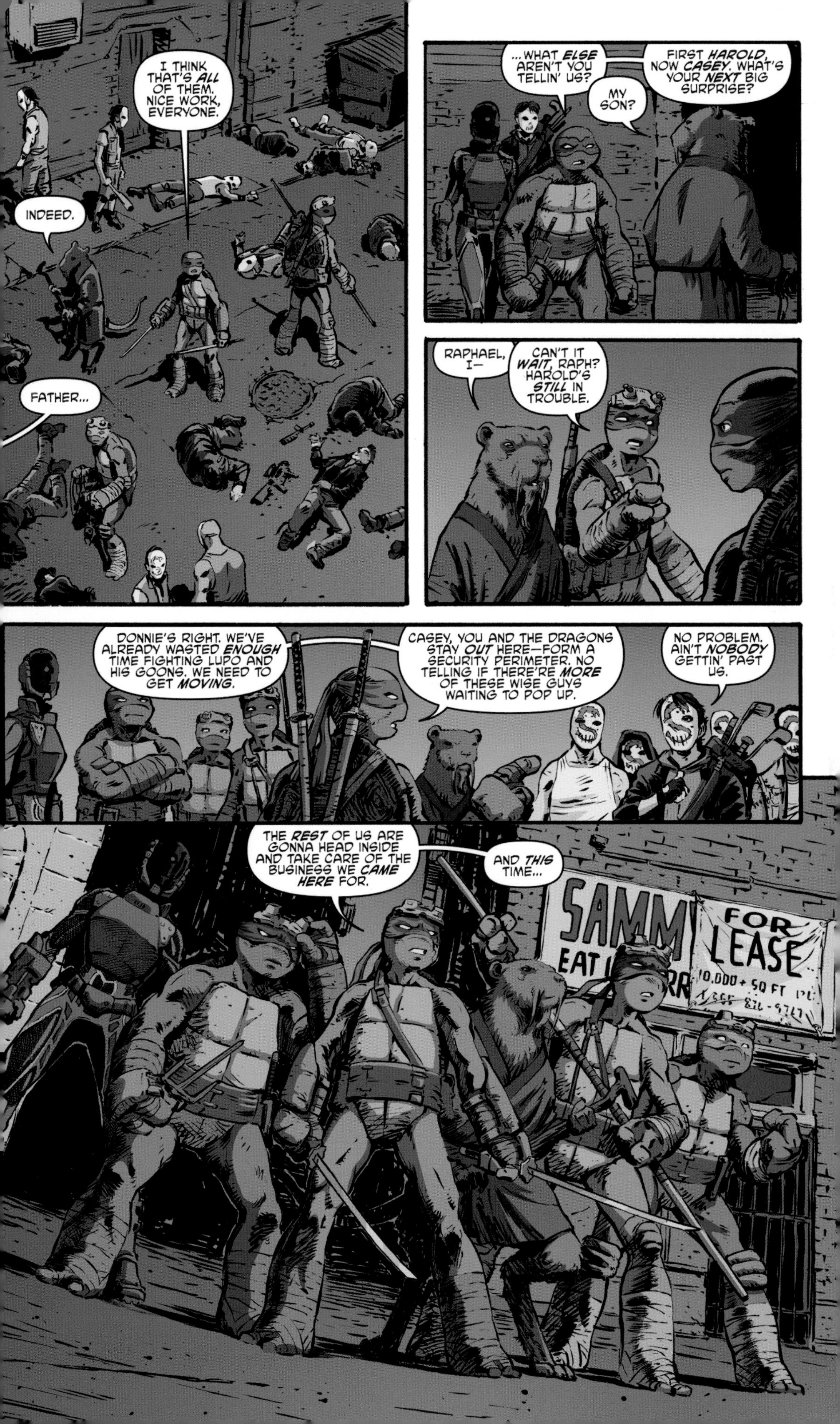
I THINK THAT'S ALL OF THEM. NICE WORK, EVERYONE.
INDEED.
FATHER...
...WHAT ELSE AREN'T YOU TELLIN' US?
MY SON?
FIRST HAROLD, NOW CASEY. WHAT'S YOUR NEXT BIG SURPRISE?
RAPHAEL, I—
CAN'T IT WAIT, RAPH? HAROLD'S STILL IN TROUBLE.
DONNIE'S RIGHT. WE'VE ALREADY WASTED ENOUGH TIME FIGHTING LUPO AND HIS GOONS. WE NEED TO GET MOVING.
CASEY, YOU AND THE DRAGONS STAY OUT HERE—FORM A SECURITY PERIMETER. NO TELLING IF THERE'RE MORE OF THESE WISE GUYS WAITING TO POP UP.
NO PROBLEM. AIN'T NOBODY GETTIN' PAST US.
THE REST OF US ARE GONNA HEAD INSIDE AND TAKE CARE OF THE BUSINESS WE CAME HERE FOR.
AND THIS TIME...
SAMM
EAT
FOR LEASE
10,000 + SQ FT

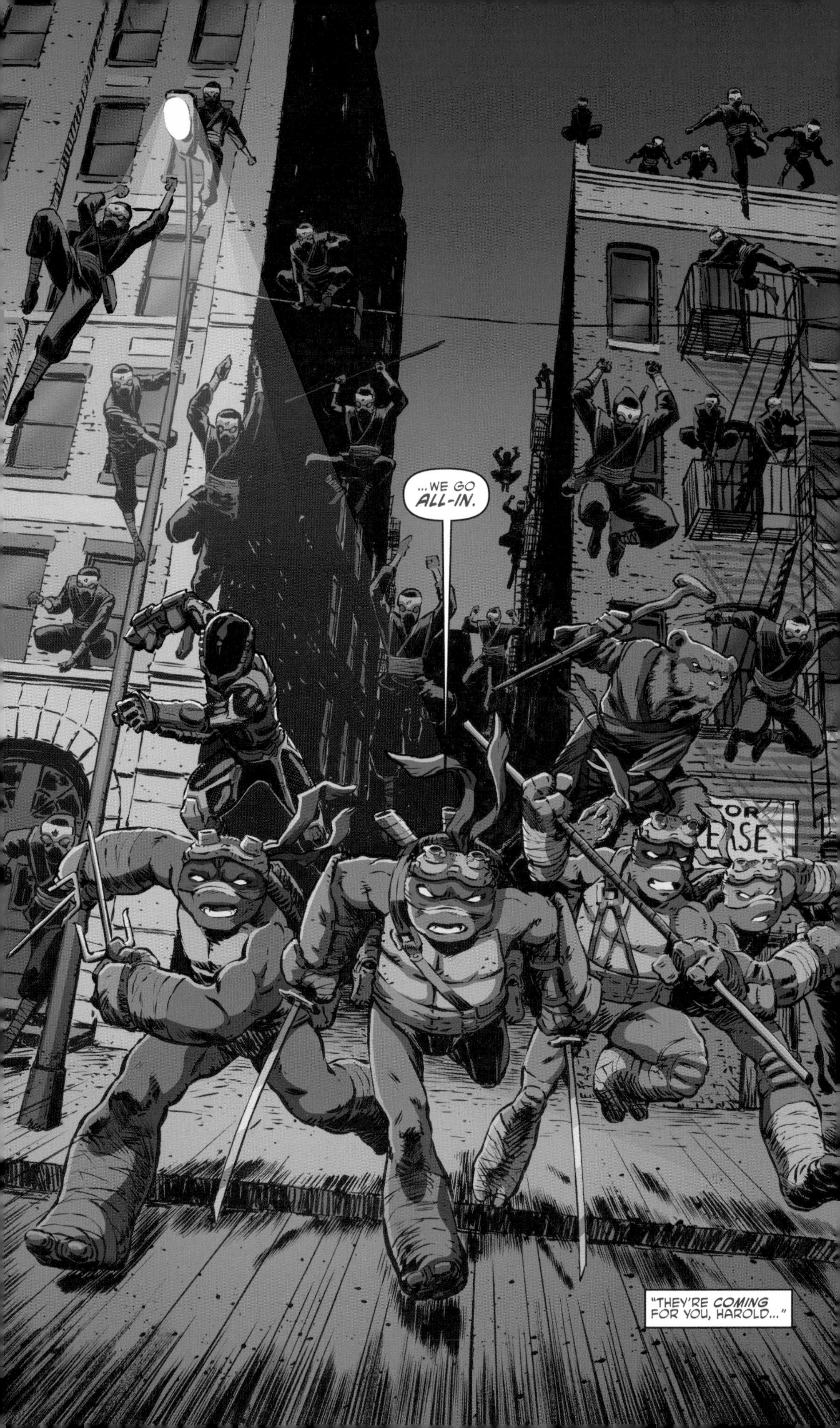

...WE GO *ALL-IN.*
FOR
RSE
"THEY'RE *COMING* FOR YOU, HAROLD..."

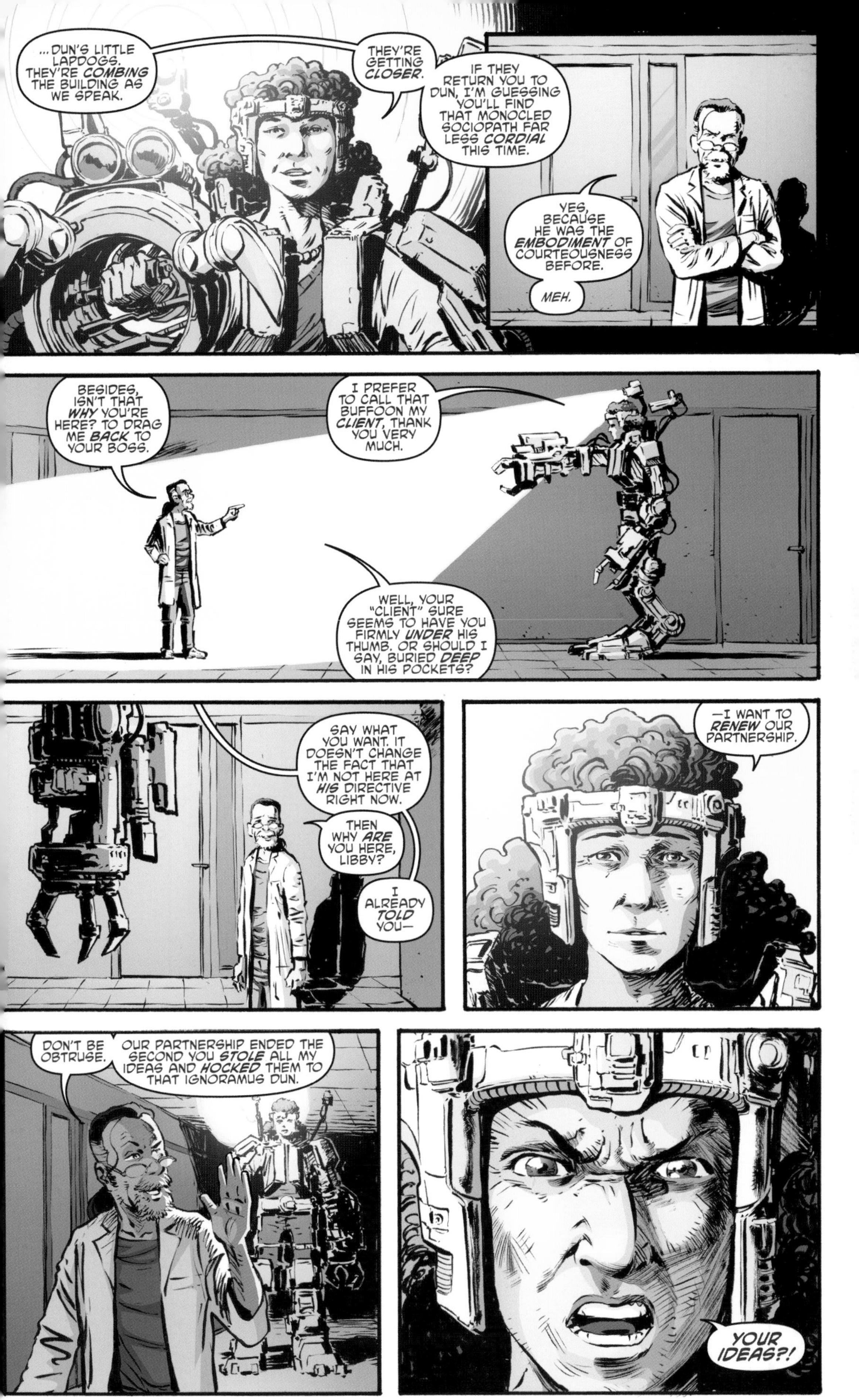
...DUN'S LITTLE LAPDOGS. THEY'RE *COMBING* THE BUILDING AS WE SPEAK.
THEY'RE GETTING *CLOSER*.
IF THEY RETURN YOU TO DUN, I'M GUESSING YOU'LL FIND THAT MONOCLED SOCIOPATH FAR LESS *CORDIAL* THIS TIME.
YES, BECAUSE HE WAS THE *EMBODIMENT* OF COURTEOUSNESS BEFORE.
MEH.
BESIDES, ISN'T THAT *WHY* YOU'RE HERE? TO DRAG ME *BACK* TO YOUR BOSS.
I PREFER TO CALL THAT BUFFOON MY *CLIENT*, THANK YOU VERY MUCH.
WELL, YOUR "CLIENT" SURE SEEMS TO HAVE YOU FIRMLY *UNDER* HIS THUMB. OR SHOULD I SAY, BURIED *DEEP* IN HIS POCKETS?
SAY WHAT YOU WANT. IT DOESN'T CHANGE THE FACT THAT I'M NOT HERE AT *HIS* DIRECTIVE RIGHT NOW.
THEN WHY *ARE* YOU HERE, LIBBY?
I ALREADY *TOLD* YOU—
—I WANT TO *RENEW* OUR PARTNERSHIP.
DON'T BE OBTRUSE.
OUR PARTNERSHIP ENDED THE SECOND YOU *STOLE* ALL MY IDEAS AND *HOCKED* THEM TO THAT IGNORAMUS DUN.
YOUR IDEAS?!

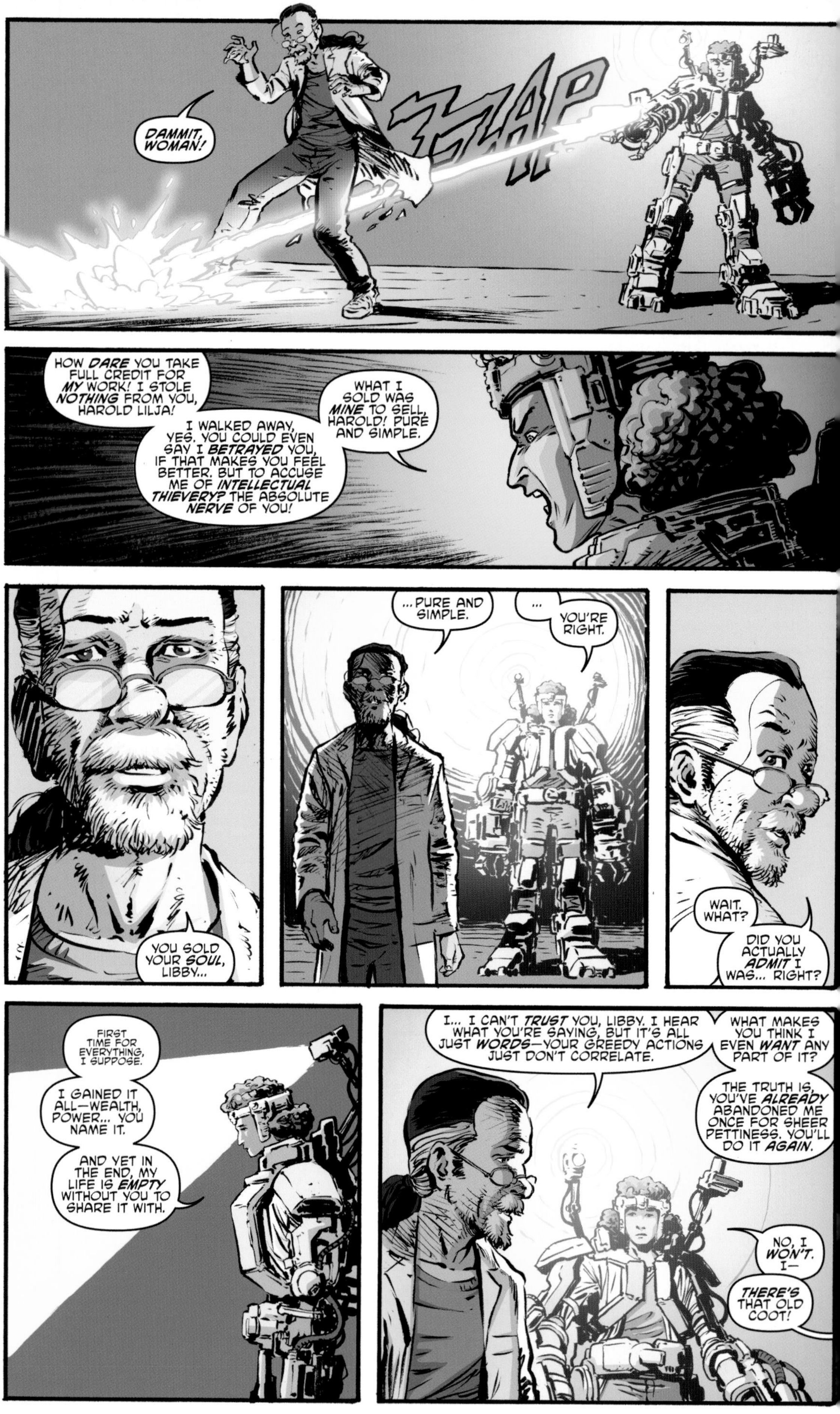
DAMMIT, WOMAN!
ZZAP
HOW DARE YOU TAKE FULL CREDIT FOR MY WORK! I STOLE NOTHING FROM YOU, HAROLD LILJA!
I WALKED AWAY, YES. YOU COULD EVEN SAY I BETRAYED YOU, IF THAT MAKES YOU FEEL BETTER. BUT TO ACCUSE ME OF INTELLECTUAL THIEVERY? THE ABSOLUTE NERVE OF YOU!
WHAT I SOLD WAS MINE TO SELL, HAROLD! PURE AND SIMPLE.
YOU SOLD YOUR SOUL, LIBBY...
...PURE AND SIMPLE.
...
YOU'RE RIGHT.
WAIT. WHAT?
DID YOU ACTUALLY ADMIT I WAS... RIGHT?
FIRST TIME FOR EVERYTHING, I SUPPOSE.
I GAINED IT ALL—WEALTH, POWER... YOU NAME IT.
AND YET IN THE END, MY LIFE IS EMPTY WITHOUT YOU TO SHARE IT WITH.
I... I CAN'T TRUST YOU, LIBBY. I HEAR WHAT YOU'RE SAYING, BUT IT'S ALL JUST WORDS—YOUR GREEDY ACTIONS JUST DON'T CORRELATE.
WHAT MAKES YOU THINK I EVEN WANT ANY PART OF IT?
THE TRUTH IS, YOU'VE ALREADY ABANDONED ME ONCE FOR SHEER PETTINESS. YOU'LL DO IT AGAIN.
NO, I WON'T. I—
THERE'S THAT OLD COOT!

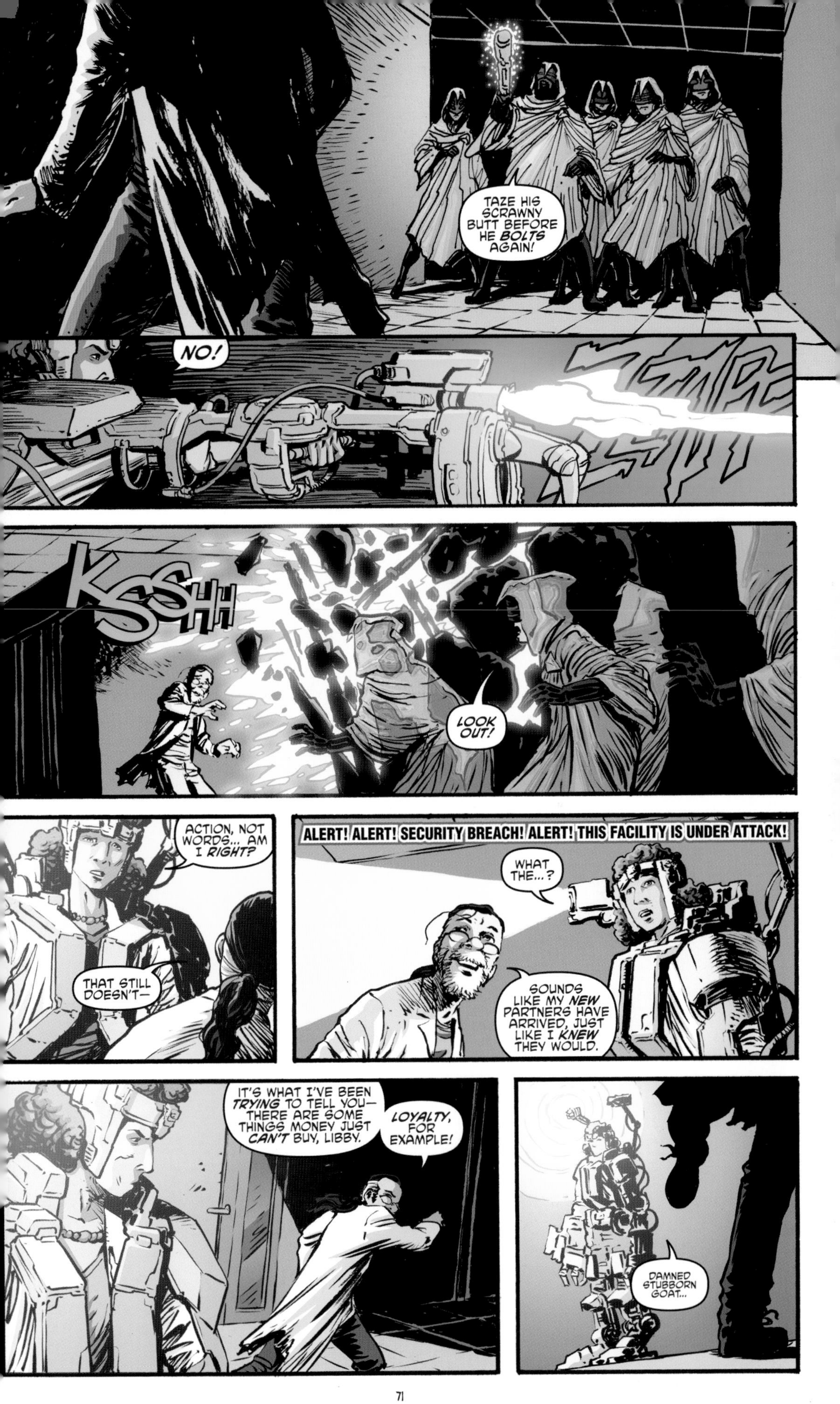
TAZE HIS SCRAWNY BUTT BEFORE HE BOLTS AGAIN!
NO!
KSSHHH
LOOK OUT!
ACTION, NOT WORDS... AM I RIGHT?
THAT STILL DOESN'T—
ALERT! ALERT! SECURITY BREACH! ALERT! THIS FACILITY IS UNDER ATTACK!
WHAT THE...?
SOUNDS LIKE MY NEW PARTNERS HAVE ARRIVED, JUST LIKE I KNEW THEY WOULD.
IT'S WHAT I'VE BEEN TRYING TO TELL YOU— THERE ARE SOME THINGS MONEY JUST CAN'T BUY, LIBBY.
LOYALTY, FOR EXAMPLE!
DAMNED STUBBORN GOAT...

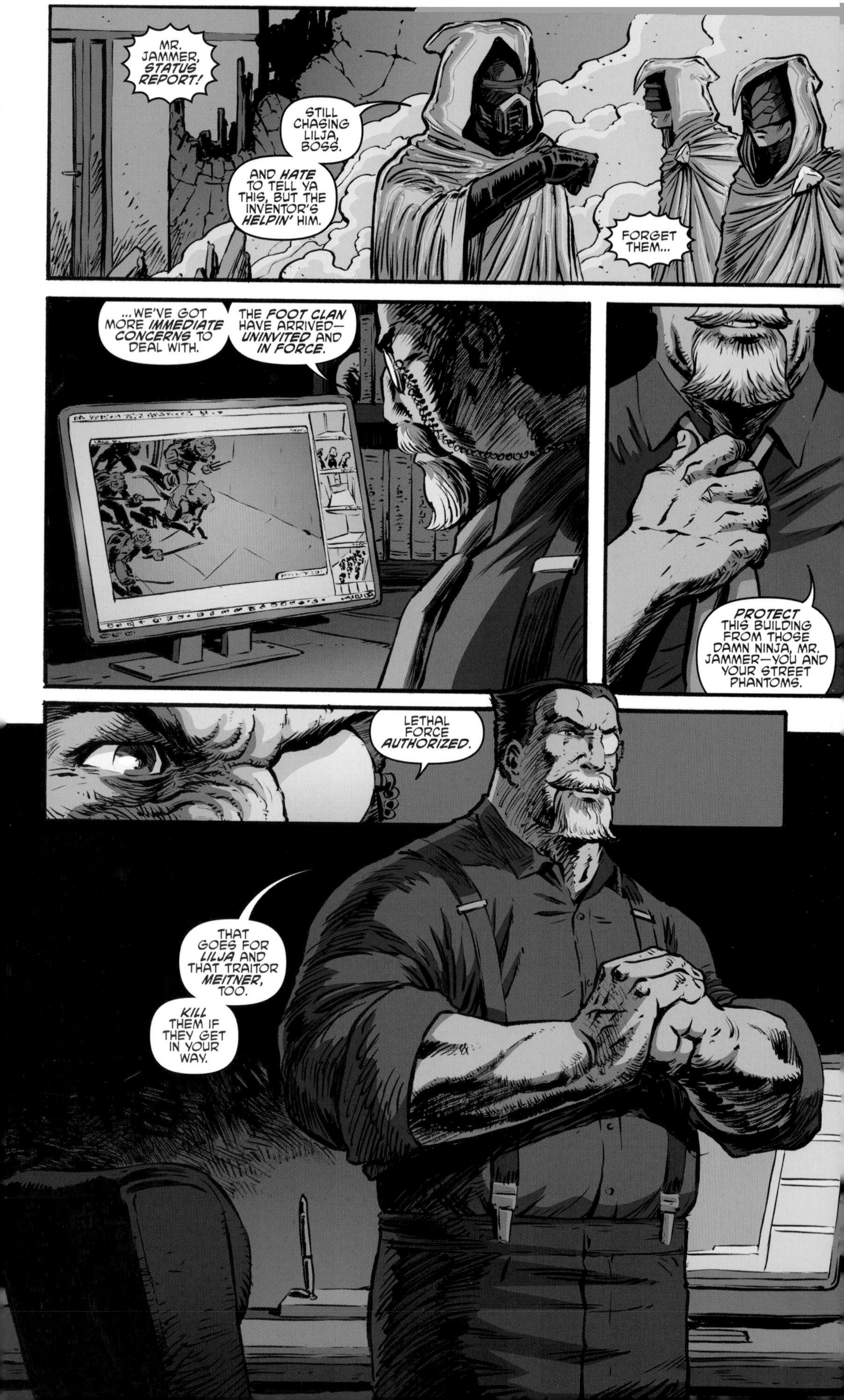
MR. JAMMER, STATUS REPORT!
STILL CHASING LILJA, BOSS.
AND HATE TO TELL YA THIS, BUT THE INVENTOR'S HELPIN' HIM.
FORGET THEM...
...WE'VE GOT MORE IMMEDIATE CONCERNS TO DEAL WITH.
THE FOOT CLAN HAVE ARRIVED— UNINVITED AND IN FORCE.
PROTECT THIS BUILDING FROM THOSE DAMN NINJA, MR. JAMMER—YOU AND YOUR STREET PHANTOMS.
LETHAL FORCE AUTHORIZED.
THAT GOES FOR LILJA AND THAT TRAITOR MEITNER, TOO.
KILL THEM IF THEY GET IN YOUR WAY.

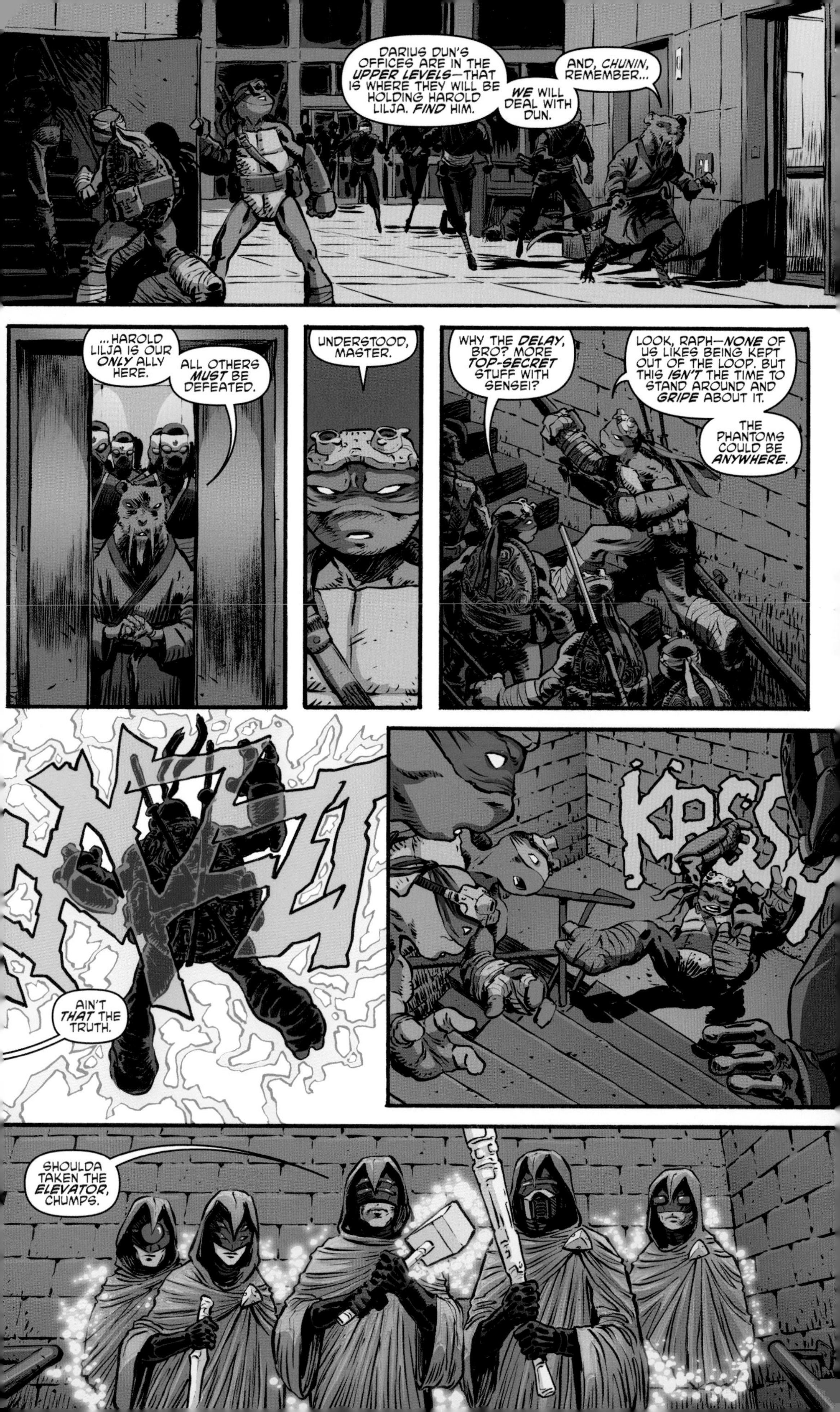
DARIUS DUN'S OFFICES ARE IN THE *UPPER LEVELS*—THAT IS WHERE THEY WILL BE HOLDING HAROLD LILJA. *FIND* HIM.
AND, *CHUNIN*, REMEMBER...
WE WILL DEAL WITH DUN.
...HAROLD LILJA IS OUR *ONLY* ALLY HERE.
ALL OTHERS *MUST* BE DEFEATED.
UNDERSTOOD, MASTER.
WHY THE *DELAY*, BRO? MORE *TOP-SECRET* STUFF WITH SENSEI?
LOOK, RAPH—*NONE* OF US LIKES BEING KEPT OUT OF THE LOOP. BUT THIS *ISN'T* THE TIME TO STAND AROUND AND *GRIPE* ABOUT IT.
THE PHANTOMS COULD BE *ANYWHERE*.
AIN'T *THAT* THE TRUTH.
KRSSH
SHOULDA TAKEN THE *ELEVATOR*, CHUMPS.

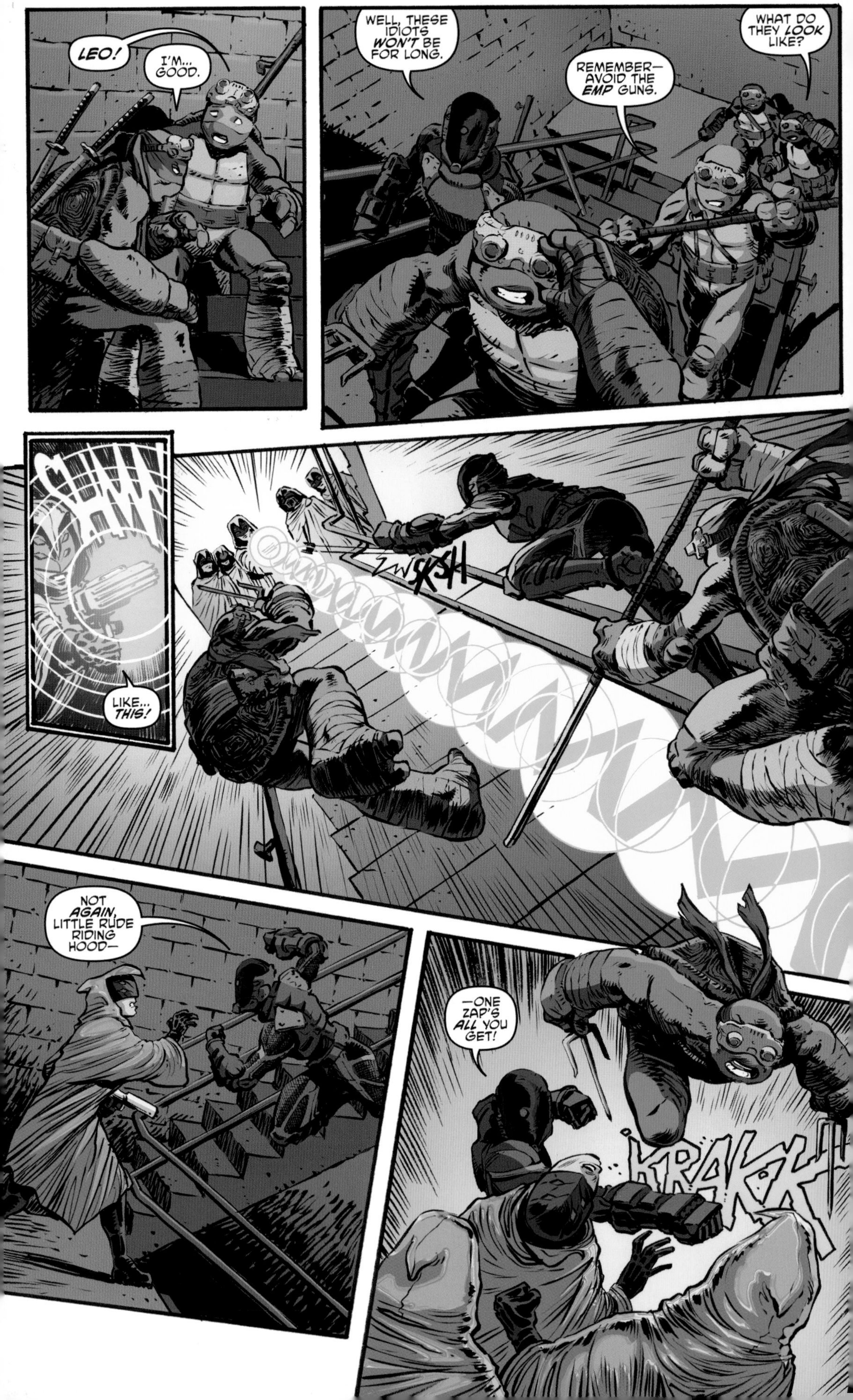
LEO!
I'M... GOOD.
WELL, THESE IDIOTS WON'T BE FOR LONG.
REMEMBER— AVOID THE EMP GUNS.
WHAT DO THEY LOOK LIKE?
LIKE... THIS!
ZWSKSH
NOT AGAIN, LITTLE RUDE RIDING HOOD—
—ONE ZAP'S ALL YOU GET!
KRAKK

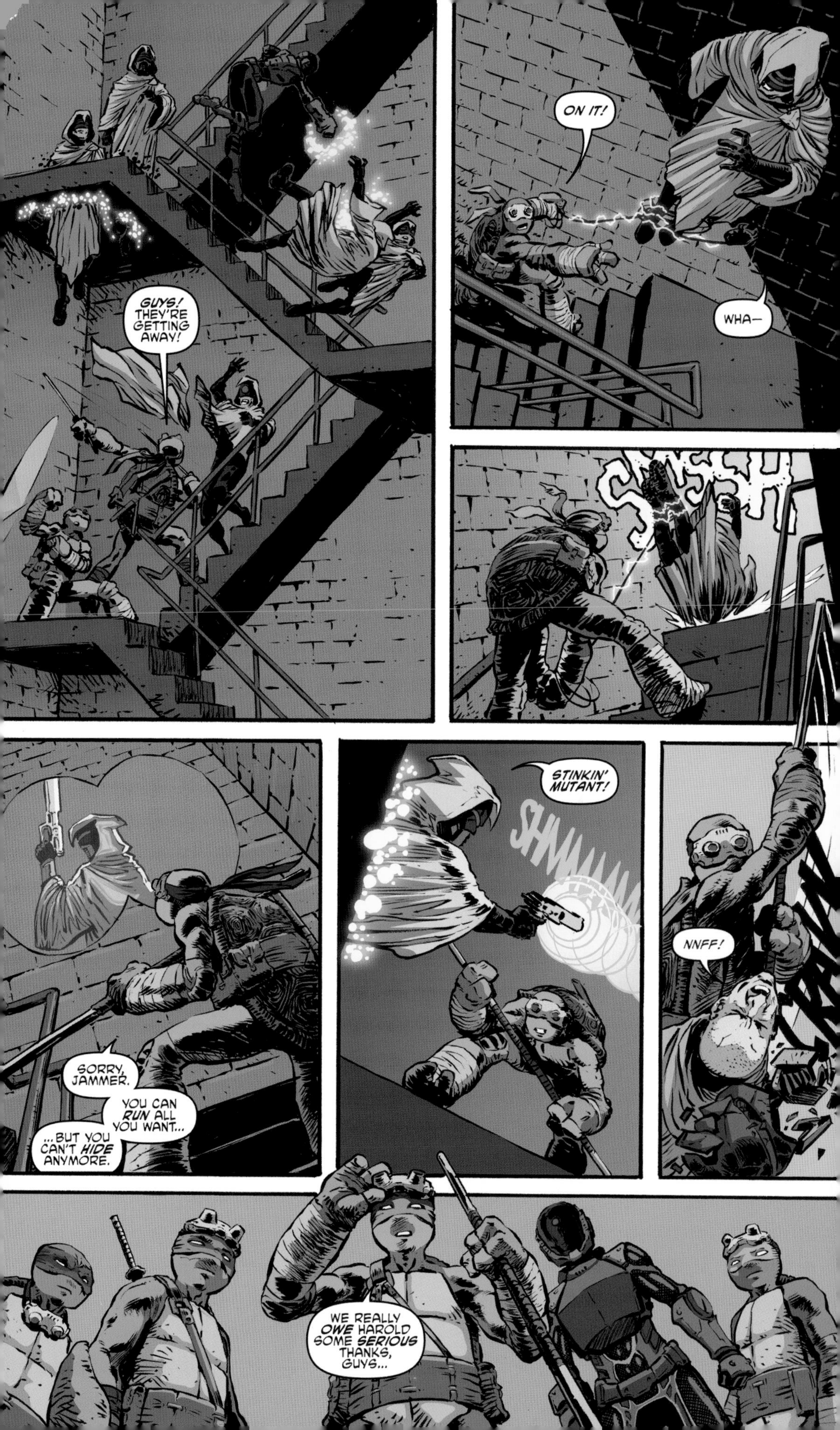
GUYS! THEY'RE GETTING AWAY!
ON IT!
WHA—
SORRY, JAMMER.
YOU CAN *RUN* ALL YOU WANT...
...BUT YOU CAN'T *HIDE* ANYMORE.
STINKIN' MUTANT!
NNFF!
WE REALLY *OWE* HAROLD SOME *SERIOUS* THANKS, GUYS...

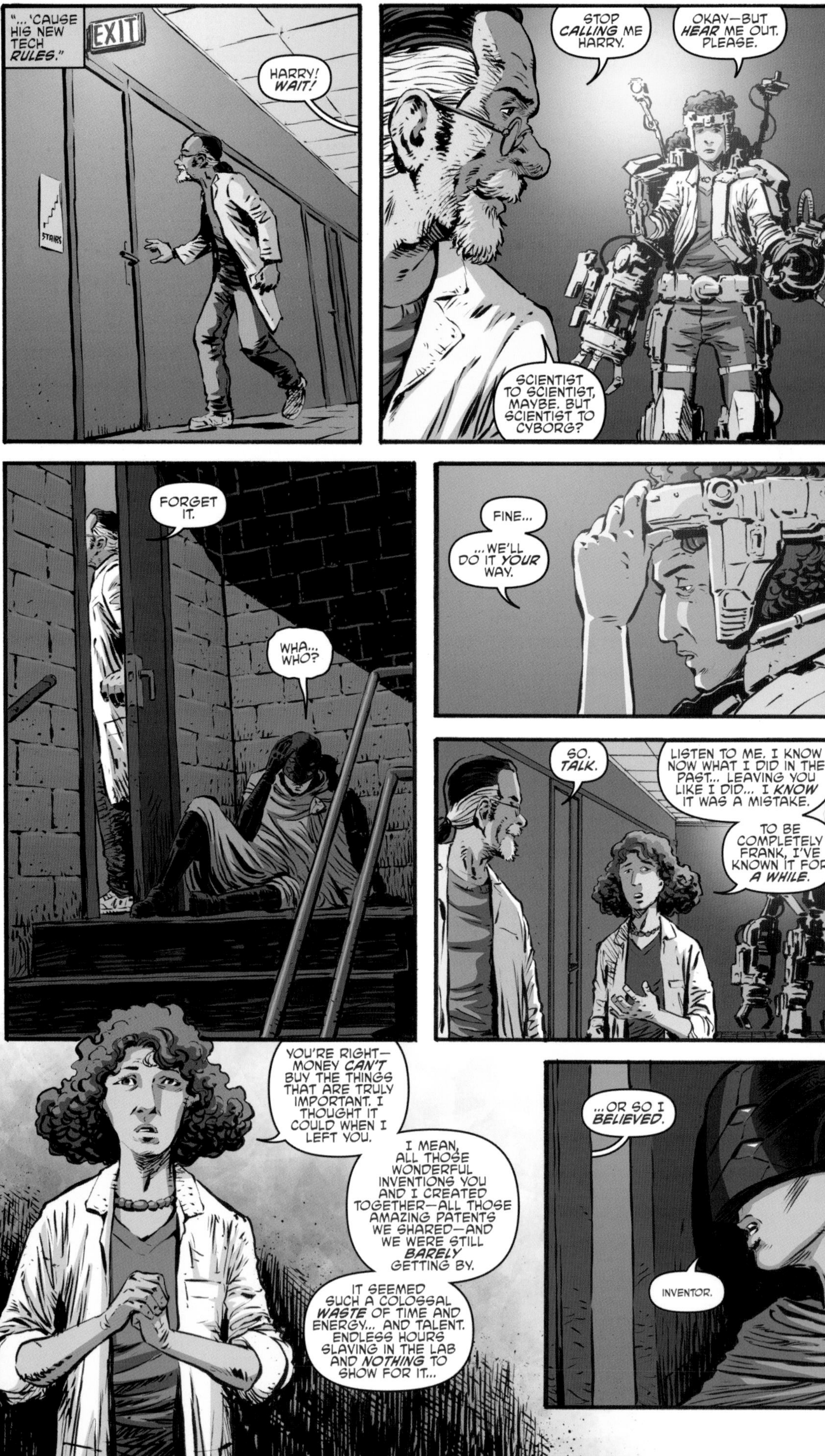
"...'CAUSE HIS NEW TECH RULES."
EXIT
HARRY! WAIT!
STAIRS
STOP CALLING ME HARRY.
OKAY—BUT HEAR ME OUT. PLEASE.
SCIENTIST TO SCIENTIST, MAYBE. BUT SCIENTIST TO CYBORG?
FORGET IT.
WHA... WHO?
FINE...
...WE'LL DO IT YOUR WAY.
SO. TALK.
LISTEN TO ME. I KNOW NOW WHAT I DID IN THE PAST... LEAVING YOU LIKE I DID... I KNOW IT WAS A MISTAKE.
TO BE COMPLETELY FRANK, I'VE KNOWN IT FOR A WHILE.
YOU'RE RIGHT—MONEY CAN'T BUY THE THINGS THAT ARE TRULY IMPORTANT. I THOUGHT IT COULD WHEN I LEFT YOU.
I MEAN, ALL THOSE WONDERFUL INVENTIONS YOU AND I CREATED TOGETHER—ALL THOSE AMAZING PATENTS WE SHARED—AND WE WERE STILL BARELY GETTING BY.
IT SEEMED SUCH A COLOSSAL WASTE OF TIME AND ENERGY... AND TALENT. ENDLESS HOURS SLAVING IN THE LAB AND NOTHING TO SHOW FOR IT...
...OR SO I BELIEVED.
INVENTOR.

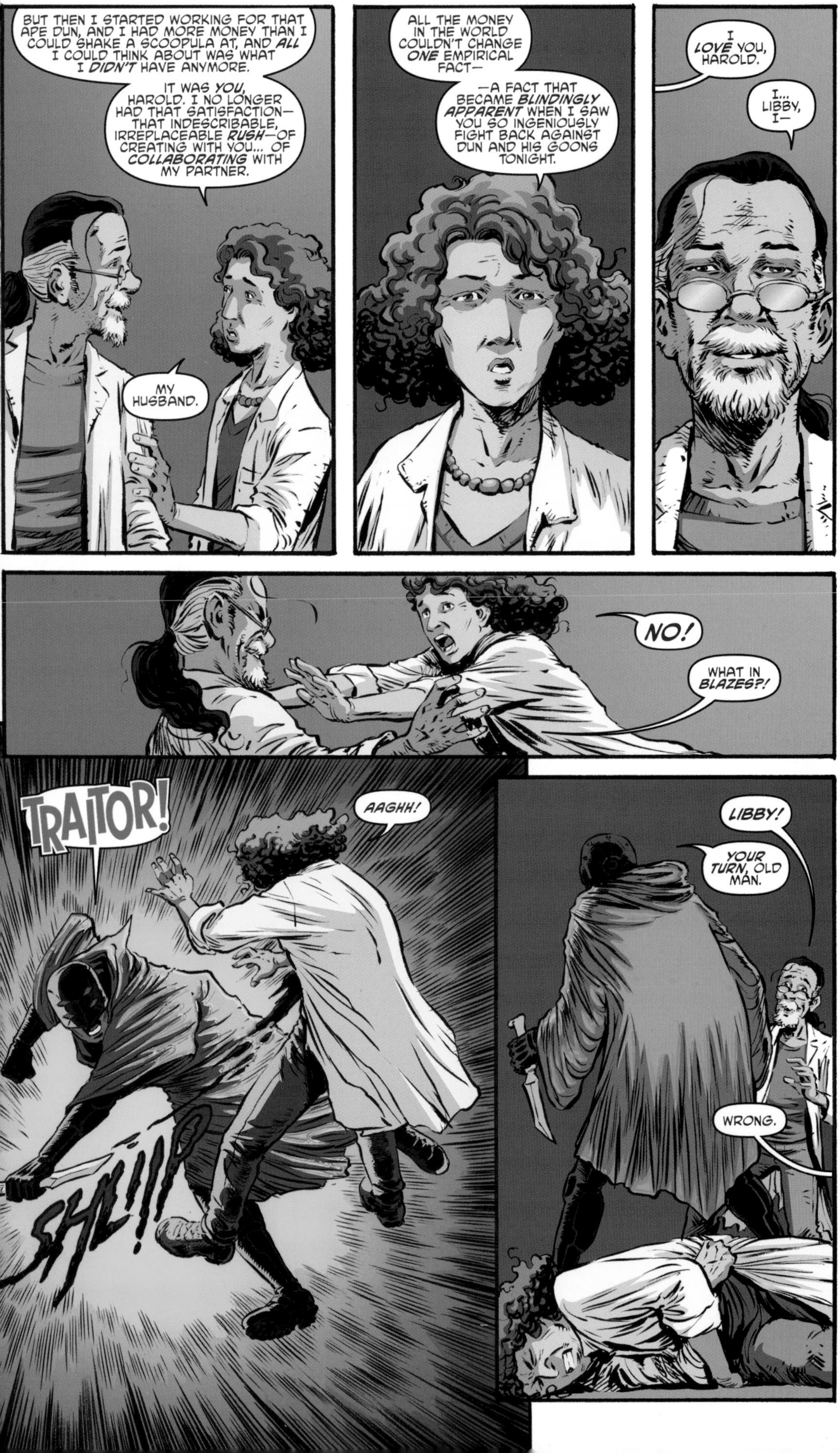
BUT THEN I STARTED WORKING FOR THAT APE DUN, AND I HAD MORE MONEY THAN I COULD SHAKE A SCOOPULA AT, AND *ALL* I COULD THINK ABOUT WAS WHAT I *DIDN'T* HAVE ANYMORE.
IT WAS *YOU*, HAROLD. I NO LONGER HAD THAT SATISFACTION—THAT INDESCRIBABLE, IRREPLACEABLE *RUSH*—OF CREATING WITH YOU... OF *COLLABORATING* WITH MY PARTNER.
MY HUSBAND.
ALL THE MONEY IN THE WORLD COULDN'T CHANGE *ONE* EMPIRICAL FACT—
—A FACT THAT BECAME *BLINDINGLY APPARENT* WHEN I SAW YOU SO INGENIOUSLY FIGHT BACK AGAINST DUN AND HIS GOONS TONIGHT.
I *LOVE* YOU, HAROLD.
I... LIBBY, I—
NO!
WHAT IN *BLAZES?!*
TRAITOR!
AAGHH!
SHLIIP
LIBBY!
YOUR TURN, OLD MAN.
WRONG.

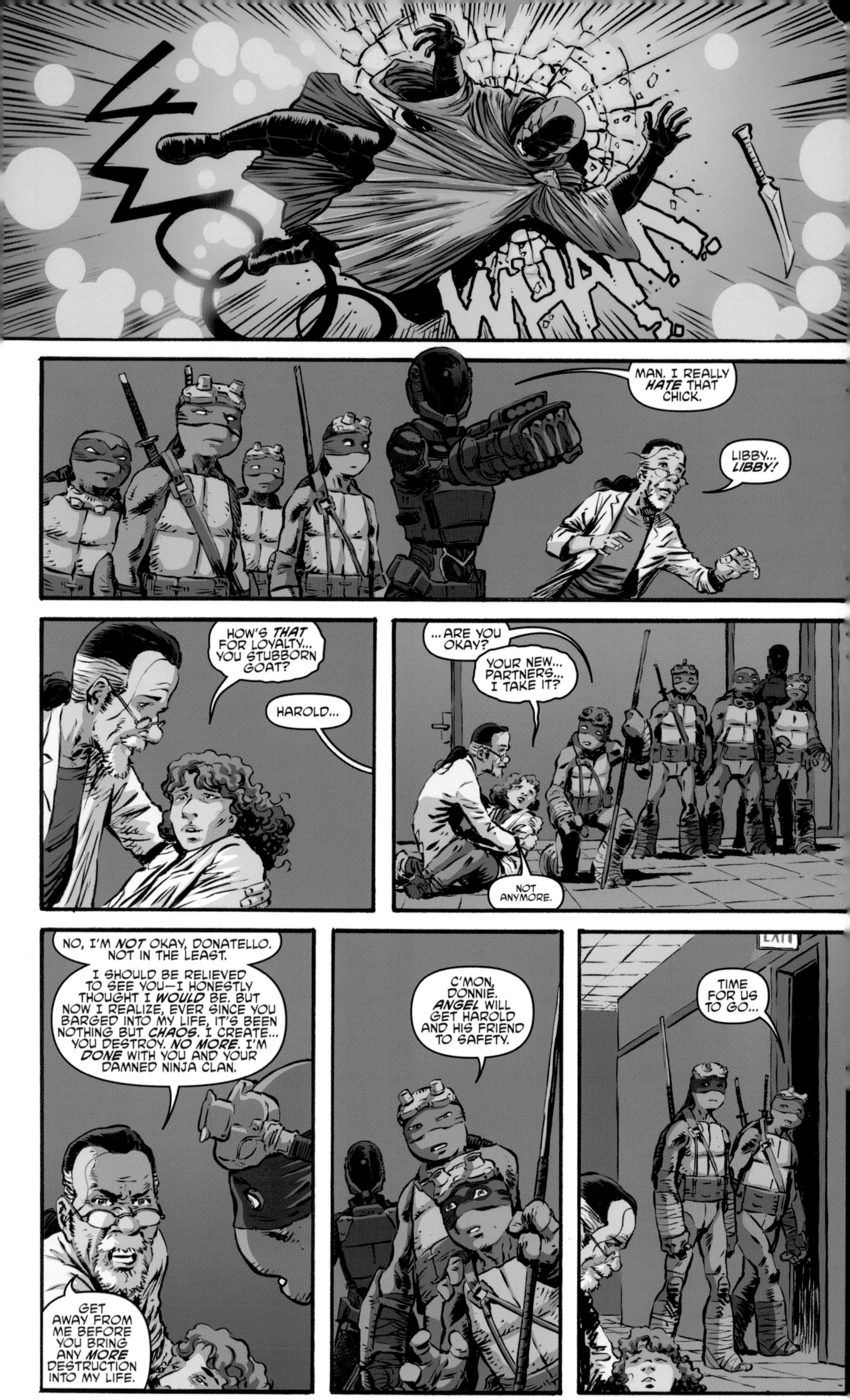

WOOOOOM
WHAM
MAN. I REALLY HATE THAT CHICK.
LIBBY... LIBBY!
HOW'S THAT FOR LOYALTY... YOU STUBBORN GOAT?
HAROLD...
...ARE YOU OKAY?
YOUR NEW... PARTNERS... I TAKE IT?
NOT ANYMORE.
NO, I'M NOT OKAY, DONATELLO. NOT IN THE LEAST.
I SHOULD BE RELIEVED TO SEE YOU—I HONESTLY THOUGHT I WOULD BE. BUT NOW I REALIZE, EVER SINCE YOU BARGED INTO MY LIFE, IT'S BEEN NOTHING BUT CHAOS. I CREATE... YOU DESTROY. NO MORE. I'M DONE WITH YOU AND YOUR DAMNED NINJA CLAN.
GET AWAY FROM ME BEFORE YOU BRING ANY MORE DESTRUCTION INTO MY LIFE.
C'MON, DONNIE. ANGEL WILL GET HAROLD AND HIS FRIEND TO SAFETY.
TIME FOR US TO GO...

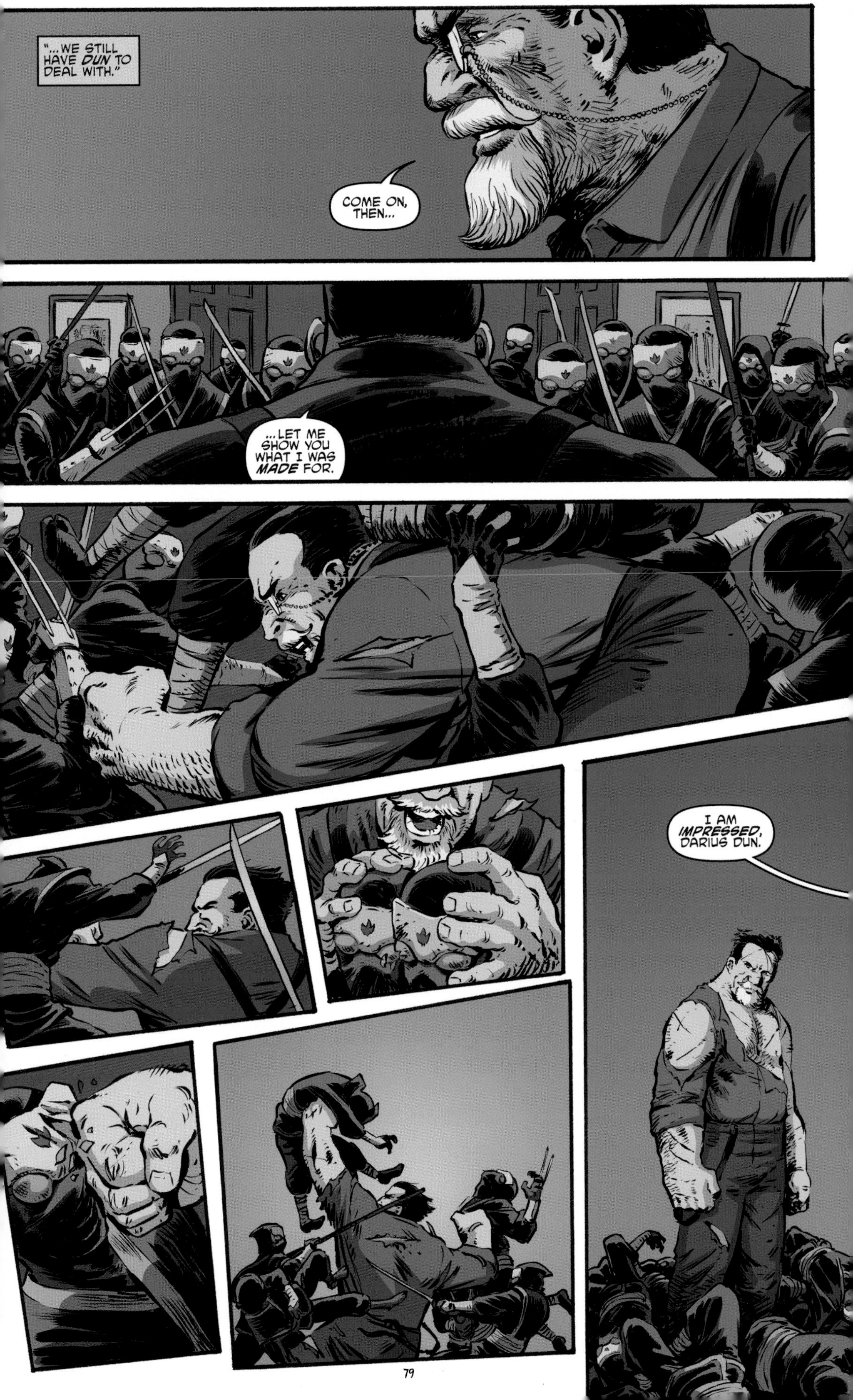
"...WE STILL HAVE *DUN* TO DEAL WITH."
COME ON, THEN...
...LET ME SHOW YOU WHAT I WAS *MADE* FOR.
I AM *IMPRESSED*, DARIUS DUN.

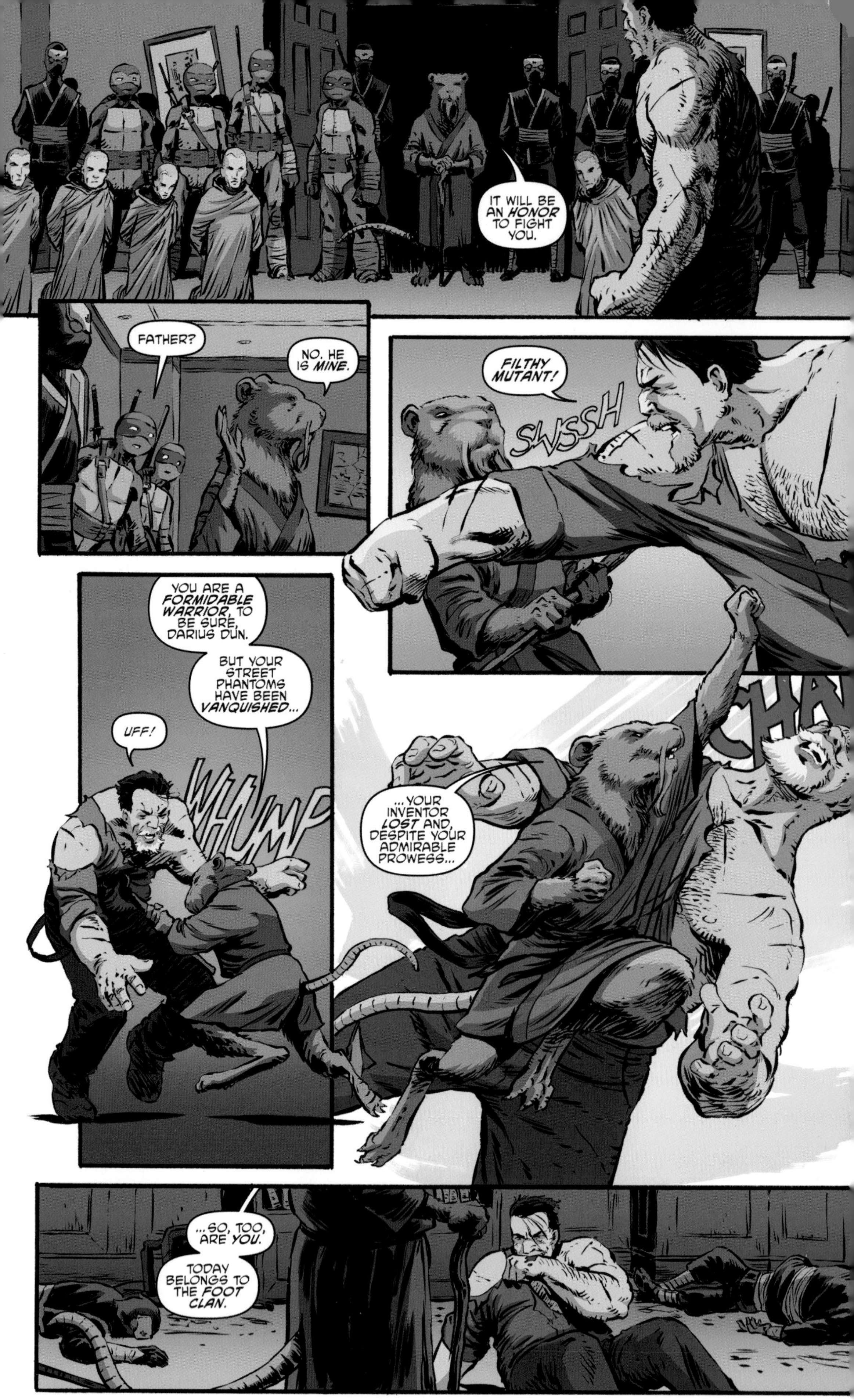
IT WILL BE AN *HONOR* TO FIGHT YOU.
FATHER?
NO. HE IS *MINE*.
FILTHY MUTANT!
SWSSH
YOU ARE A *FORMIDABLE WARRIOR*, TO BE SURE, DARIUS DUN.
BUT YOUR STREET PHANTOMS HAVE BEEN *VANQUISHED*...
UFF!
WHUMP
...YOUR INVENTOR *LOST* AND, DESPITE YOUR ADMIRABLE PROWESS...
...SO, TOO, ARE *YOU*.
TODAY BELONGS TO THE *FOOT CLAN*.

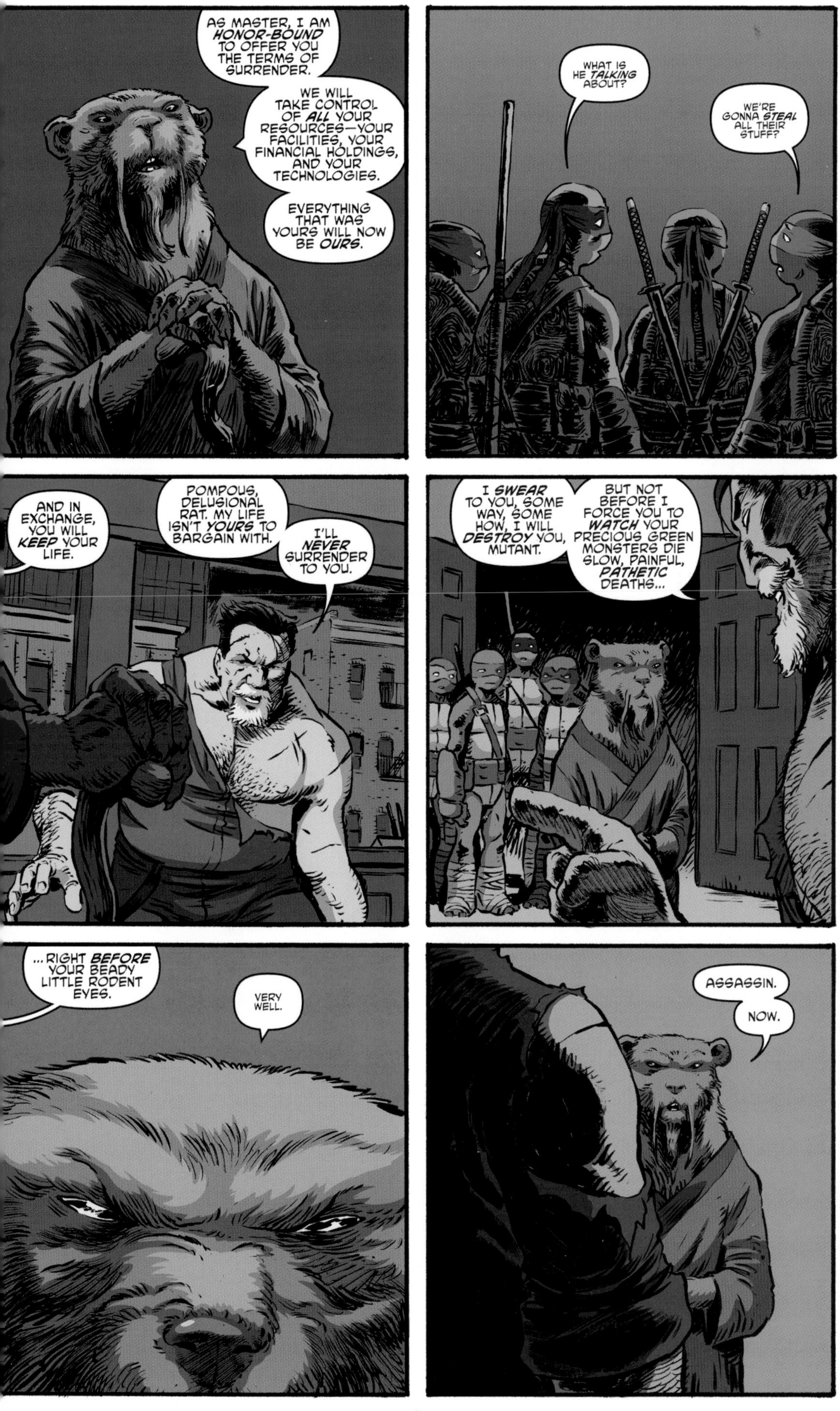
AS MASTER, I AM HONOR-BOUND TO OFFER YOU THE TERMS OF SURRENDER.
WE WILL TAKE CONTROL OF ALL YOUR RESOURCES—YOUR FACILITIES, YOUR FINANCIAL HOLDINGS, AND YOUR TECHNOLOGIES.
EVERYTHING THAT WAS YOURS WILL NOW BE OURS.
WHAT IS HE TALKING ABOUT?
WE'RE GONNA STEAL ALL THEIR STUFF?
AND IN EXCHANGE, YOU WILL KEEP YOUR LIFE.
POMPOUS, DELUSIONAL RAT. MY LIFE ISN'T YOURS TO BARGAIN WITH.
I'LL NEVER SURRENDER TO YOU.
I SWEAR TO YOU, SOME WAY, SOME HOW, I WILL DESTROY YOU, MUTANT.
BUT NOT BEFORE I FORCE YOU TO WATCH YOUR PRECIOUS GREEN MONSTERS DIE SLOW, PAINFUL, PATHETIC DEATHS...
...RIGHT BEFORE YOUR BEADY LITTLE RODENT EYES.
VERY WELL.
ASSASSIN.
NOW.

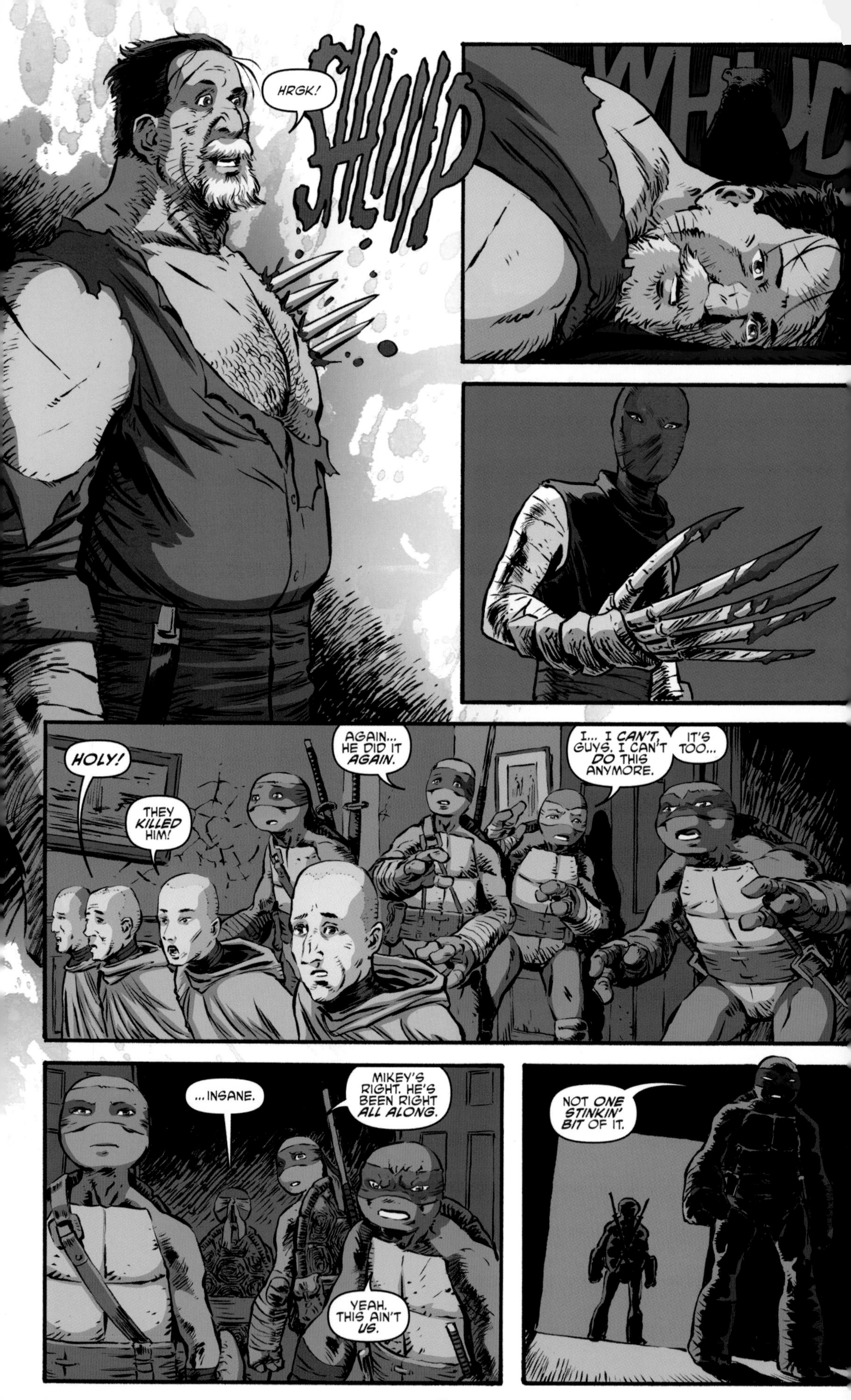
HRGK!
SHUUD
WHUD
HOLY!
THEY KILLED HIM!
AGAIN... HE DID IT AGAIN.
I... I CAN'T, GUYS. I CAN'T DO THIS ANYMORE.
IT'S TOO...
...INSANE.
MIKEY'S RIGHT. HE'S BEEN RIGHT ALL ALONG.
YEAH. THIS AIN'T US.
NOT ONE STINKIN' BIT OF IT.

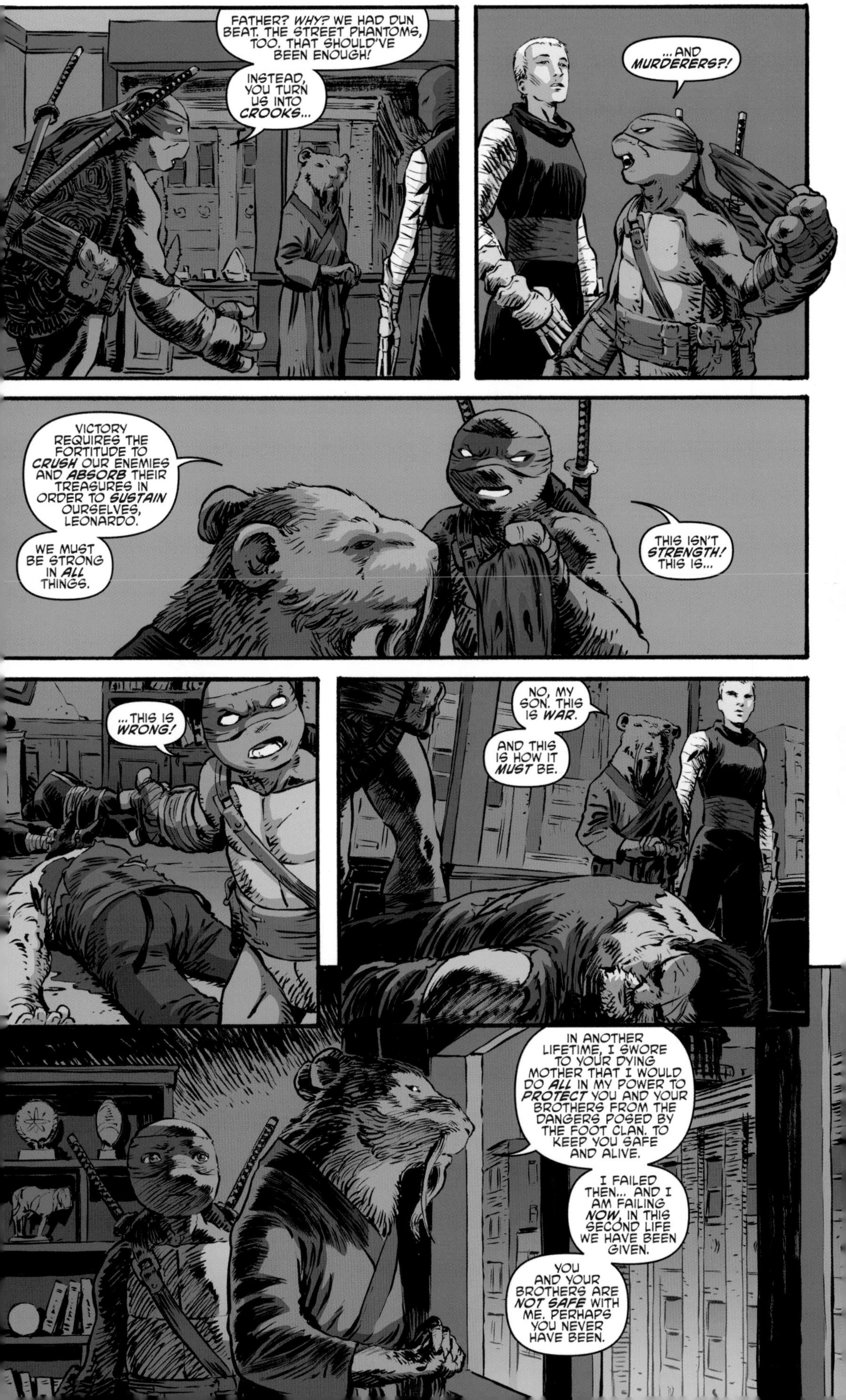
FATHER? WHY? WE HAD DUN BEAT. THE STREET PHANTOMS, TOO. THAT SHOULD'VE BEEN ENOUGH!
INSTEAD, YOU TURN US INTO CROOKS...
...AND MURDERERS?!
VICTORY REQUIRES THE FORTITUDE TO CRUSH OUR ENEMIES AND ABSORB THEIR TREASURES IN ORDER TO SUSTAIN OURSELVES, LEONARDO.
WE MUST BE STRONG IN ALL THINGS.
THIS ISN'T STRENGTH! THIS IS...
...THIS IS WRONG!
NO, MY SON. THIS IS WAR.
AND THIS IS HOW IT MUST BE.
IN ANOTHER LIFETIME, I SWORE TO YOUR DYING MOTHER THAT I WOULD DO ALL IN MY POWER TO PROTECT YOU AND YOUR BROTHERS FROM THE DANGERS POSED BY THE FOOT CLAN. TO KEEP YOU SAFE AND ALIVE.
I FAILED THEN... AND I AM FAILING NOW, IN THIS SECOND LIFE WE HAVE BEEN GIVEN.
YOU AND YOUR BROTHERS ARE NOT SAFE WITH ME. PERHAPS YOU NEVER HAVE BEEN.

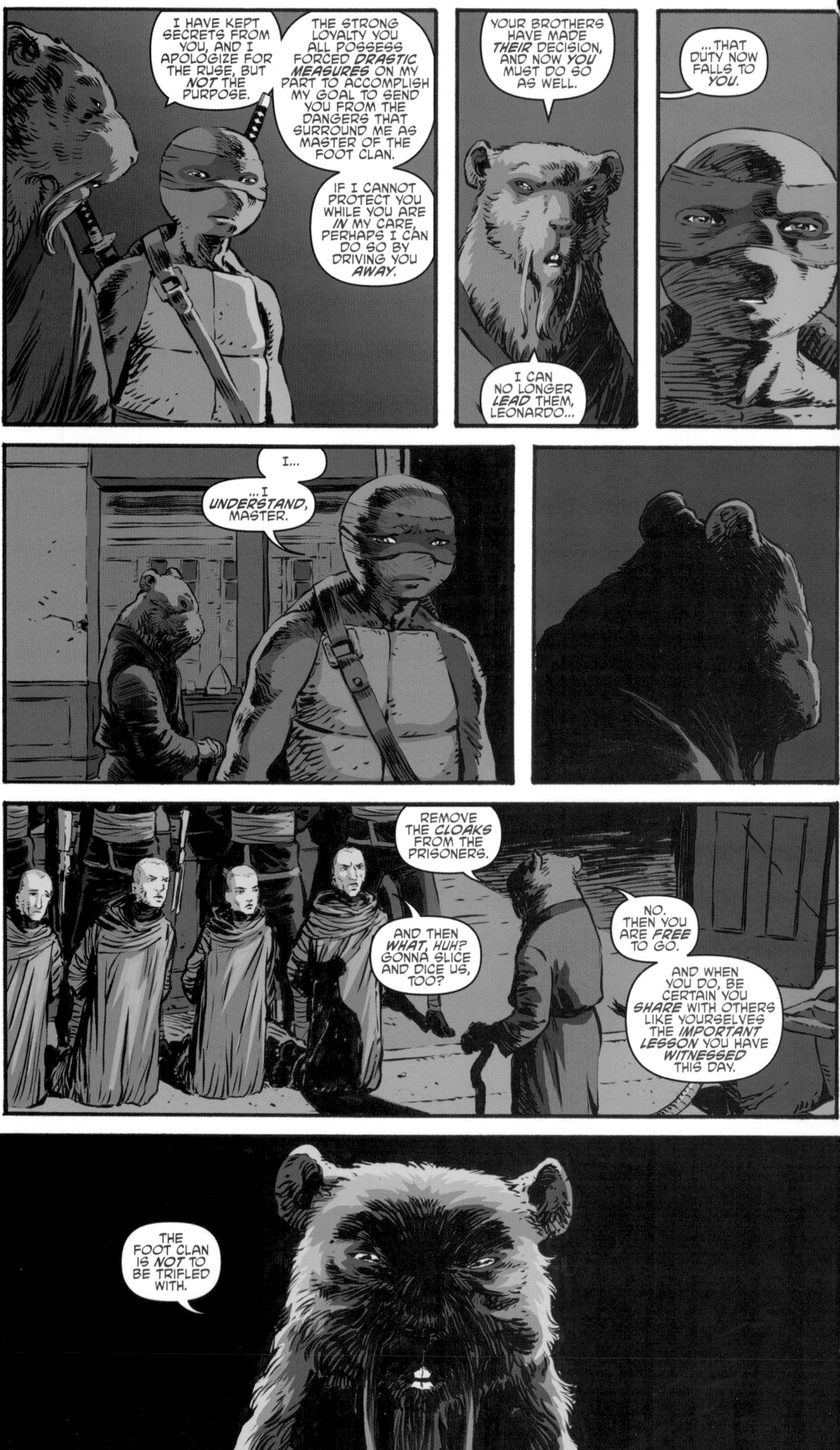
I HAVE KEPT SECRETS FROM YOU, AND I APOLOGIZE FOR THE RUSE, BUT *NOT* THE PURPOSE.
THE STRONG LOYALTY YOU ALL POSSESS FORCED *DRASTIC MEASURES* ON MY PART TO ACCOMPLISH MY GOAL TO SEND YOU FROM THE DANGERS THAT SURROUND ME AS MASTER OF THE FOOT CLAN.
IF I CANNOT PROTECT YOU WHILE YOU ARE *IN* MY CARE, PERHAPS I CAN DO SO BY DRIVING YOU *AWAY*.
YOUR BROTHERS HAVE MADE *THEIR* DECISION, AND NOW *YOU* MUST DO SO AS WELL.
I CAN NO LONGER *LEAD* THEM, LEONARDO...
...THAT DUTY NOW FALLS TO *YOU*.
I...
...I *UNDERSTAND*, MASTER.
REMOVE THE *CLOAKS* FROM THE PRISONERS.
AND THEN *WHAT, HUH?* GONNA SLICE AND DICE US, TOO?
NO. THEN YOU ARE *FREE* TO GO.
AND WHEN YOU DO, BE CERTAIN YOU *SHARE* WITH OTHERS LIKE YOURSELVES THE *IMPORTANT LESSON* YOU HAVE *WITNESSED* THIS DAY.
THE FOOT CLAN IS *NOT* TO BE TRIFLED WITH.

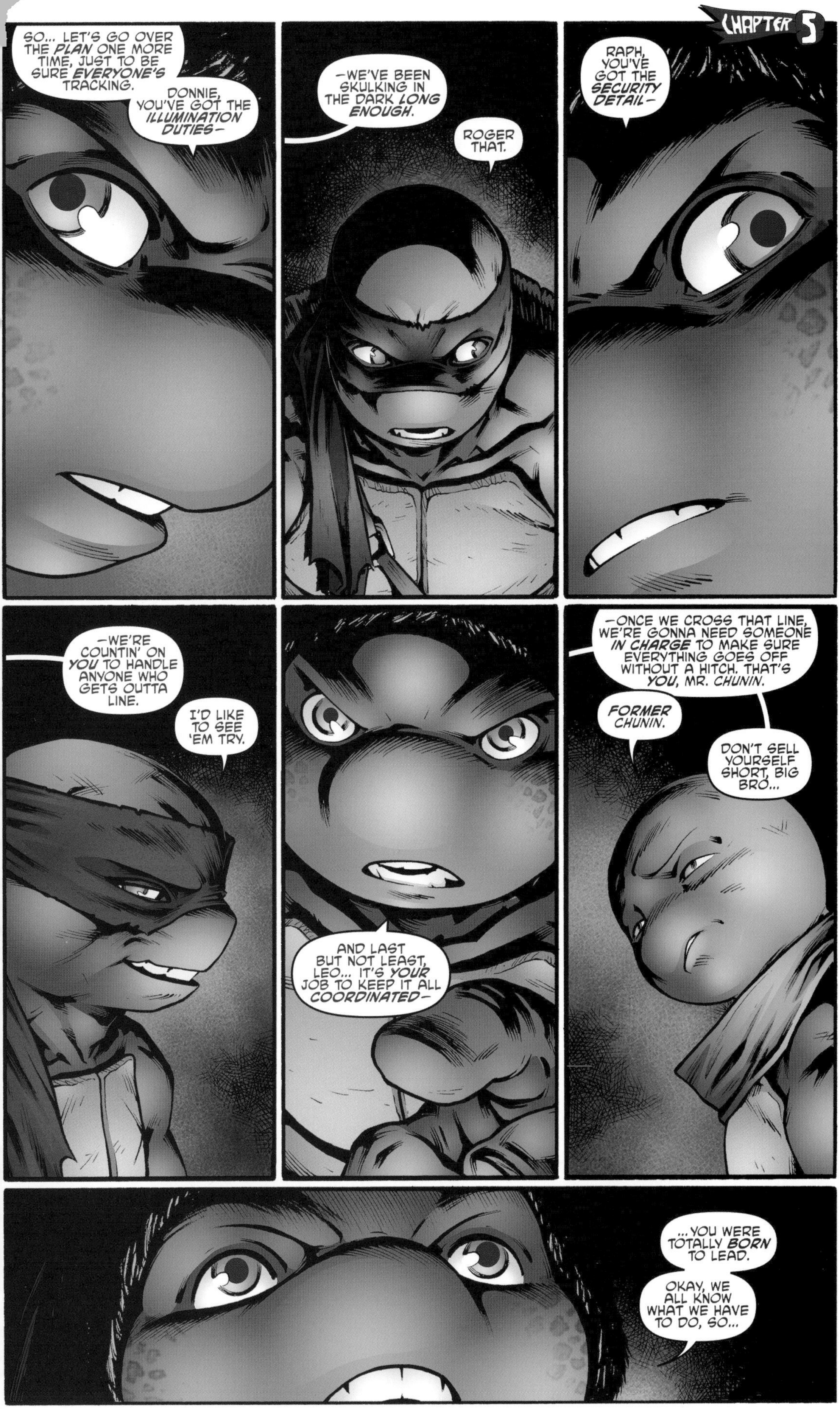
CHAPTER 5
SO... LET'S GO OVER THE PLAN ONE MORE TIME, JUST TO BE SURE EVERYONE'S TRACKING.
DONNIE, YOU'VE GOT THE ILLUMINATION DUTIES—
—WE'VE BEEN SKULKING IN THE DARK LONG ENOUGH.
ROGER THAT.
RAPH, YOU'VE GOT THE SECURITY DETAIL—
—WE'RE COUNTIN' ON YOU TO HANDLE ANYONE WHO GETS OUTTA LINE.
I'D LIKE TO SEE 'EM TRY.
AND LAST BUT NOT LEAST, LEO... IT'S YOUR JOB TO KEEP IT ALL COORDINATED—
—ONCE WE CROSS THAT LINE, WE'RE GONNA NEED SOMEONE IN CHARGE TO MAKE SURE EVERYTHING GOES OFF WITHOUT A HITCH. THAT'S YOU, MR. CHUNIN.
FORMER CHUNIN.
DON'T SELL YOURSELF SHORT, BIG BRO...
...YOU WERE TOTALLY BORN TO LEAD.
OKAY, WE ALL KNOW WHAT WE HAVE TO DO, SO...

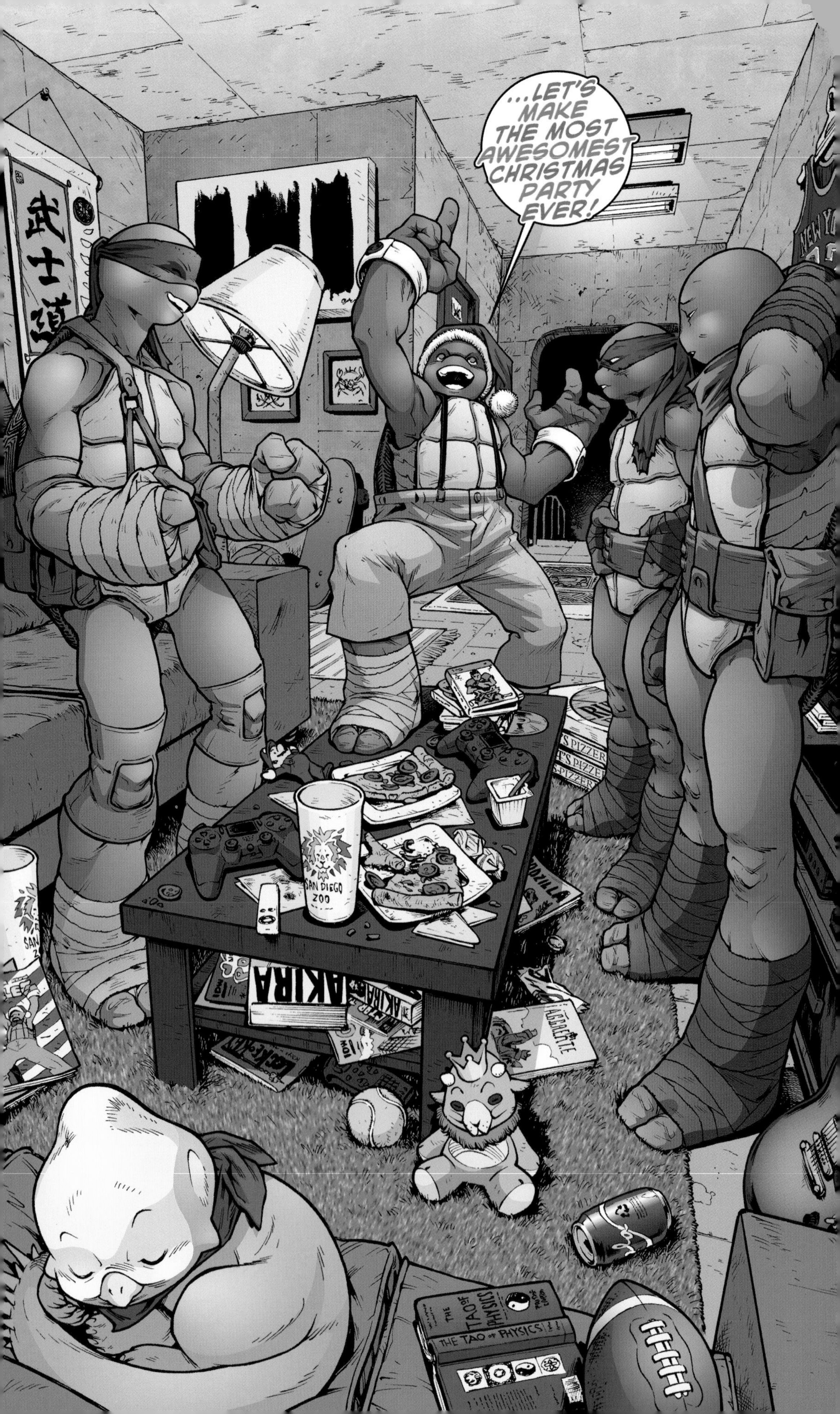
...LET'S MAKE THE MOST AWESOMEST CHRISTMAS PARTY EVER!
武士道
NEW YORK
SAN DIEGO ZOO
AKIRA
GODZILLA
THE TAO OF PHYSICS

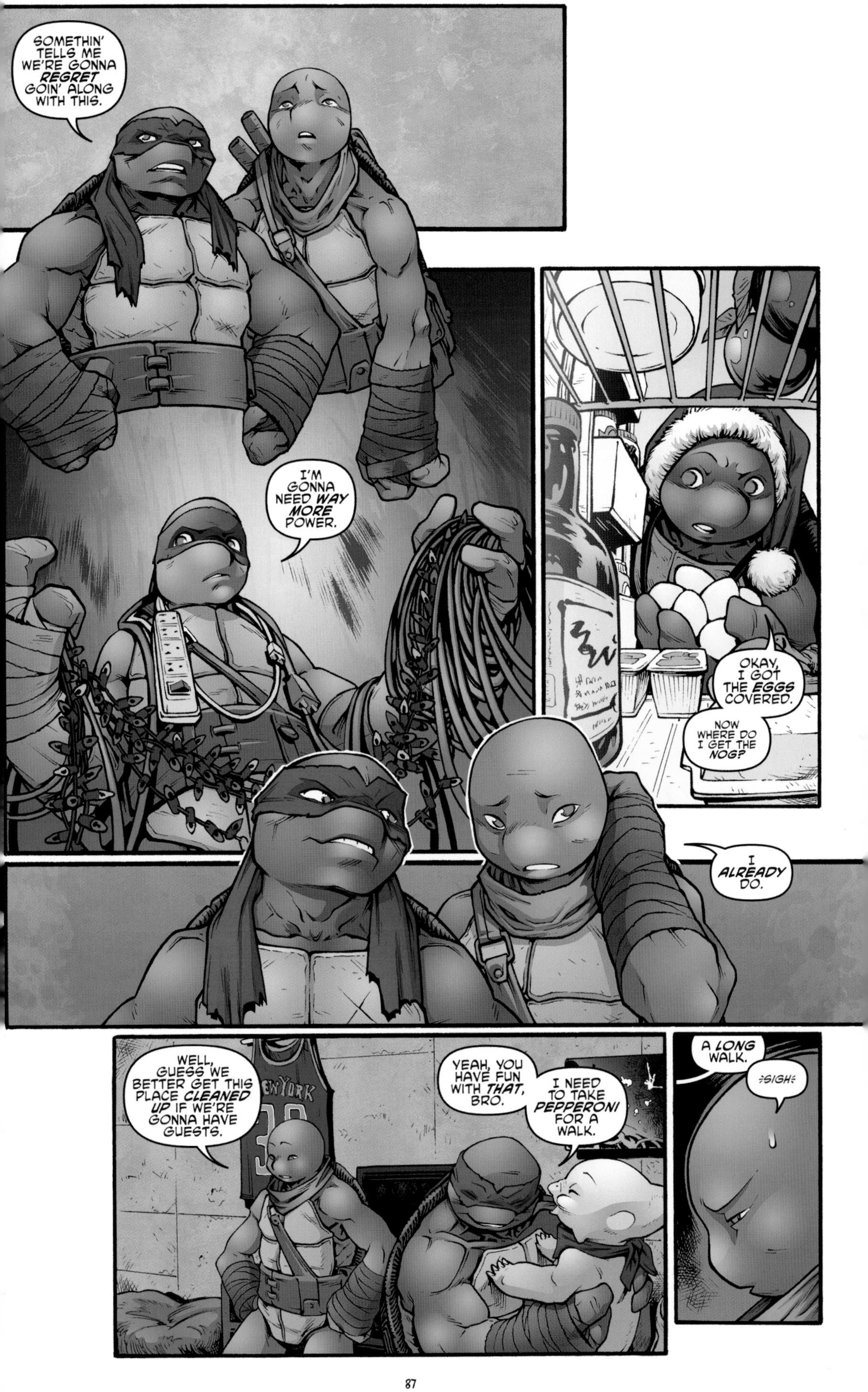
SOMETHIN' TELLS ME WE'RE GONNA REGRET GOIN' ALONG WITH THIS.
I'M GONNA NEED WAY MORE POWER.
OKAY, I GOT THE EGGS COVERED.
NOW WHERE DO I GET THE NOG?
I ALREADY DO.
WELL, GUESS WE BETTER GET THIS PLACE CLEANED UP IF WE'RE GONNA HAVE GUESTS.
NEW YORK
YEAH, YOU HAVE FUN WITH THAT, BRO.
I NEED TO TAKE PEPPERONI FOR A WALK.
A LONG WALK.
SIGH

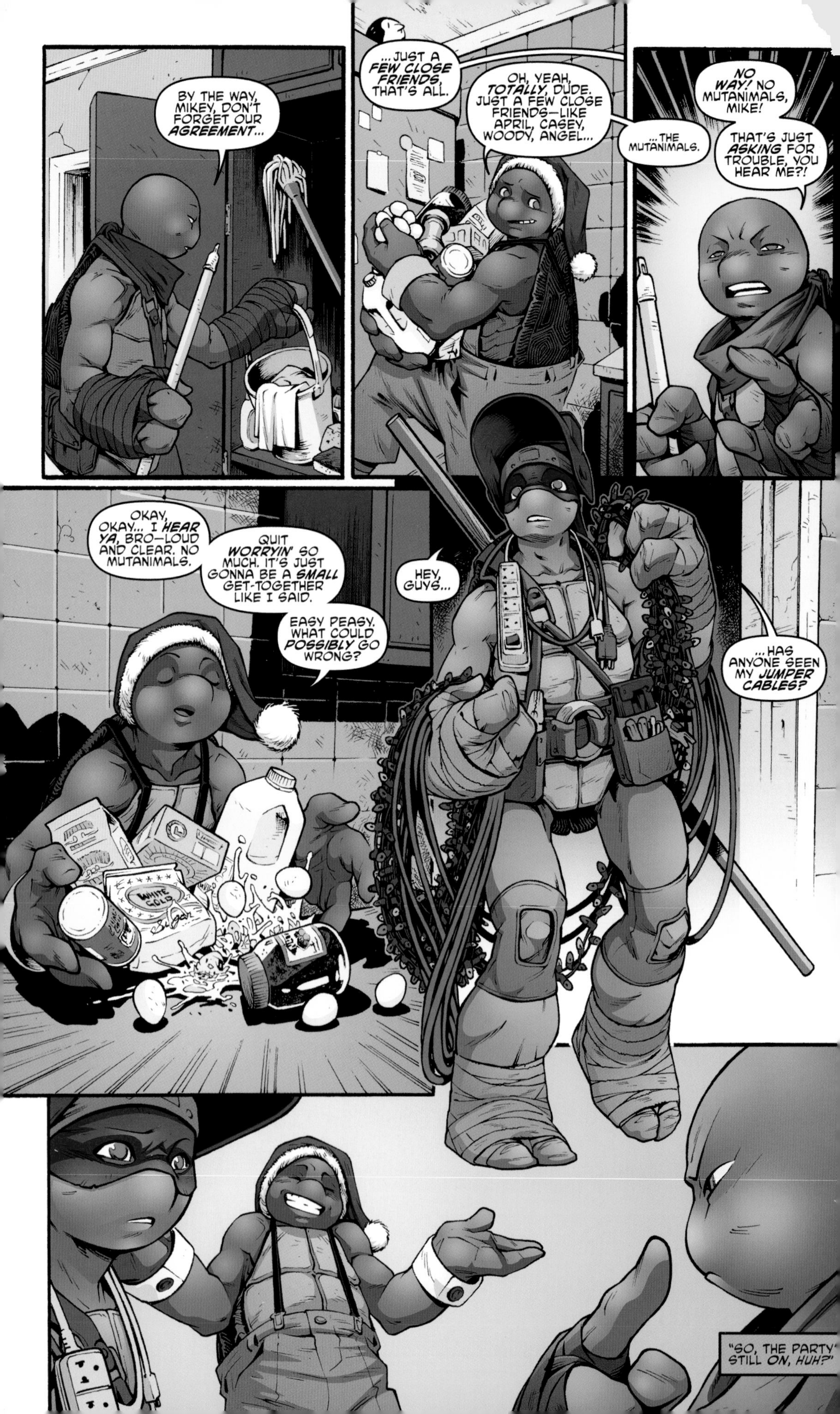
BY THE WAY, MIKEY, DON'T FORGET OUR AGREEMENT...
...JUST A FEW CLOSE FRIENDS, THAT'S ALL.
OH, YEAH, TOTALLY, DUDE. JUST A FEW CLOSE FRIENDS—LIKE APRIL, CASEY, WOODY, ANGEL...
...THE MUTANIMALS.
NO WAY! NO MUTANIMALS, MIKE!
THAT'S JUST ASKING FOR TROUBLE, YOU HEAR ME?!
OKAY, OKAY... I HEAR YA, BRO—LOUD AND CLEAR. NO MUTANIMALS.
QUIT WORRYIN' SO MUCH. IT'S JUST GONNA BE A SMALL GET-TOGETHER LIKE I SAID.
EASY PEASY. WHAT COULD POSSIBLY GO WRONG?
HEY, GUYS...
...HAS ANYONE SEEN MY JUMPER CABLES?
"SO, THE PARTY STILL ON, HUH?"

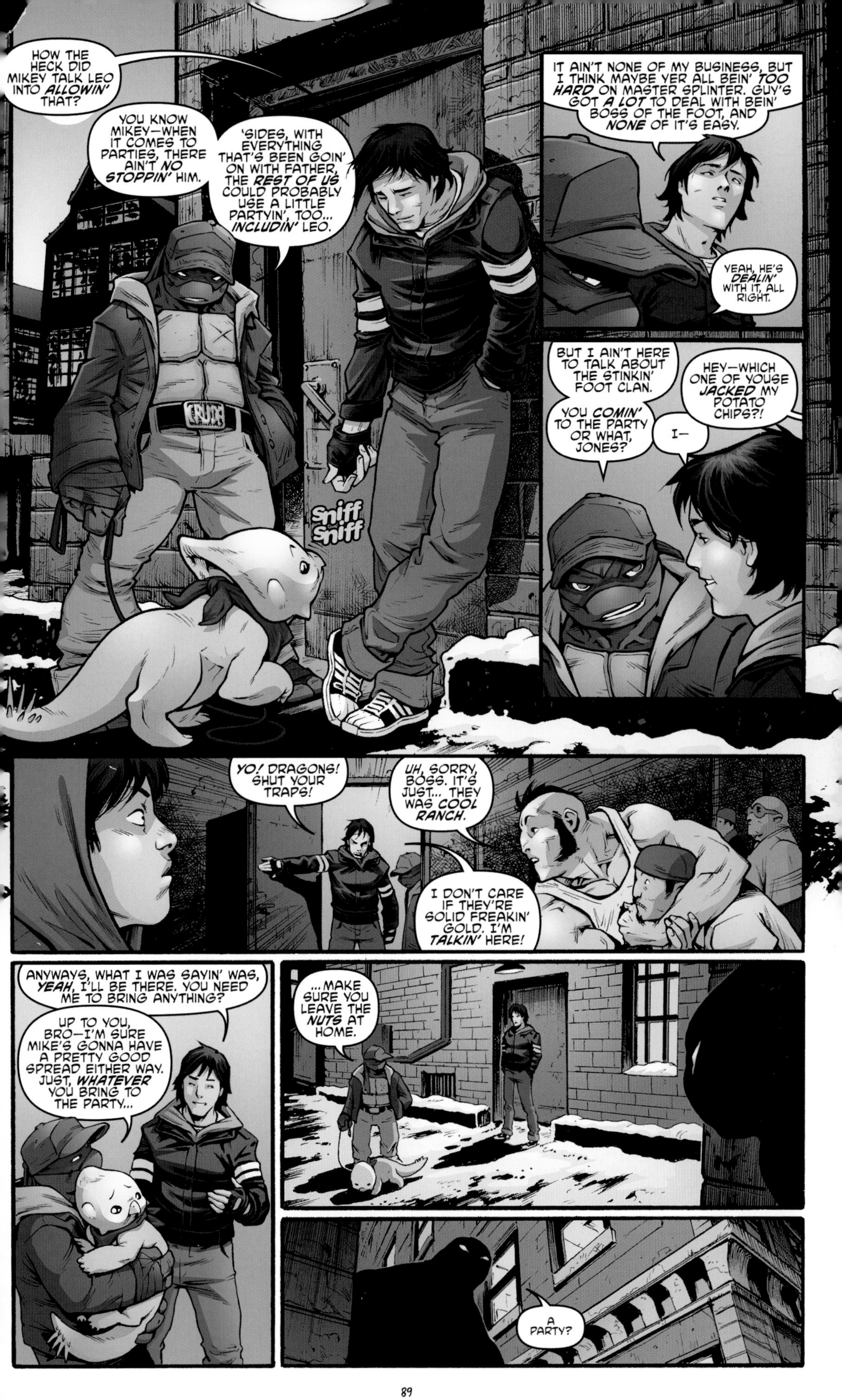
HOW THE HECK DID MIKEY TALK LEO INTO ALLOWIN' THAT?
YOU KNOW MIKEY—WHEN IT COMES TO PARTIES, THERE AIN'T NO STOPPIN' HIM.
'SIDES, WITH EVERYTHING THAT'S BEEN GOIN' ON WITH FATHER, THE REST OF US COULD PROBABLY USE A LITTLE PARTYIN', TOO... INCLUDIN' LEO.
Sniff Sniff
IT AIN'T NONE OF MY BUSINESS, BUT I THINK MAYBE YER ALL BEIN' TOO HARD ON MASTER SPLINTER. GUY'S GOT A LOT TO DEAL WITH BEIN' BOSS OF THE FOOT, AND NONE OF IT'S EASY.
YEAH, HE'S DEALIN' WITH IT, ALL RIGHT.
BUT I AIN'T HERE TO TALK ABOUT THE STINKIN' FOOT CLAN.
YOU COMIN' TO THE PARTY OR WHAT, JONES?
I—
HEY—WHICH ONE OF YOUSE JACKED MY POTATO CHIPS?!
YO! DRAGONS! SHUT YOUR TRAPS!
UH, SORRY, BOSS. IT'S JUST... THEY WAS COOL RANCH.
I DON'T CARE IF THEY'RE SOLID FREAKIN' GOLD. I'M TALKIN' HERE!
ANYWAYS, WHAT I WAS SAYIN' WAS, YEAH, I'LL BE THERE. YOU NEED ME TO BRING ANYTHING?
UP TO YOU, BRO—I'M SURE MIKE'S GONNA HAVE A PRETTY GOOD SPREAD EITHER WAY. JUST, WHATEVER YOU BRING TO THE PARTY...
...MAKE SURE YOU LEAVE THE NUTS AT HOME.
A PARTY?

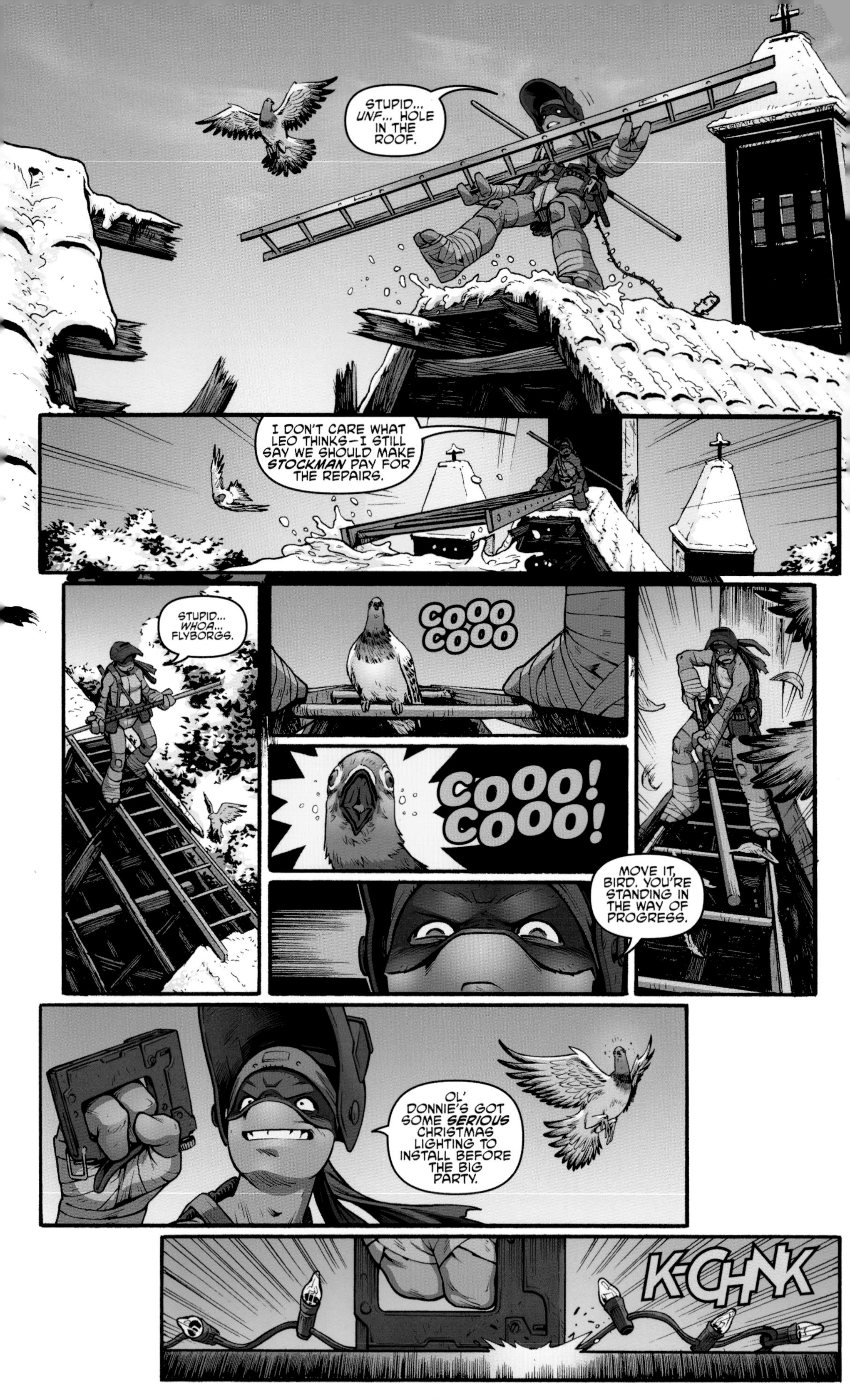
STUPID... UNF... HOLE IN THE ROOF.
I DON'T CARE WHAT LEO THINKS—I STILL SAY WE SHOULD MAKE STOCKMAN PAY FOR THE REPAIRS.
STUPID... WHOA... FLYBORGS.
COOO COOO
COOO! COOO!
MOVE IT, BIRD. YOU'RE STANDING IN THE WAY OF PROGRESS.
OL' DONNIE'S GOT SOME SERIOUS CHRISTMAS LIGHTING TO INSTALL BEFORE THE BIG PARTY.
K-CHNK

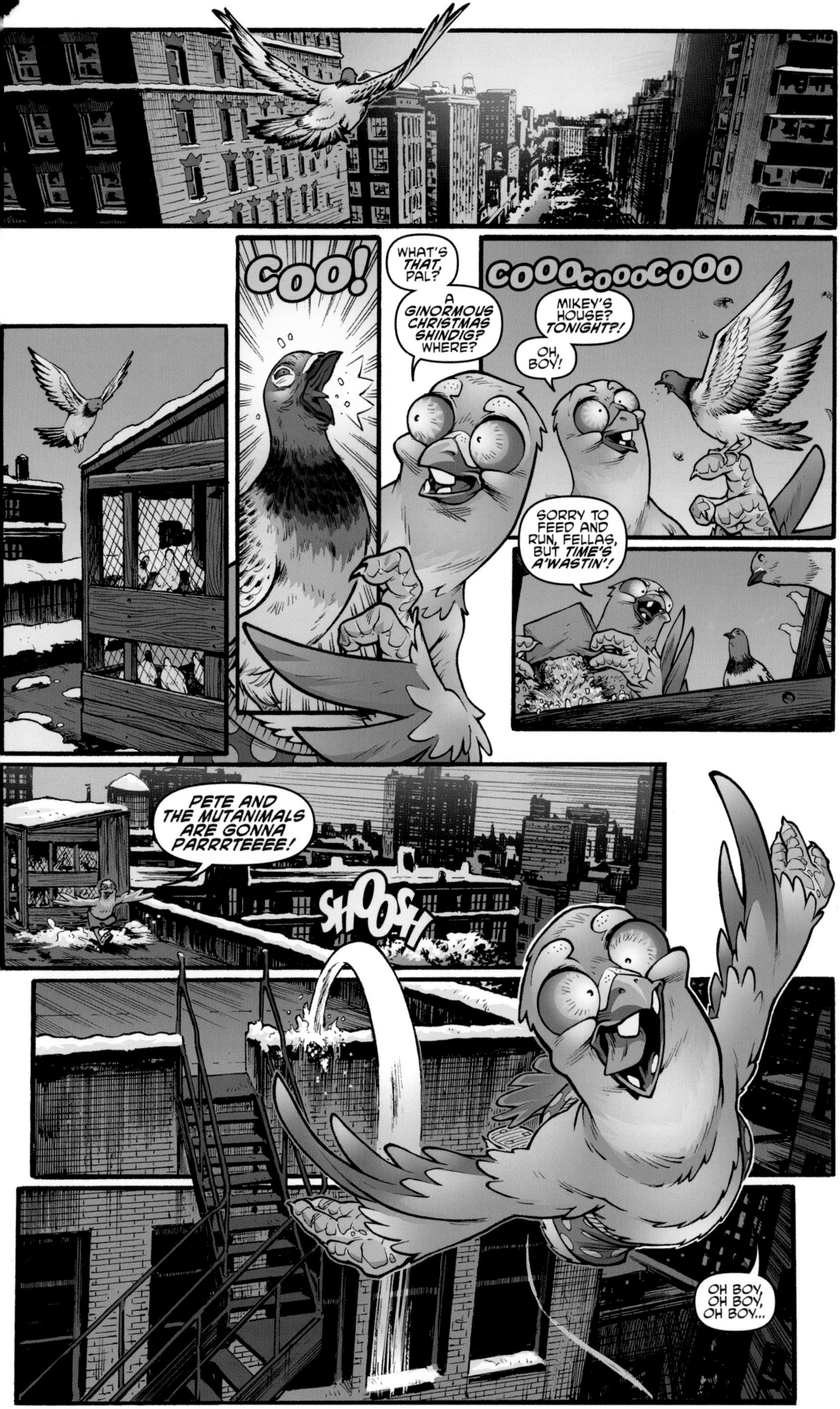
COO!
WHAT'S THAT, PAL?
A GINORMOUS CHRISTMAS SHINDIG? WHERE?
COOOCOOOCOOO
MIKEY'S HOUSE? TONIGHT?!
OH, BOY!
SORRY TO FEED AND RUN, FELLAS, BUT TIME'S A'WASTIN'!
PETE AND THE MUTANIMALS ARE GONNA PARRRTEEEE!
SHOOSH
OH BOY, OH BOY, OH BOY...

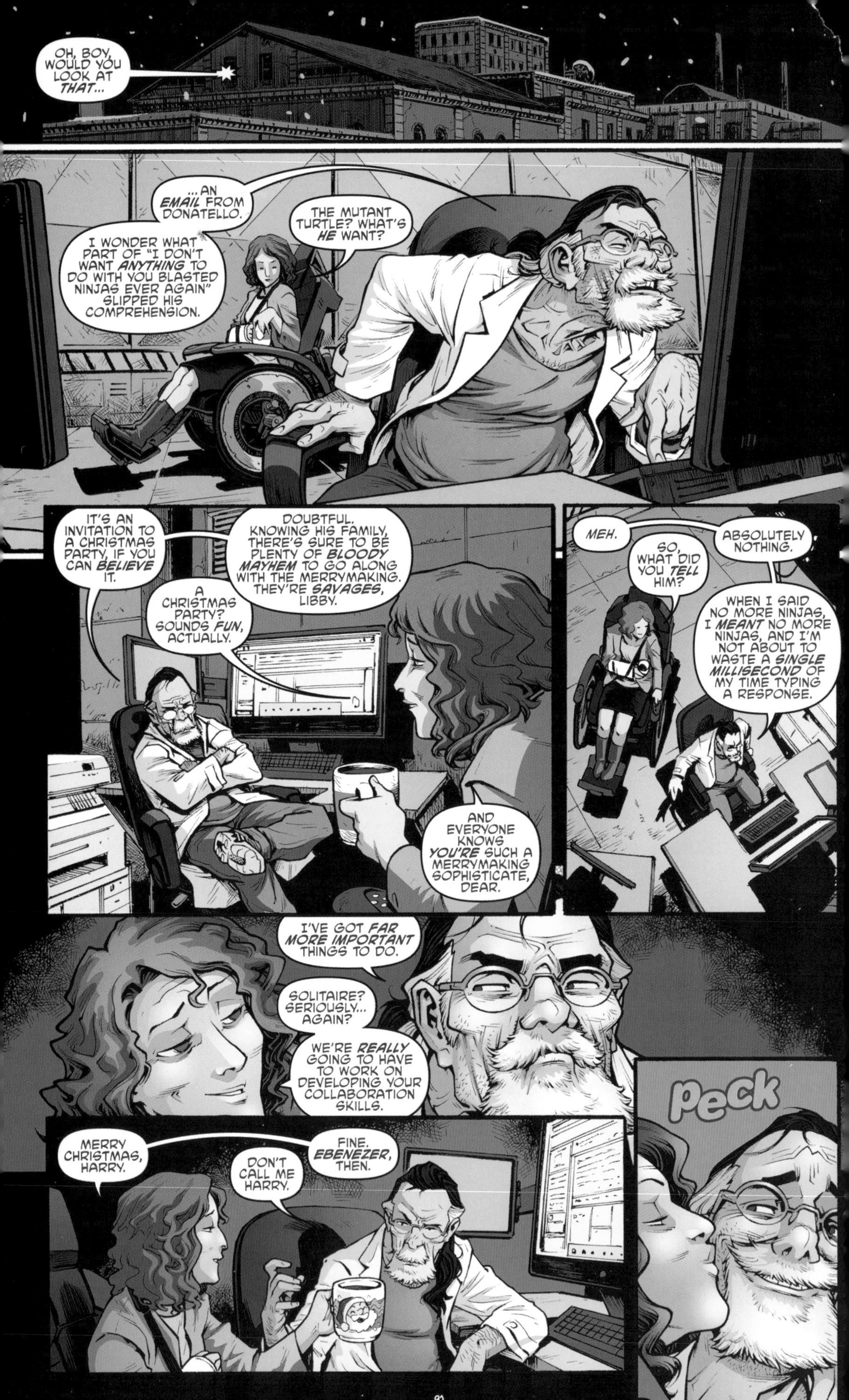
OH, BOY, WOULD YOU LOOK AT THAT...
...AN EMAIL FROM DONATELLO.
THE MUTANT TURTLE? WHAT'S HE WANT?
I WONDER WHAT PART OF "I DON'T WANT ANYTHING TO DO WITH YOU BLASTED NINJAS EVER AGAIN" SLIPPED HIS COMPREHENSION.
IT'S AN INVITATION TO A CHRISTMAS PARTY, IF YOU CAN BELIEVE IT.
A CHRISTMAS PARTY? SOUNDS FUN, ACTUALLY.
DOUBTFUL. KNOWING HIS FAMILY, THERE'S SURE TO BE PLENTY OF BLOODY MAYHEM TO GO ALONG WITH THE MERRYMAKING. THEY'RE SAVAGES, LIBBY.
AND EVERYONE KNOWS YOU'RE SUCH A MERRYMAKING SOPHISTICATE, DEAR.
MEH.
SO, WHAT DID YOU TELL HIM?
ABSOLUTELY NOTHING.
WHEN I SAID NO MORE NINJAS, I MEANT NO MORE NINJAS, AND I'M NOT ABOUT TO WASTE A SINGLE MILLISECOND OF MY TIME TYPING A RESPONSE.
I'VE GOT FAR MORE IMPORTANT THINGS TO DO.
SOLITAIRE? SERIOUSLY... AGAIN?
WE'RE REALLY GOING TO HAVE TO WORK ON DEVELOPING YOUR COLLABORATION SKILLS.
MERRY CHRISTMAS, HARRY.
DON'T CALL ME HARRY.
FINE. EBENEZER, THEN.
peck

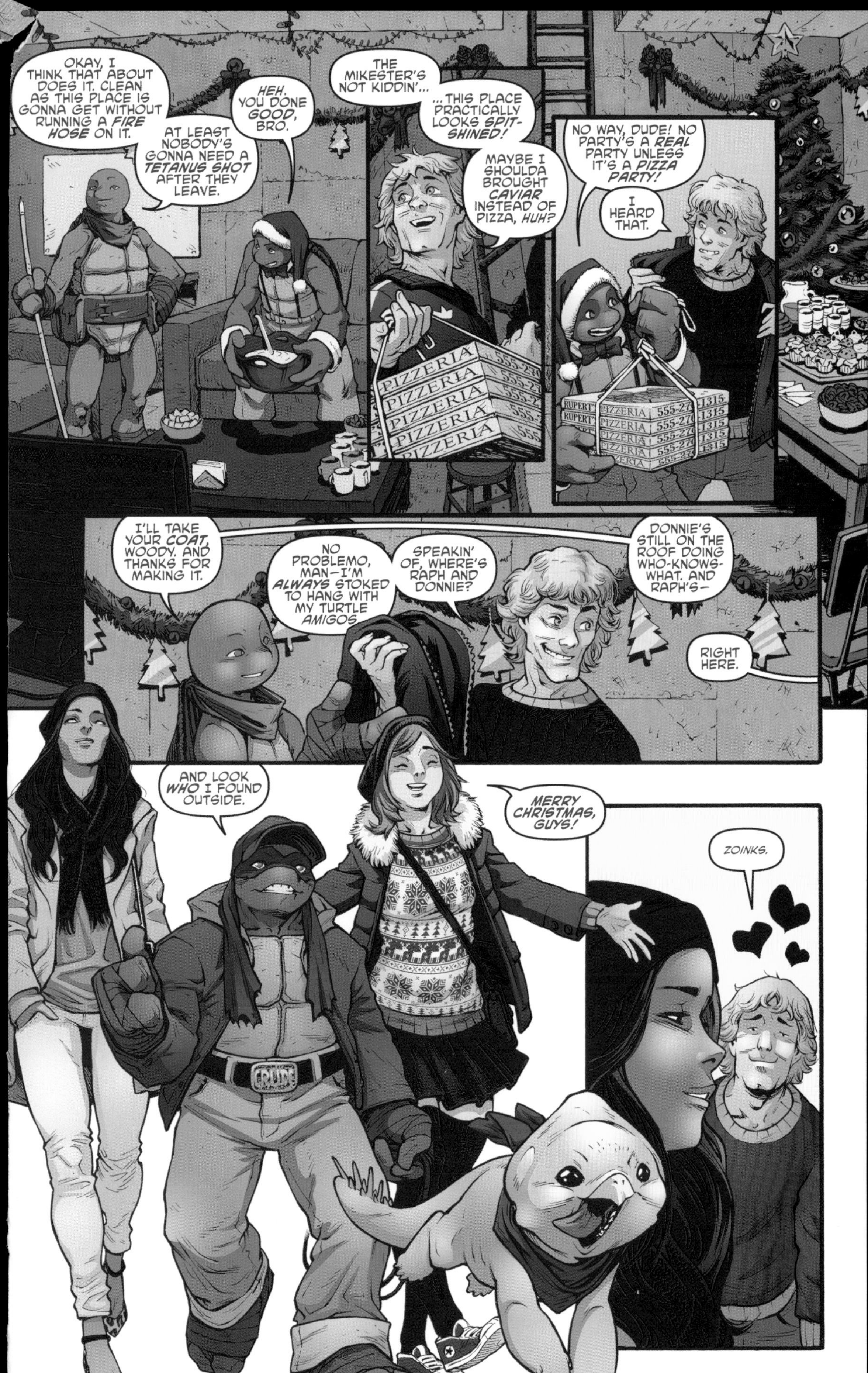

OKAY, I THINK THAT ABOUT DOES IT. CLEAN AS THIS PLACE IS GONNA GET WITHOUT RUNNING A FIRE HOSE ON IT.
AT LEAST NOBODY'S GONNA NEED A TETANUS SHOT AFTER THEY LEAVE.
HEH. YOU DONE GOOD, BRO.
THE MIKESTER'S NOT KIDDIN'...
...THIS PLACE PRACTICALLY LOOKS SPIT-SHINED!
MAYBE I SHOULDA BROUGHT CAVIAR INSTEAD OF PIZZA, HUH?
PIZZERIA
NO WAY, DUDE! NO PARTY'S A REAL PARTY UNLESS IT'S A PIZZA PARTY!
I HEARD THAT.
RUPERT'S PIZZERIA 555-2701315
I'LL TAKE YOUR COAT, WOODY. AND THANKS FOR MAKING IT.
NO PROBLEMO, MAN—I'M ALWAYS STOKED TO HANG WITH MY TURTLE AMIGOS.
SPEAKIN' OF, WHERE'S RAPH AND DONNIE?
DONNIE'S STILL ON THE ROOF DOING WHO-KNOWS-WHAT. AND RAPH'S—
RIGHT HERE.
AND LOOK WHO I FOUND OUTSIDE.
MERRY CHRISTMAS, GUYS!
CRUDE
ZOINKS.

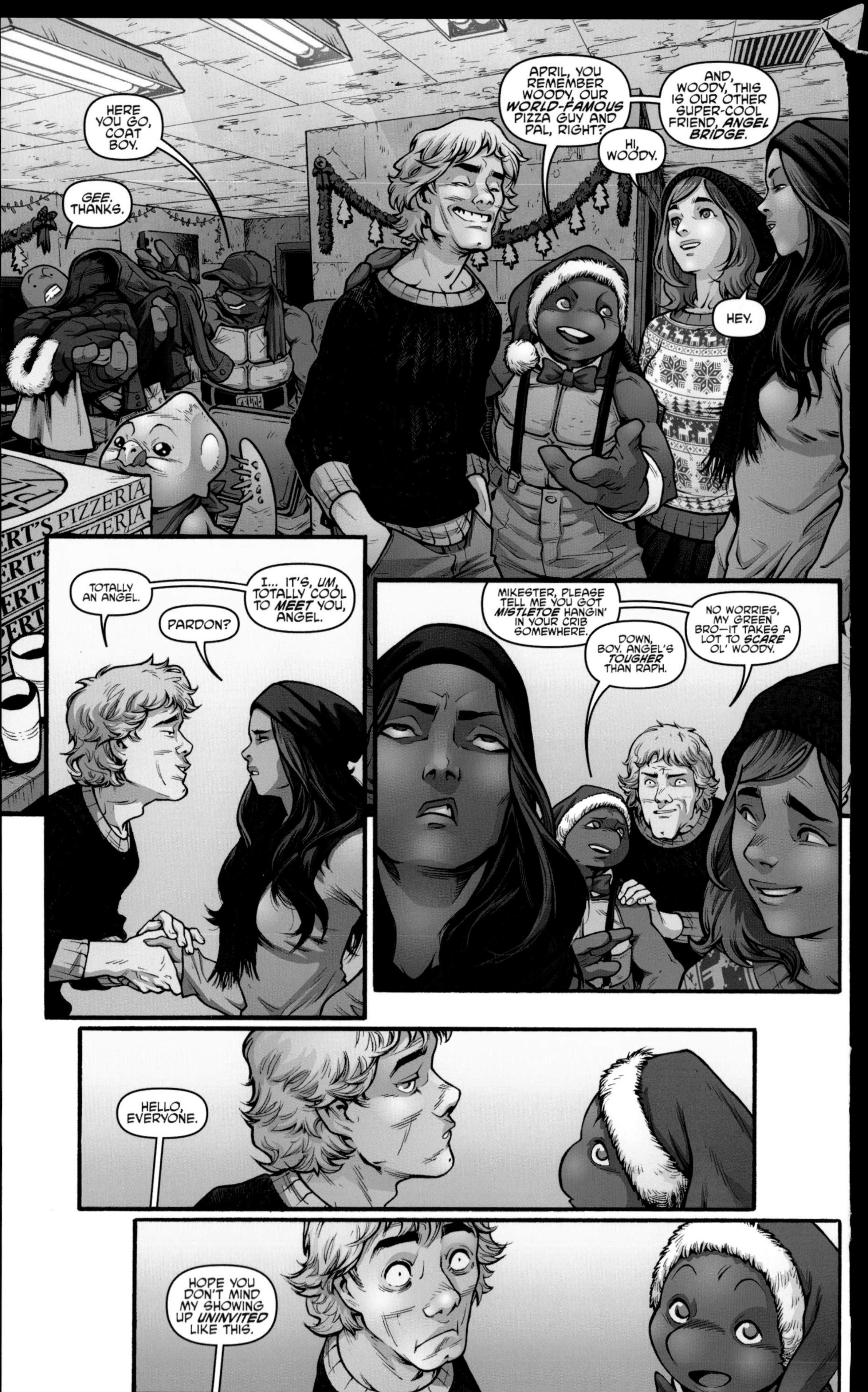
HERE YOU GO, COAT BOY.
GEE. THANKS.
APRIL, YOU REMEMBER WOODY, OUR WORLD-FAMOUS PIZZA GUY AND PAL, RIGHT?
HI, WOODY.
AND, WOODY, THIS IS OUR OTHER SUPER-COOL FRIEND, ANGEL BRIDGE.
HEY.
ERT'S PIZZERIA
TOTALLY AN ANGEL.
I... IT'S, UM, TOTALLY COOL TO MEET YOU, ANGEL.
PARDON?
MIKESTER, PLEASE TELL ME YOU GOT MISTLETOE HANGIN' IN YOUR CRIB SOMEWHERE.
NO WORRIES, MY GREEN BRO—IT TAKES A LOT TO SCARE OL' WOODY.
DOWN, BOY. ANGEL'S TOUGHER THAN RAPH.
HELLO, EVERYONE.
HOPE YOU DON'T MIND MY SHOWING UP UNINVITED LIKE THIS.

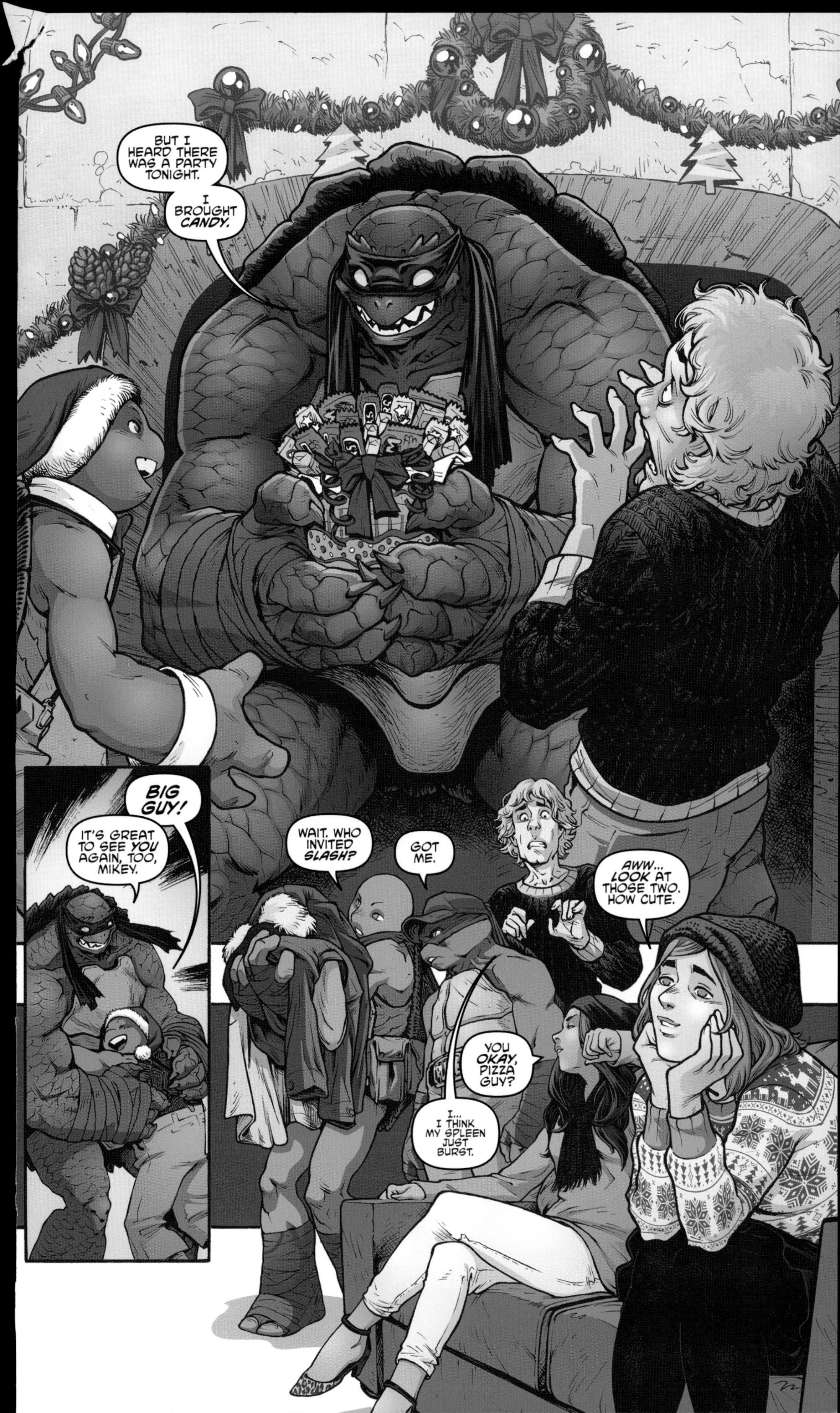
BUT I HEARD THERE WAS A PARTY TONIGHT.
I BROUGHT *CANDY.*
BIG GUY!
IT'S GREAT TO SEE *YOU* AGAIN, TOO, MIKEY.
WAIT. WHO INVITED *SLASH?*
GOT ME.
AWW... LOOK AT THOSE TWO. HOW CUTE.
YOU *OKAY,* PIZZA GUY?
I... I THINK MY SPLEEN JUST BURST.

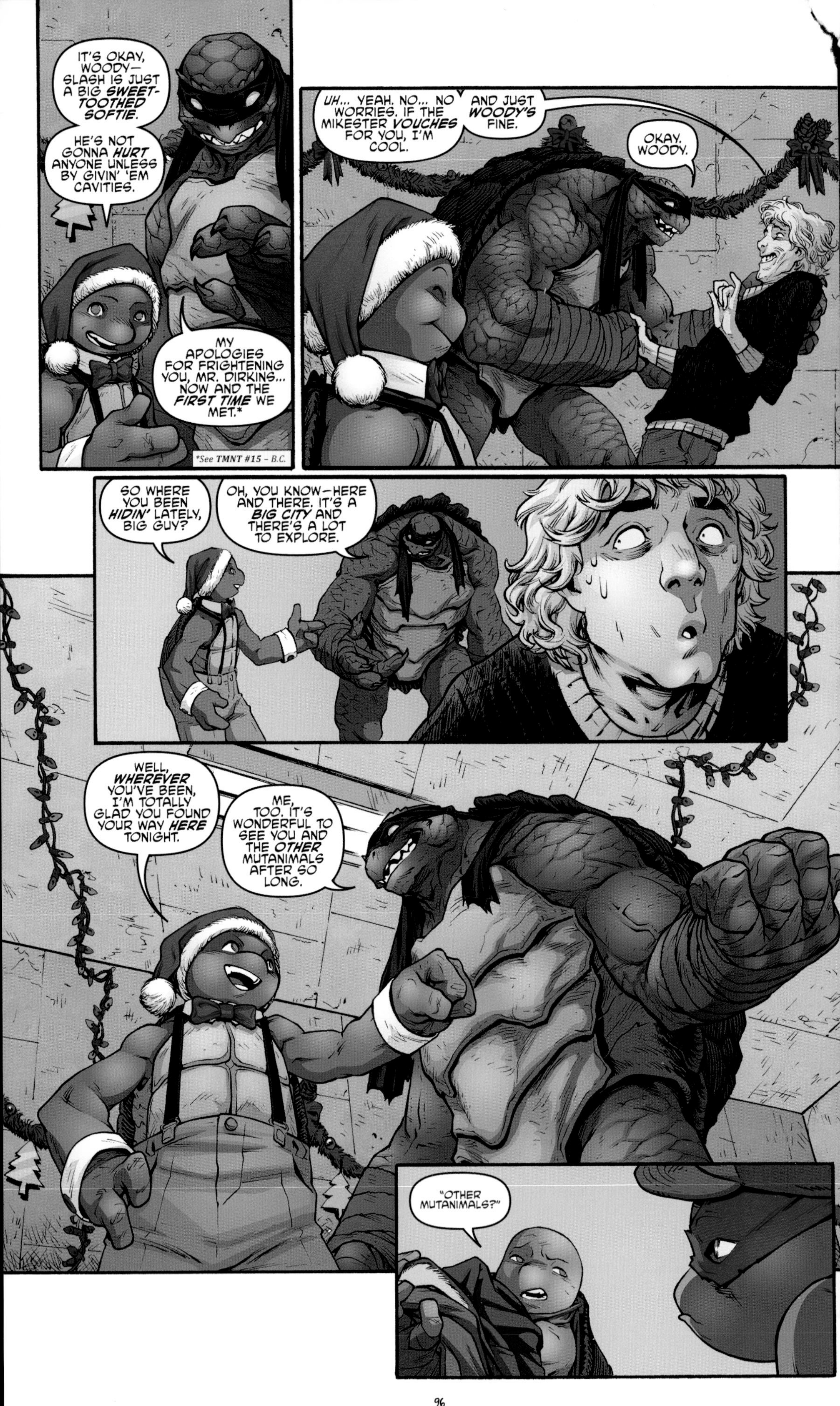
IT'S OKAY, WOODY— SLASH IS JUST A BIG SWEET-TOOTHED SOFTIE.
HE'S NOT GONNA HURT ANYONE UNLESS BY GIVIN' 'EM CAVITIES.
MY APOLOGIES FOR FRIGHTENING YOU, MR. DIRKINS... NOW AND THE FIRST TIME WE MET.*
*See TMNT #15 – B.C.
UH... YEAH. NO... NO WORRIES. IF THE MIKESTER VOUCHES FOR YOU, I'M COOL.
AND JUST WOODY'S FINE.
OKAY. WOODY.
SO WHERE YOU BEEN HIDIN' LATELY, BIG GUY?
OH, YOU KNOW—HERE AND THERE. IT'S A BIG CITY AND THERE'S A LOT TO EXPLORE.
WELL, WHEREVER YOU'VE BEEN, I'M TOTALLY GLAD YOU FOUND YOUR WAY HERE TONIGHT.
ME, TOO. IT'S WONDERFUL TO SEE YOU AND THE OTHER MUTANIMALS AFTER SO LONG.
"OTHER MUTANIMALS?"

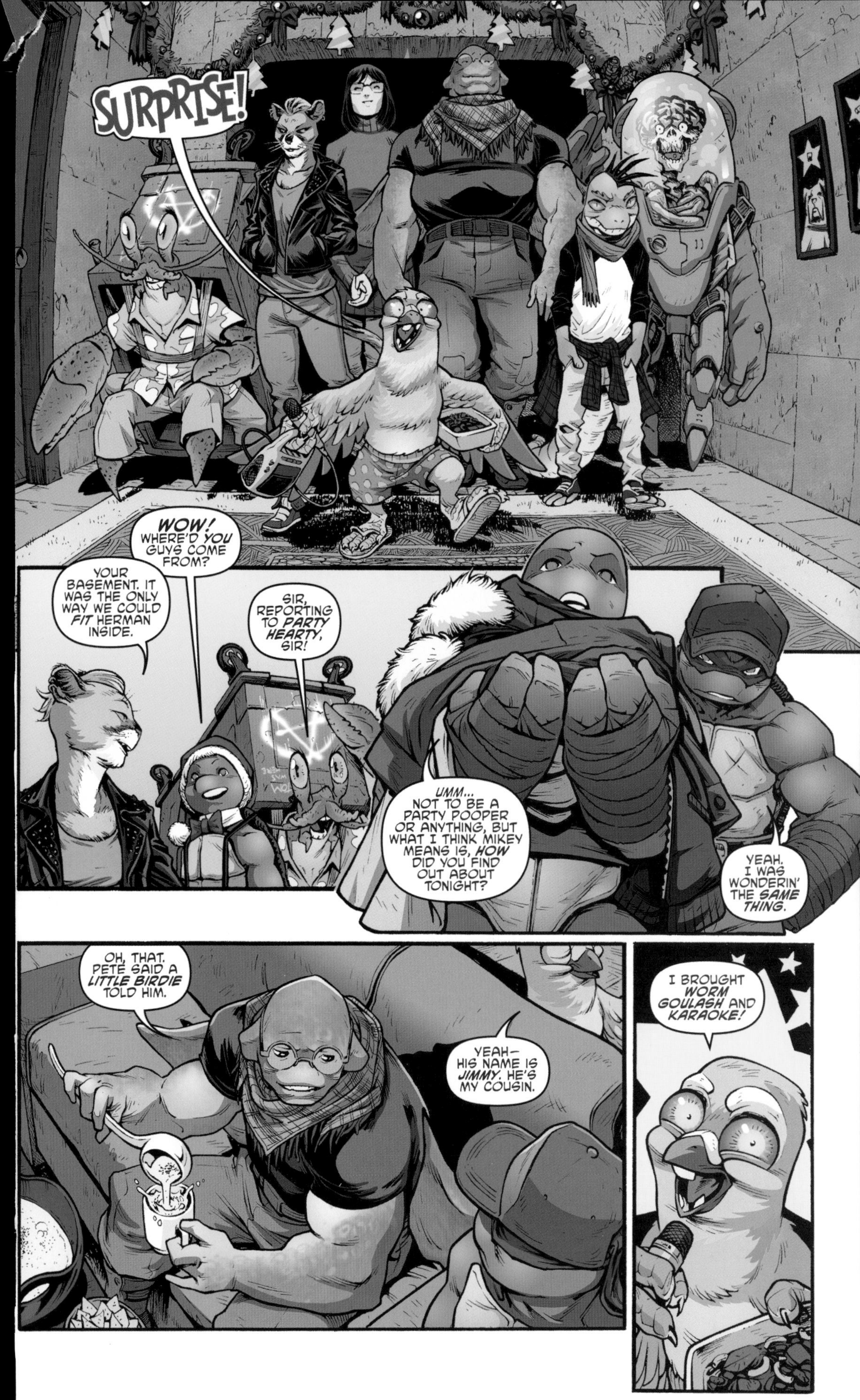
SURPRISE!
WOW! WHERE'D YOU GUYS COME FROM?
YOUR BASEMENT. IT WAS THE ONLY WAY WE COULD FIT HERMAN INSIDE.
SIR, REPORTING TO PARTY HEARTY, SIR!
UMM... NOT TO BE A PARTY POOPER OR ANYTHING, BUT WHAT I THINK MIKEY MEANS IS, HOW DID YOU FIND OUT ABOUT TONIGHT?
YEAH. I WAS WONDERIN' THE SAME THING.
OH, THAT. PETE SAID A LITTLE BIRDIE TOLD HIM.
YEAH— HIS NAME IS JIMMY. HE'S MY COUSIN.
I BROUGHT WORM GOULASH AND KARAOKE!

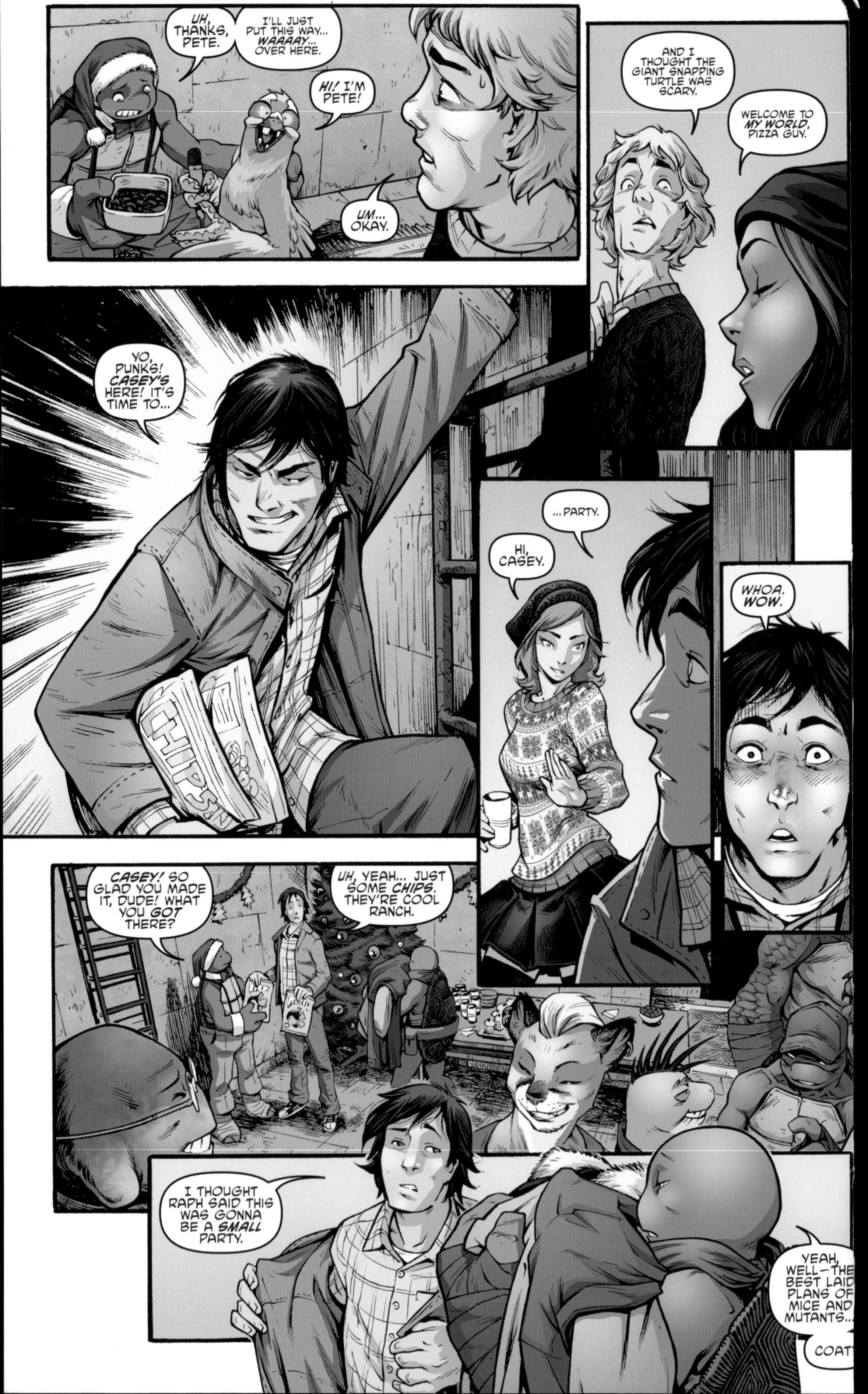

UH, THANKS, PETE.
I'LL JUST PUT THIS WAY... WAAAAY... OVER HERE.
HI! I'M PETE!
UM... OKAY.
AND I THOUGHT THE GIANT SNAPPING TURTLE WAS SCARY.
WELCOME TO MY WORLD, PIZZA GUY.
YO, PUNKS! CASEY'S HERE! IT'S TIME TO...
CHIPS
...PARTY.
HI, CASEY.
WHOA. WOW.
CASEY! SO GLAD YOU MADE IT, DUDE! WHAT YOU GOT THERE?
UH, YEAH... JUST SOME CHIPS. THEY'RE COOL RANCH.
I THOUGHT RAPH SAID THIS WAS GONNA BE A SMALL PARTY.
YEAH, WELL--THE BEST LAID PLANS OF MICE AND MUTANTS...
COAT

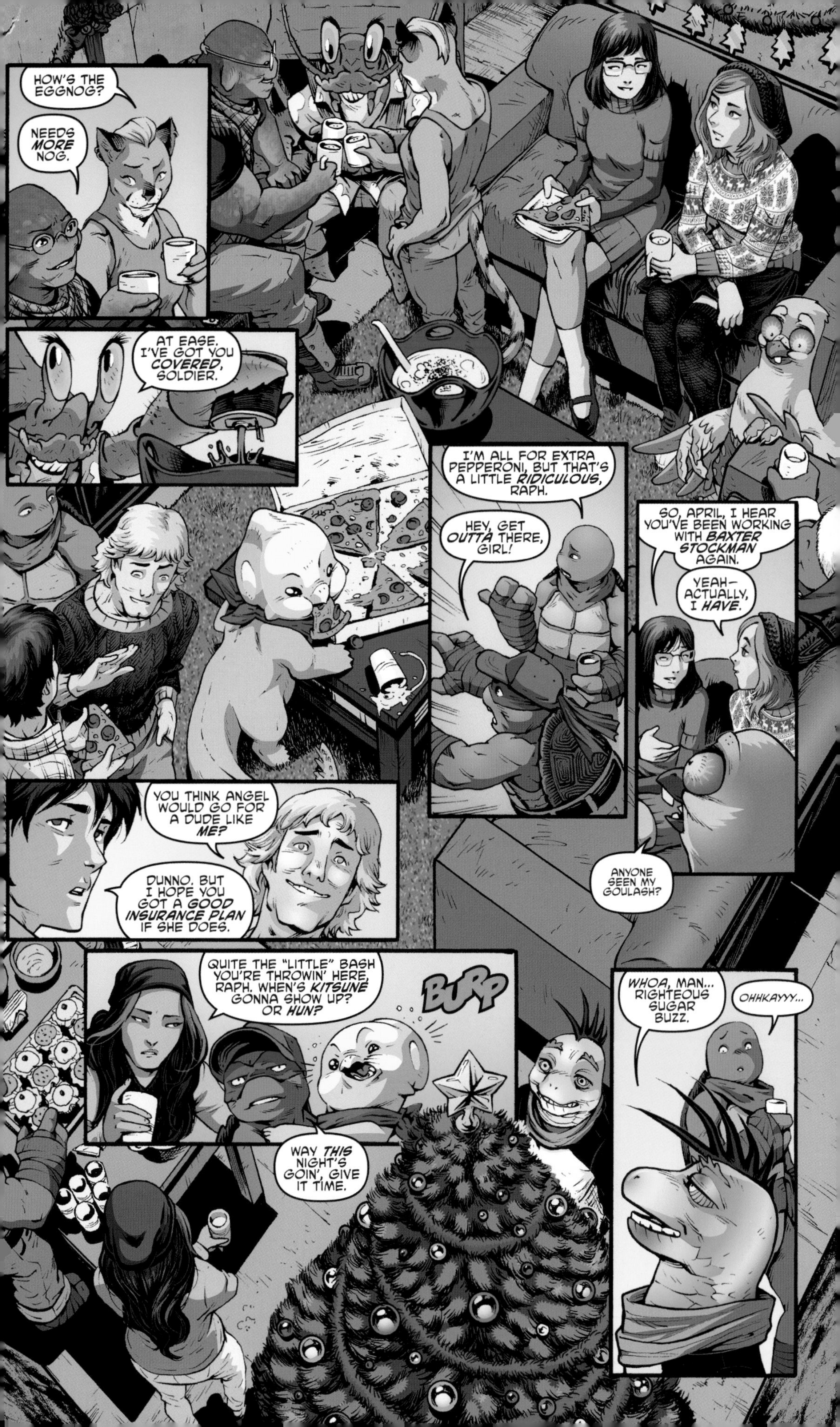
HOW'S THE EGGNOG?
NEEDS *MORE* NOG.
AT EASE. I'VE GOT YOU *COVERED*, SOLDIER.
I'M ALL FOR EXTRA PEPPERONI, BUT THAT'S A LITTLE *RIDICULOUS*, RAPH.
HEY, GET *OUTTA* THERE, GIRL!
SO, APRIL, I HEAR YOU'VE BEEN WORKING WITH *BAXTER STOCKMAN* AGAIN.
YEAH— ACTUALLY, I *HAVE*.
YOU THINK ANGEL WOULD GO FOR A DUDE LIKE *ME?*
DUNNO. BUT I HOPE YOU GOT A *GOOD INSURANCE PLAN* IF SHE DOES.
ANYONE SEEN MY GOULASH?
QUITE THE "LITTLE" BASH YOU'RE THROWIN' HERE, RAPH. WHEN'S *KITSUNE* GONNA SHOW UP? OR *HUN?*
BURP
WAY *THIS* NIGHT'S GOIN', GIVE IT TIME.
WHOA, MAN... RIGHTEOUS SUGAR BUZZ.
OHHKAYYY...

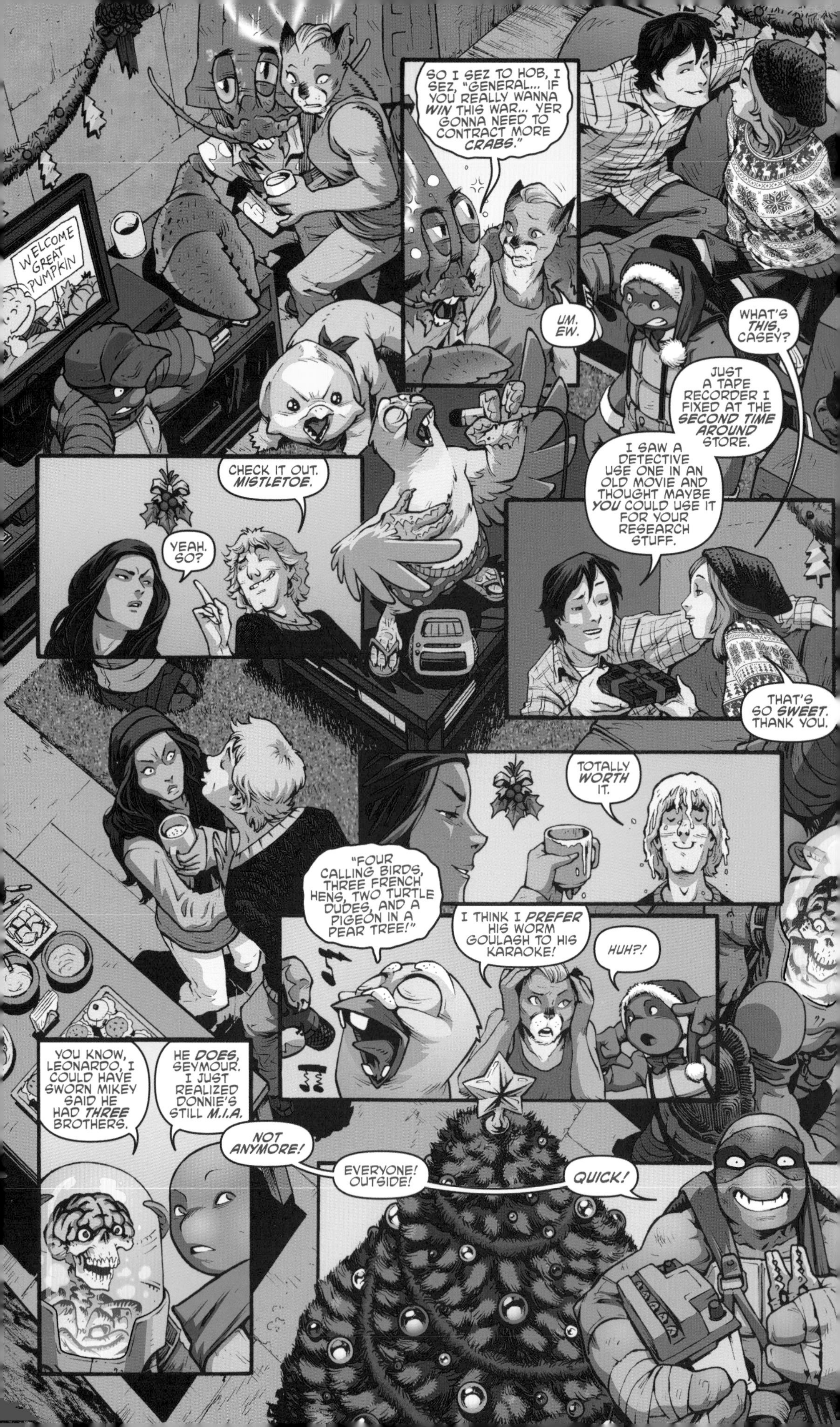

WELCOME GREAT PUMPKIN
SO I SEZ TO HOB, I SEZ, "GENERAL... IF YOU REALLY WANNA WIN THIS WAR... YER GONNA NEED TO CONTRACT MORE CRABS."
UM. EW.
WHAT'S THIS, CASEY?
JUST A TAPE RECORDER I FIXED AT THE SECOND TIME AROUND STORE.
I SAW A DETECTIVE USE ONE IN AN OLD MOVIE AND THOUGHT MAYBE YOU COULD USE IT FOR YOUR RESEARCH STUFF.
CHECK IT OUT. MISTLETOE.
YEAH. SO?
THAT'S SO SWEET. THANK YOU.
TOTALLY WORTH IT.
"FOUR CALLING BIRDS, THREE FRENCH HENS, TWO TURTLE DUDES, AND A PIGEON IN A PEAR TREE!"
I THINK I PREFER HIS WORM GOULASH TO HIS KARAOKE!
HUH?!
YOU KNOW, LEONARDO, I COULD HAVE SWORN MIKEY SAID HE HAD THREE BROTHERS.
HE DOES, SEYMOUR. I JUST REALIZED DONNIE'S STILL M.I.A.
NOT ANYMORE!
EVERYONE! OUTSIDE!
QUICK!

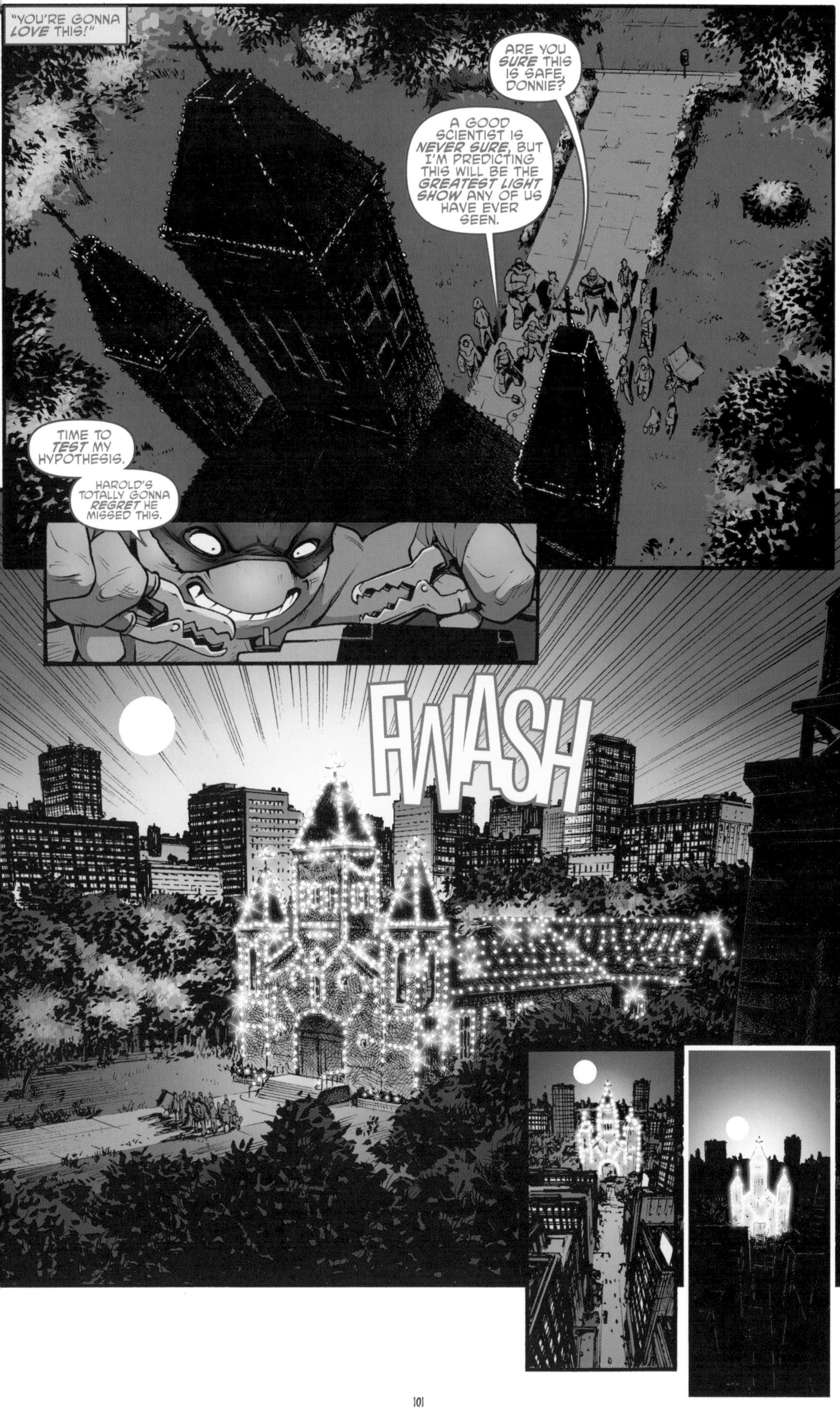
"YOU'RE GONNA *LOVE* THIS!"
ARE YOU *SURE* THIS IS SAFE, DONNIE?
A GOOD SCIENTIST IS *NEVER SURE*, BUT I'M PREDICTING THIS WILL BE THE *GREATEST LIGHT SHOW* ANY OF US HAVE EVER SEEN.
TIME TO *TEST* MY HYPOTHESIS.
HAROLD'S TOTALLY GONNA *REGRET* HE MISSED THIS.
FWASH

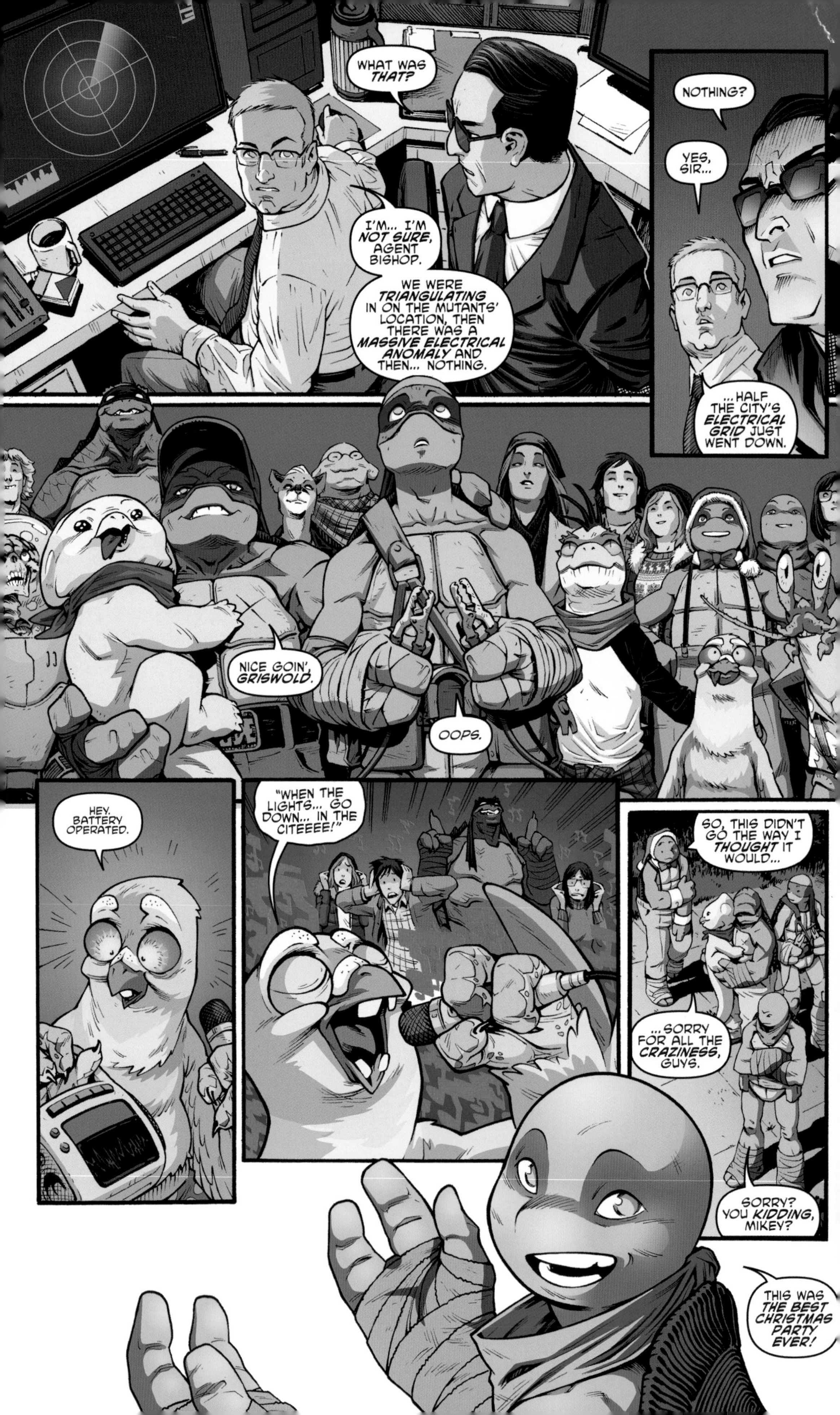
WHAT WAS THAT?
I'M... I'M NOT SURE, AGENT BISHOP.
WE WERE TRIANGULATING IN ON THE MUTANTS' LOCATION, THEN THERE WAS A MASSIVE ELECTRICAL ANOMALY AND THEN... NOTHING.
NOTHING?
YES, SIR...
...HALF THE CITY'S ELECTRICAL GRID JUST WENT DOWN.
NICE GOIN', GRISWOLD.
OOPS.
HEY. BATTERY OPERATED.
"WHEN THE LIGHTS... GO DOWN... IN THE CITEEEE!"
SO, THIS DIDN'T GO THE WAY I THOUGHT IT WOULD...
...SORRY FOR ALL THE CRAZINESS, GUYS.
SORRY? YOU KIDDING, MIKEY?
THIS WAS THE BEST CHRISTMAS PARTY EVER!

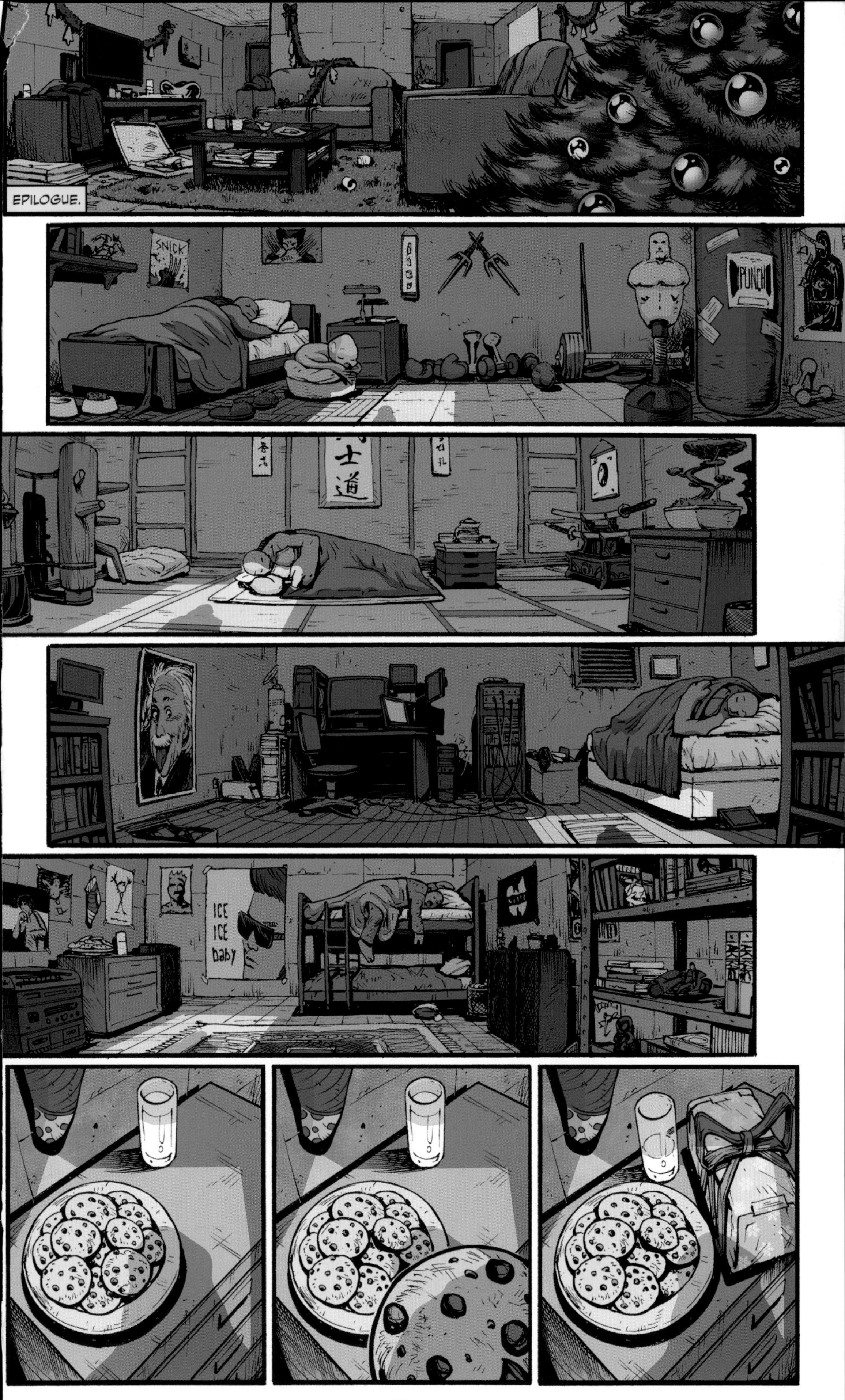
EPILOGUE.
SNICK
PUNCH
ICE ICE baby

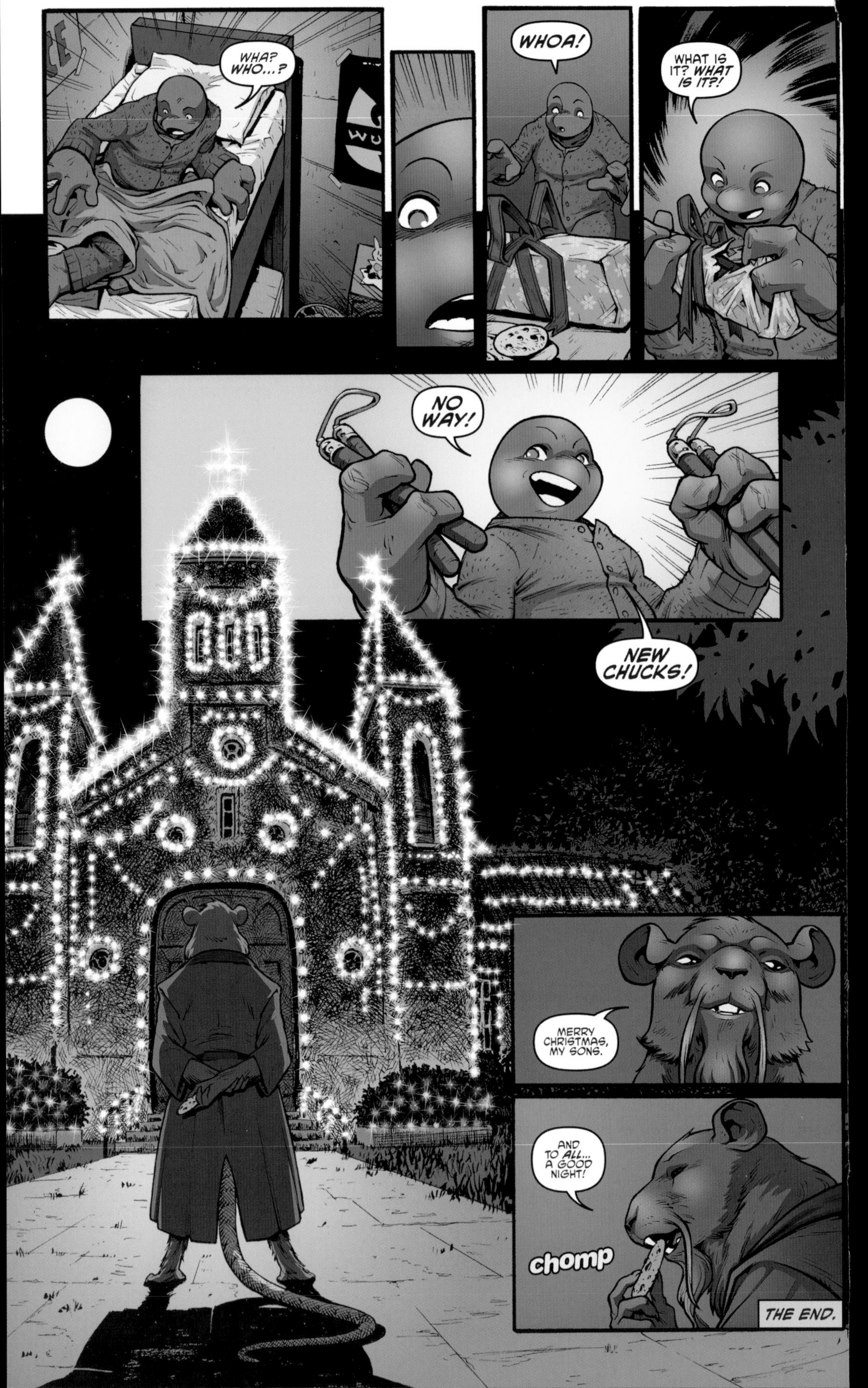
WHA? WHO...?
WHOA!
WHAT IS IT? WHAT IS IT?!
NO WAY!
NEW CHUCKS!
MERRY CHRISTMAS, MY SONS.
AND TO ALL... A GOOD NIGHT!
chomp
THE END.

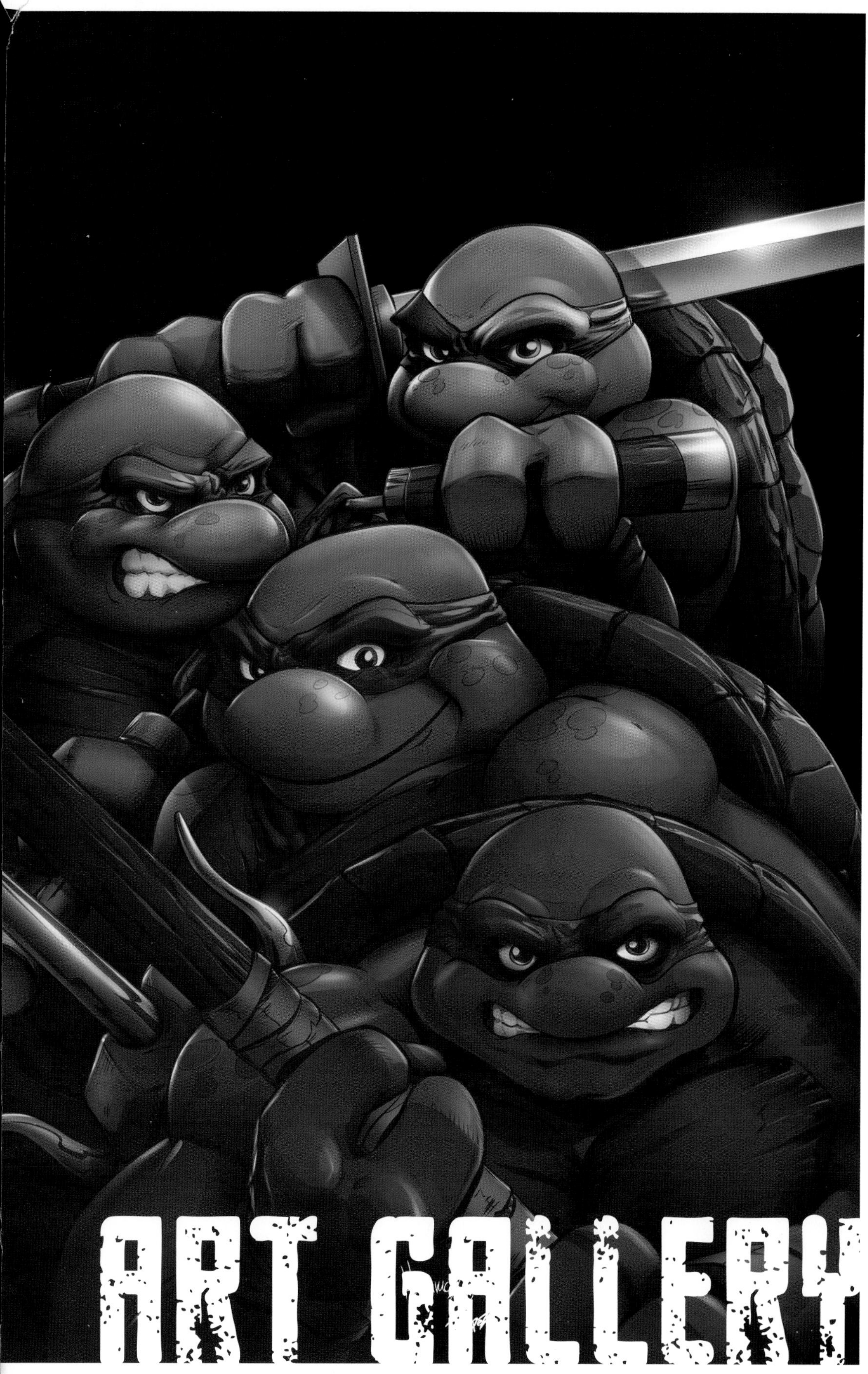

ART GALLERY
ART BY DAN HAMMOND

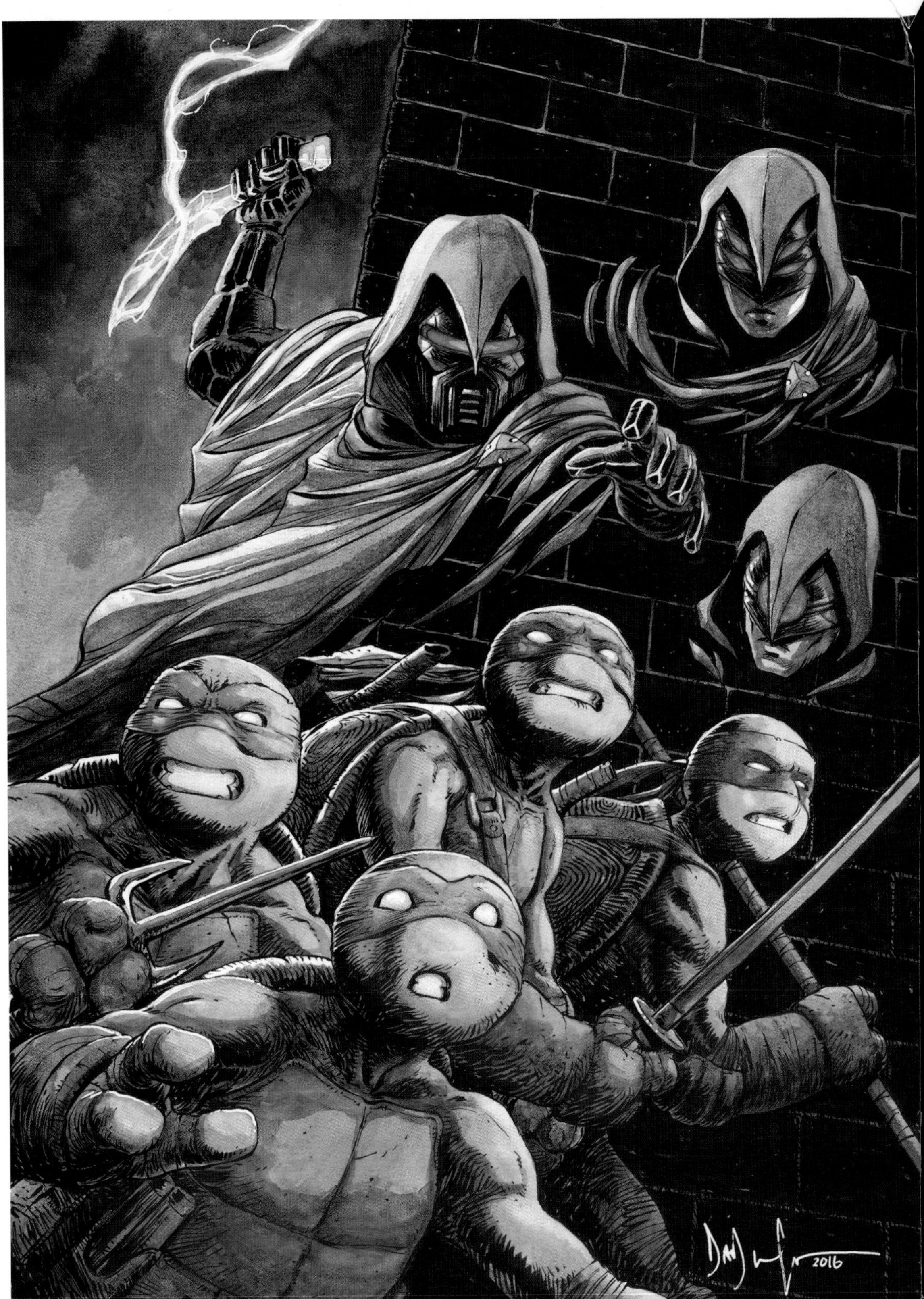
2016

ART BY DAVE WACHTER

OPPOSITE PAGE: ART BY KEVIN EASTMAN

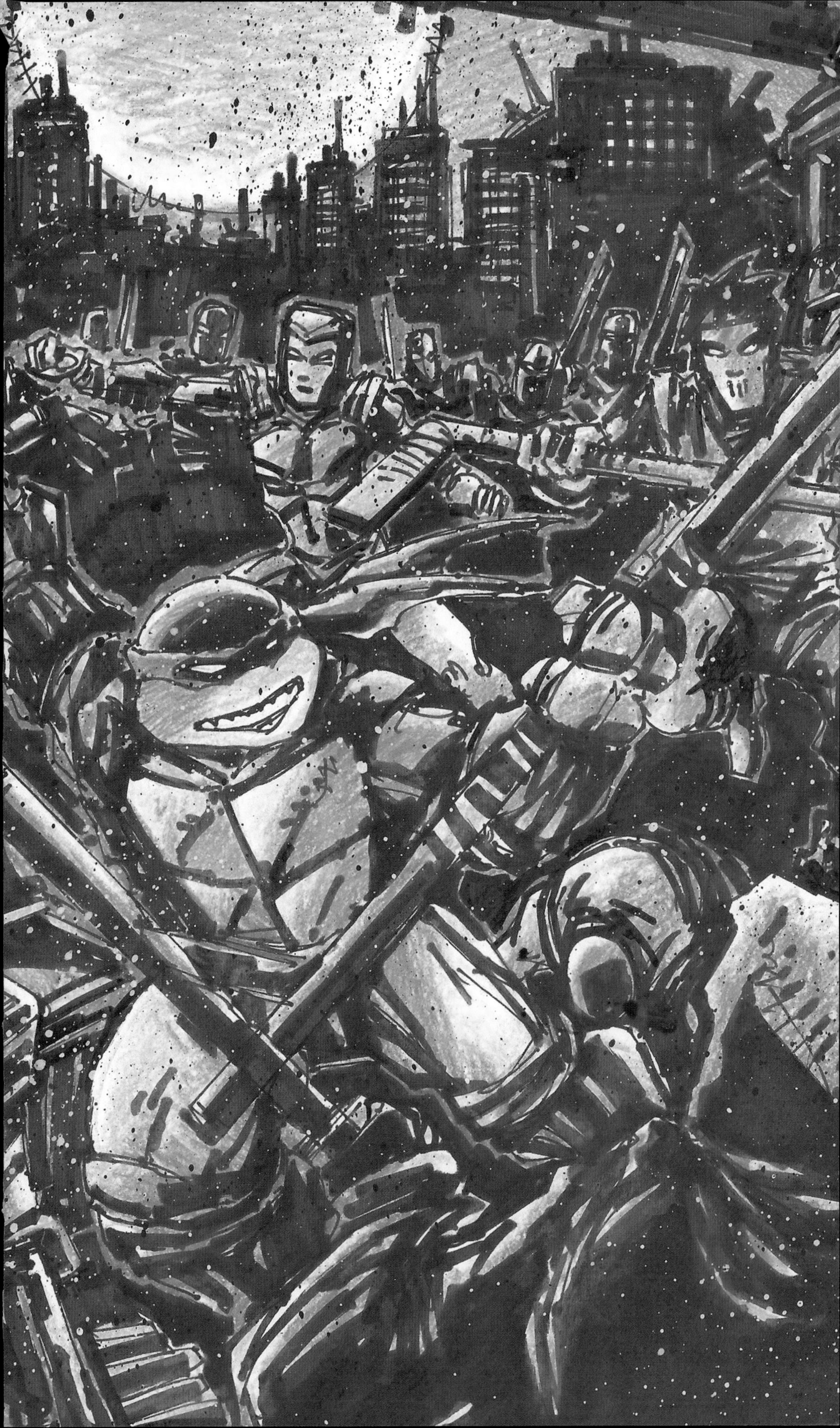

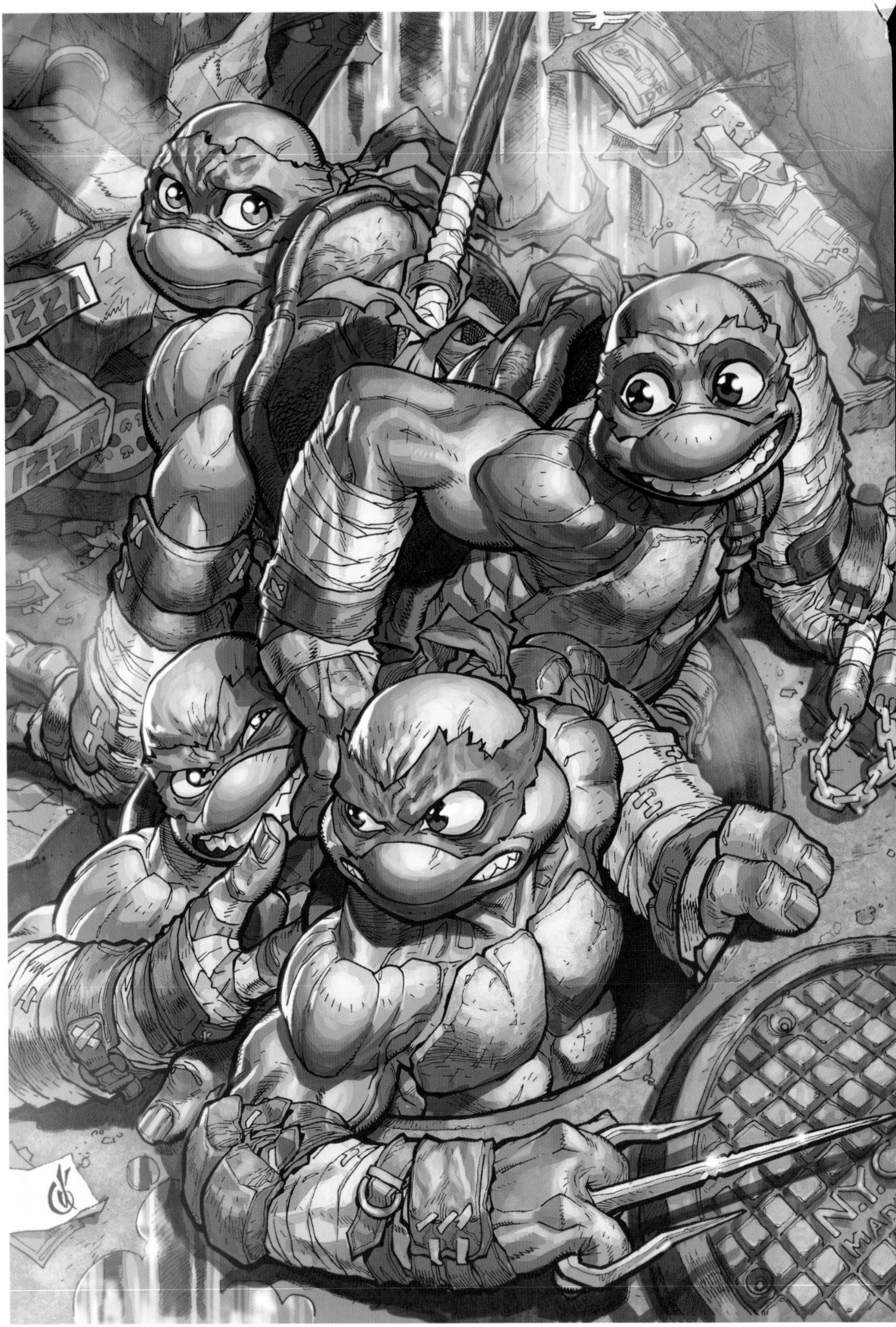

ART BY CARLOS D'ANDA

OPPOSITE PAGE: ART BY KEVIN EASTMAN · COLORS BY TOMI VARGA

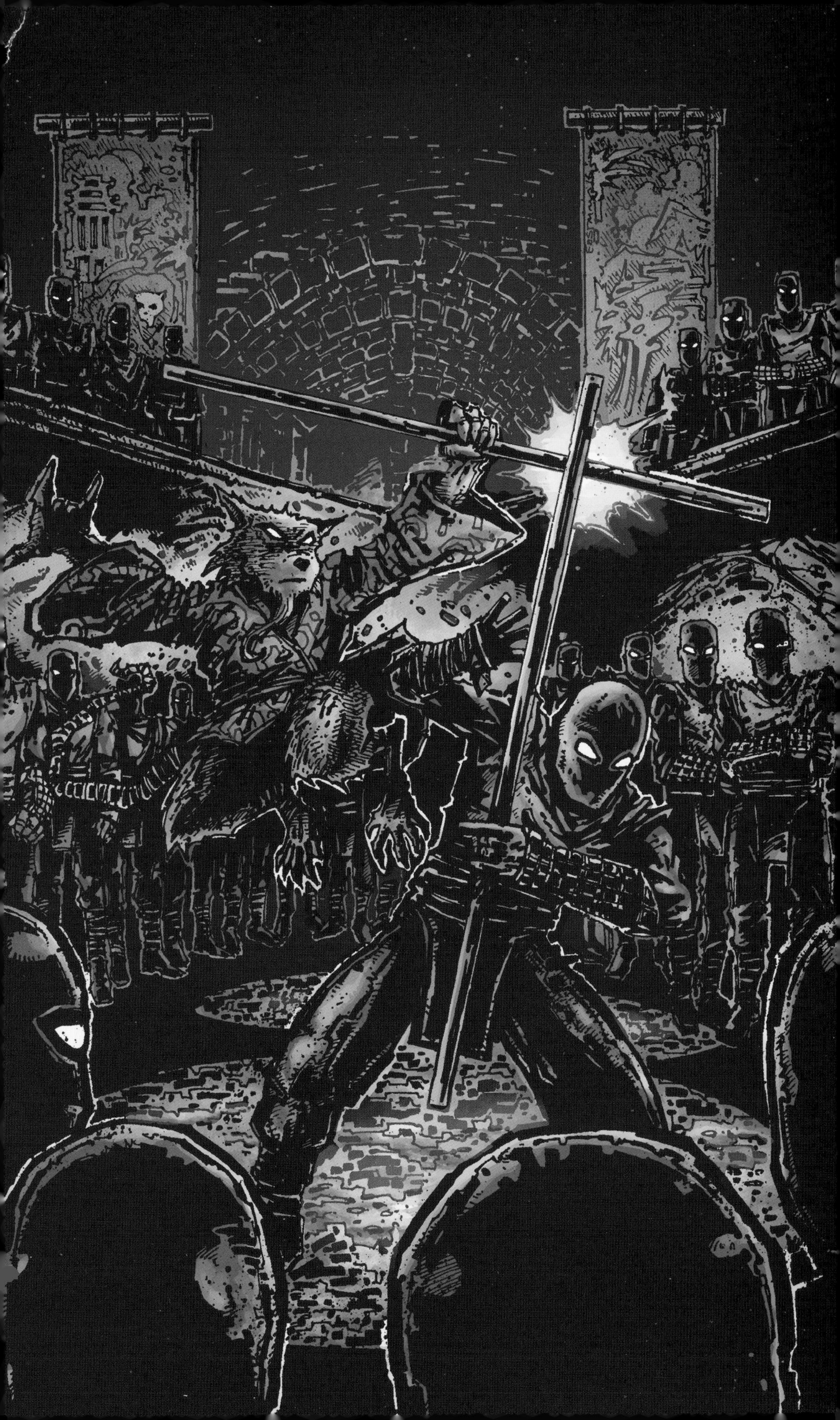

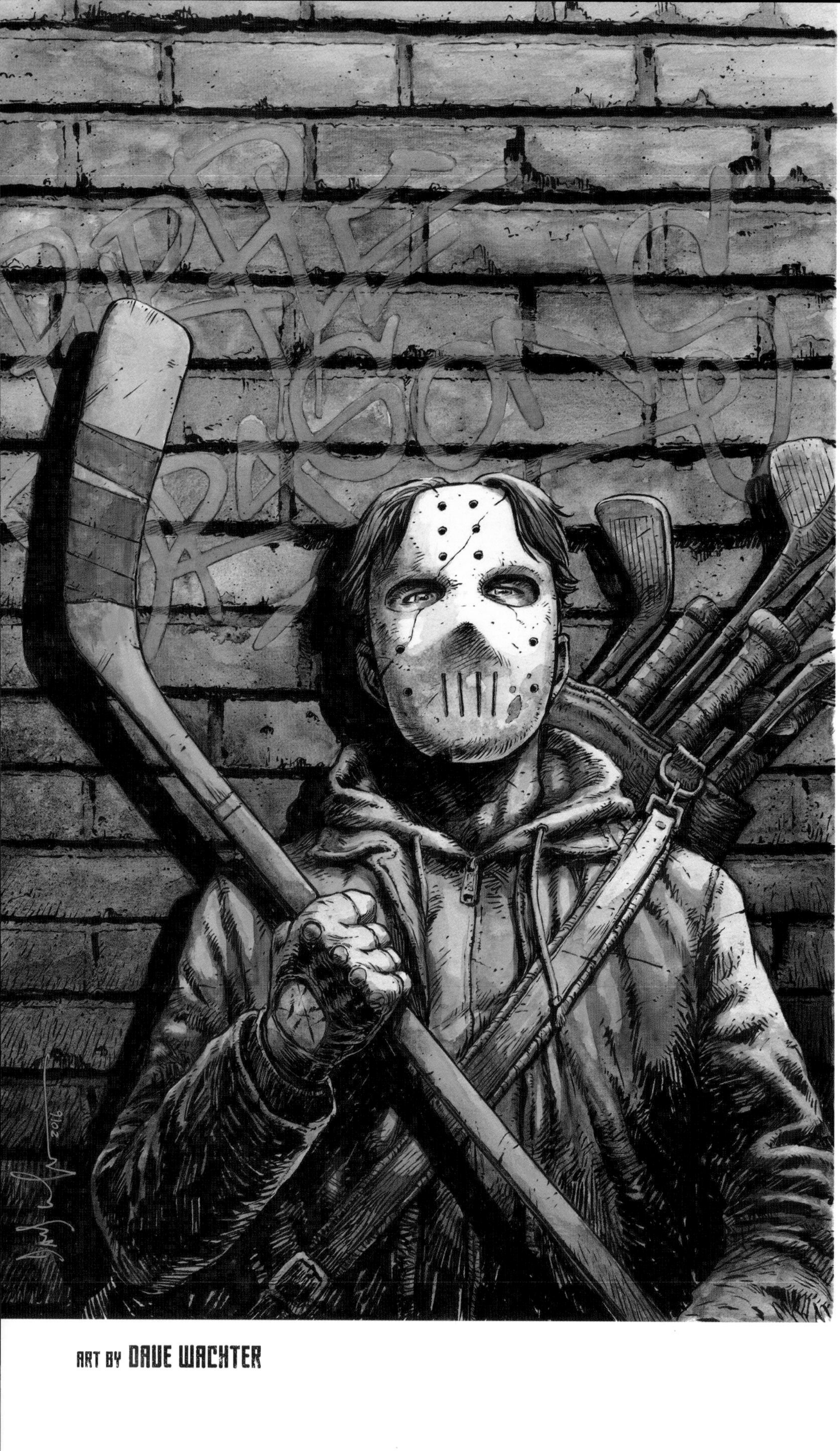

ART BY **DAVE WACHTER**

OPPOSITE PAGE: ART BY **KEVIN EASTMAN**

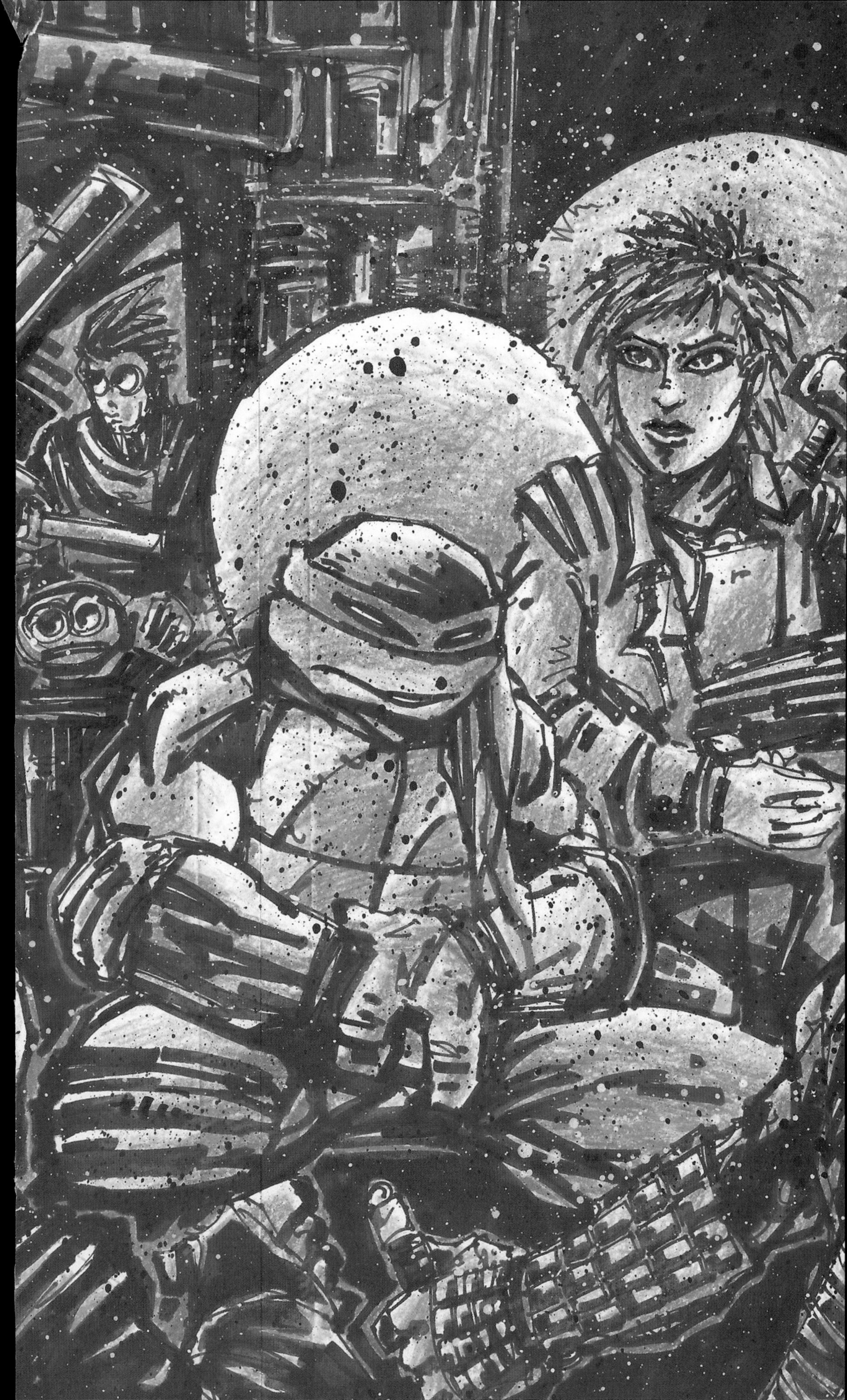

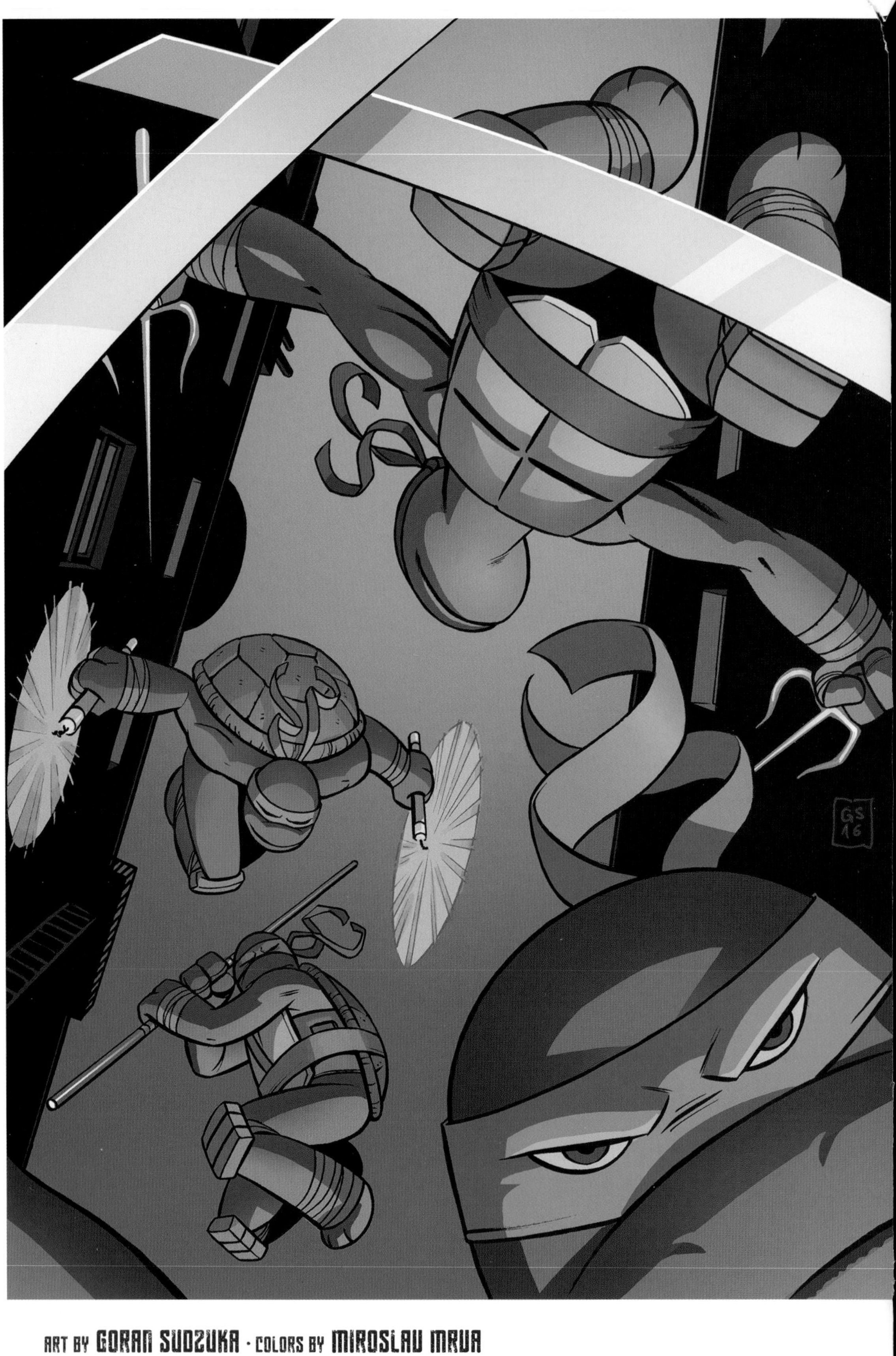
GS
16

ART BY GORAN SUDŽUKA · COLORS BY MIROSLAV MRVA

OPPOSITE PAGE: ART BY KEVIN EASTMAN · COLORS BY TOMI VARGA

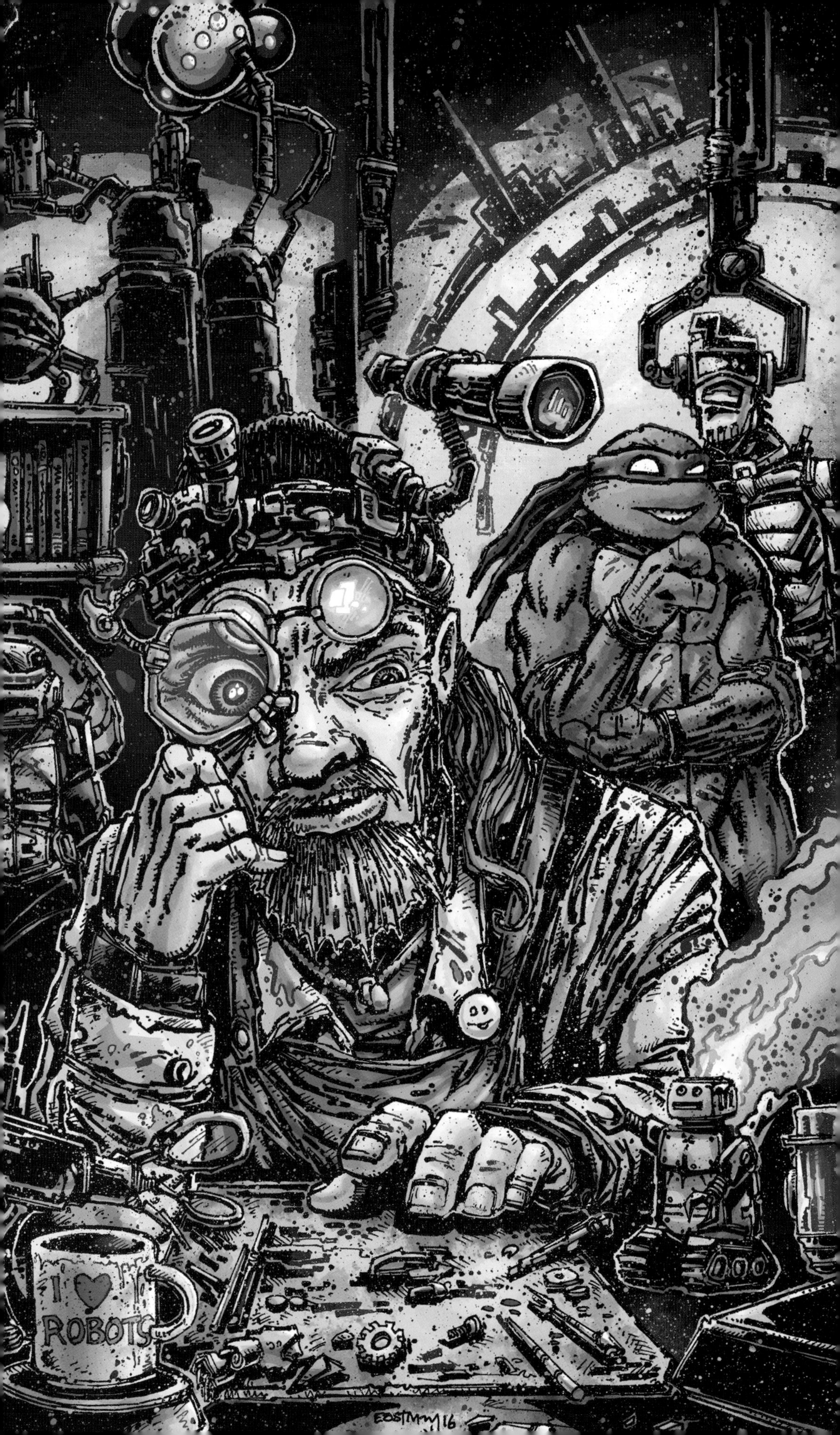
I ♥ ROBOTS

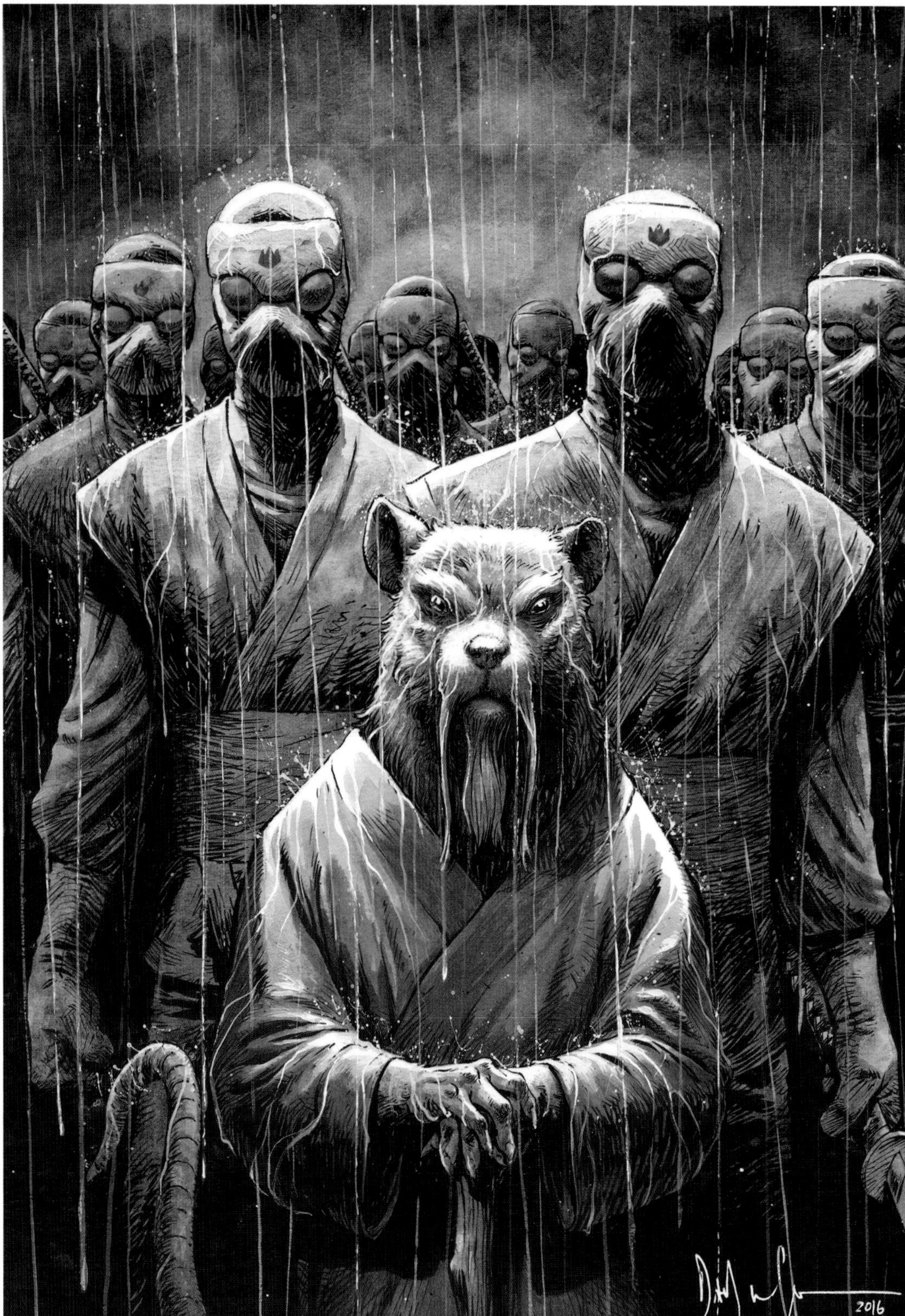
2016

ART BY DAVE WACHTER

ART BY ALEX KOTKIN

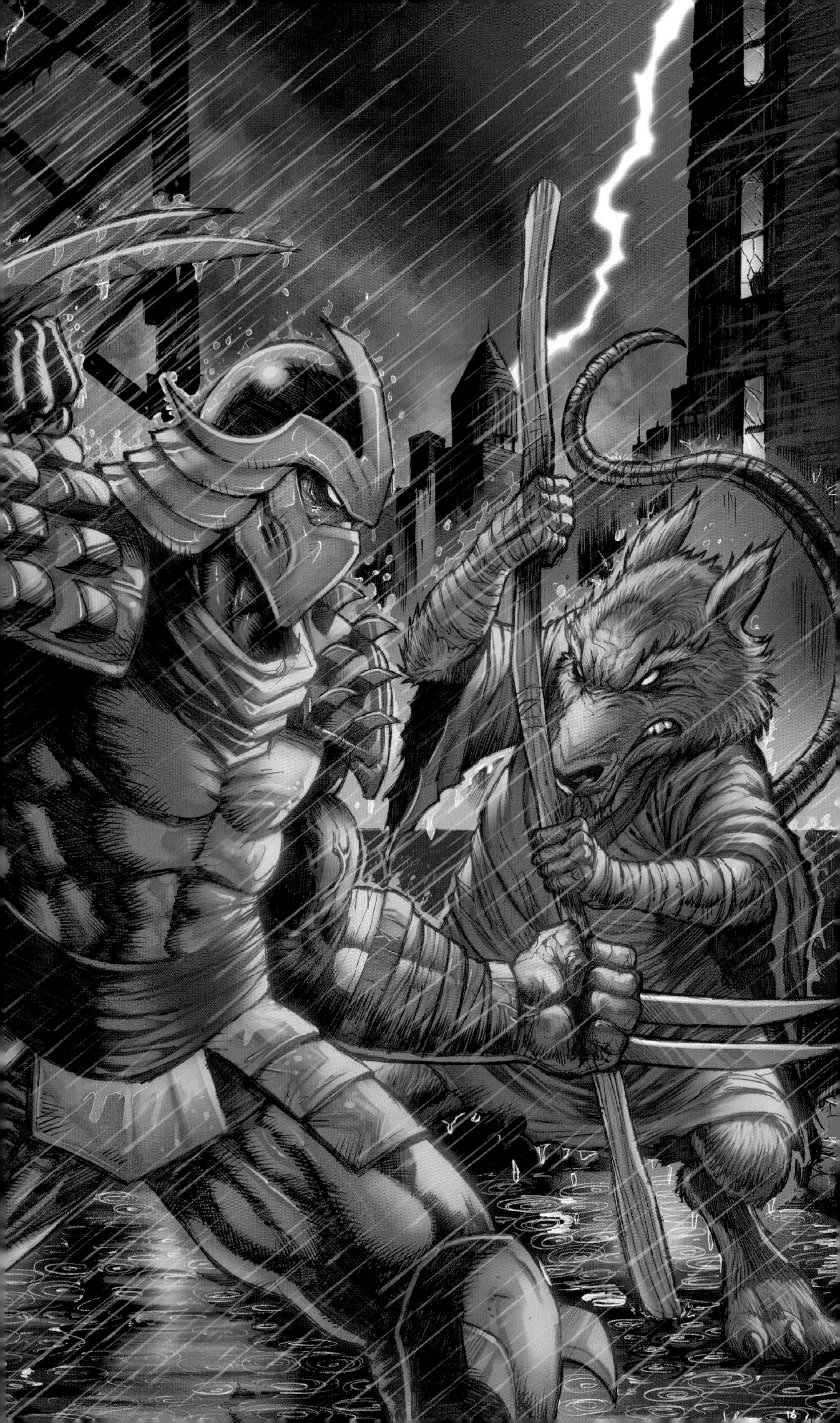

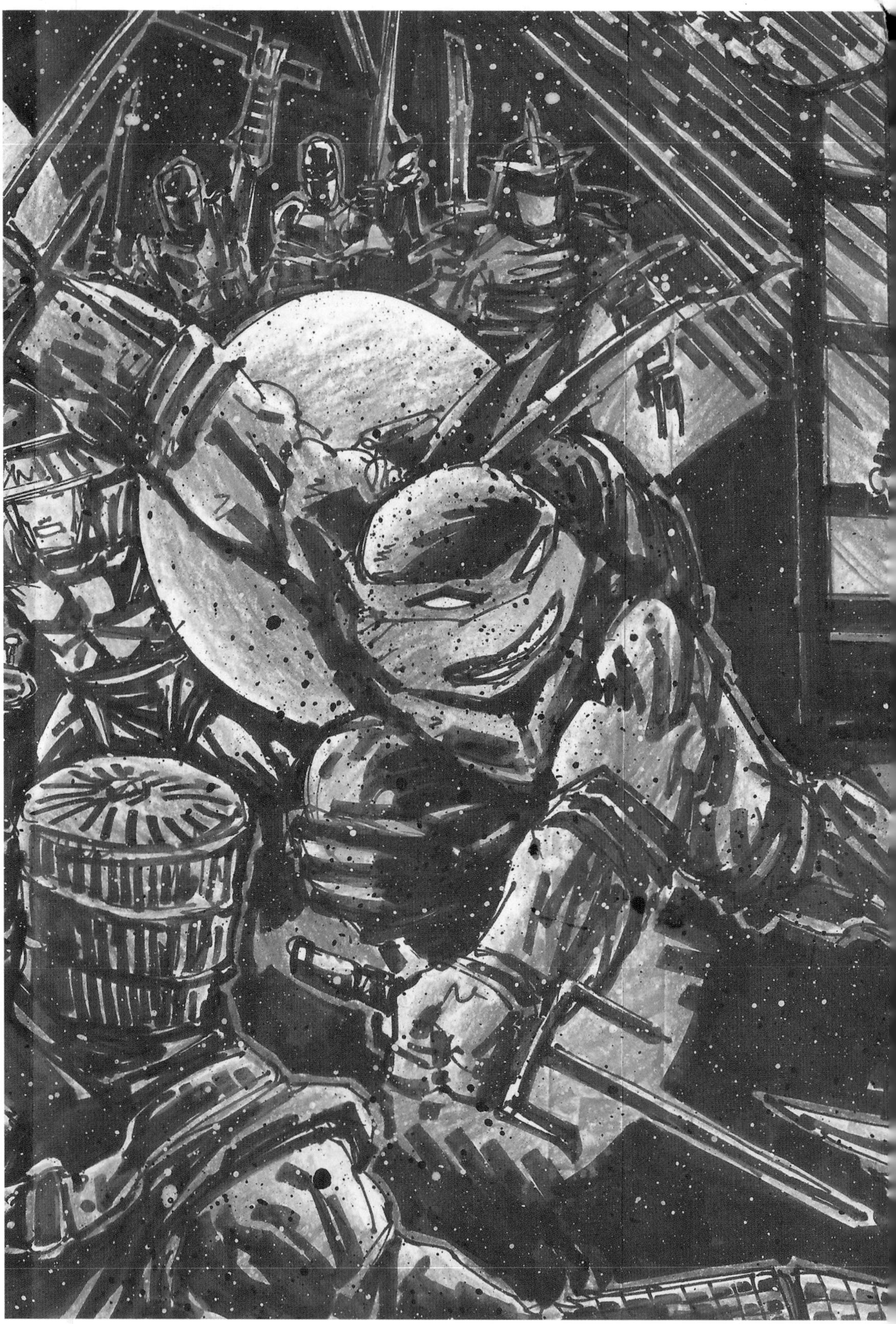

ART BY KEVIN EASTMAN

OPPOSITE PAGE: ART BY ROD THORNTON

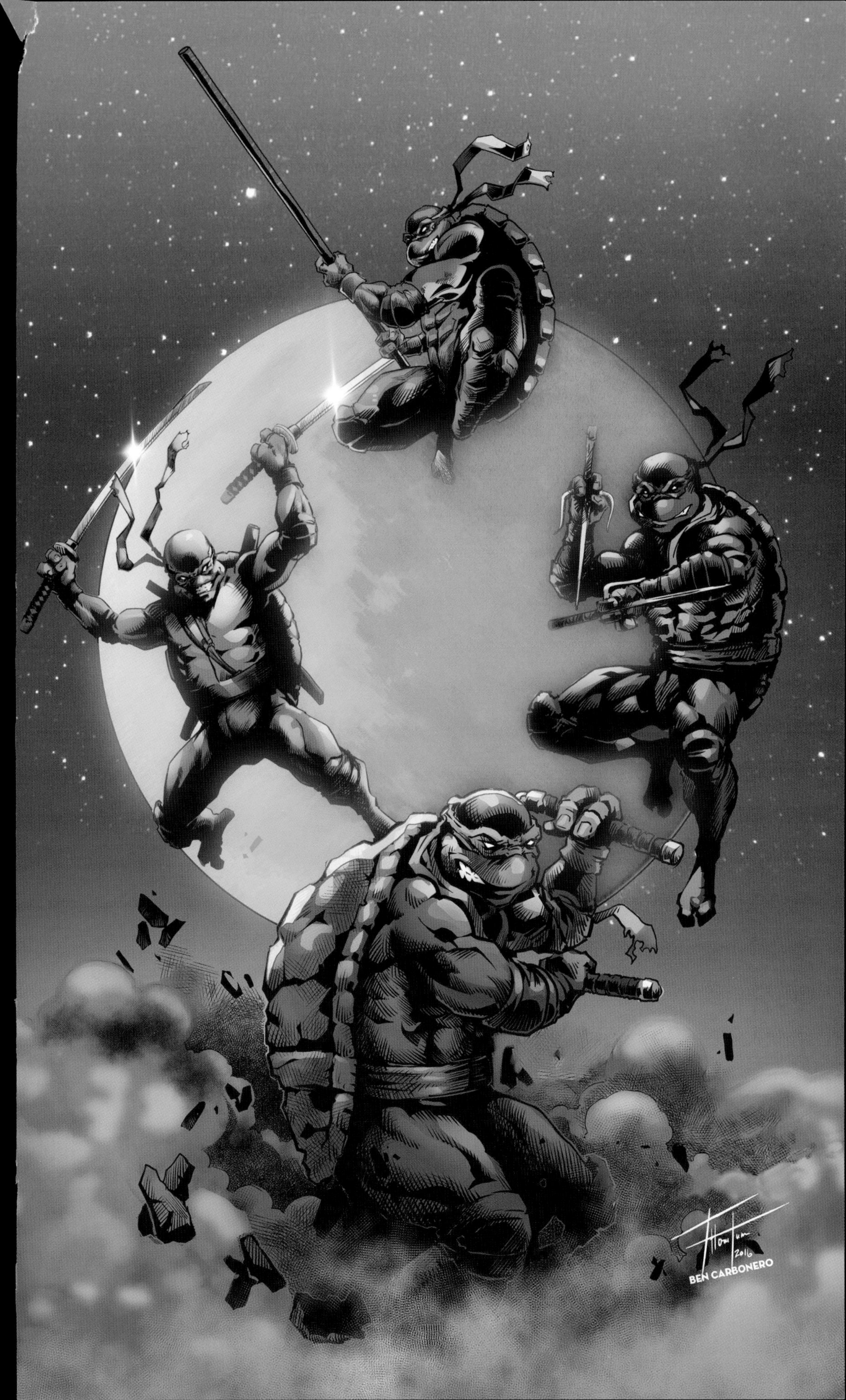

BEN CARBONERO

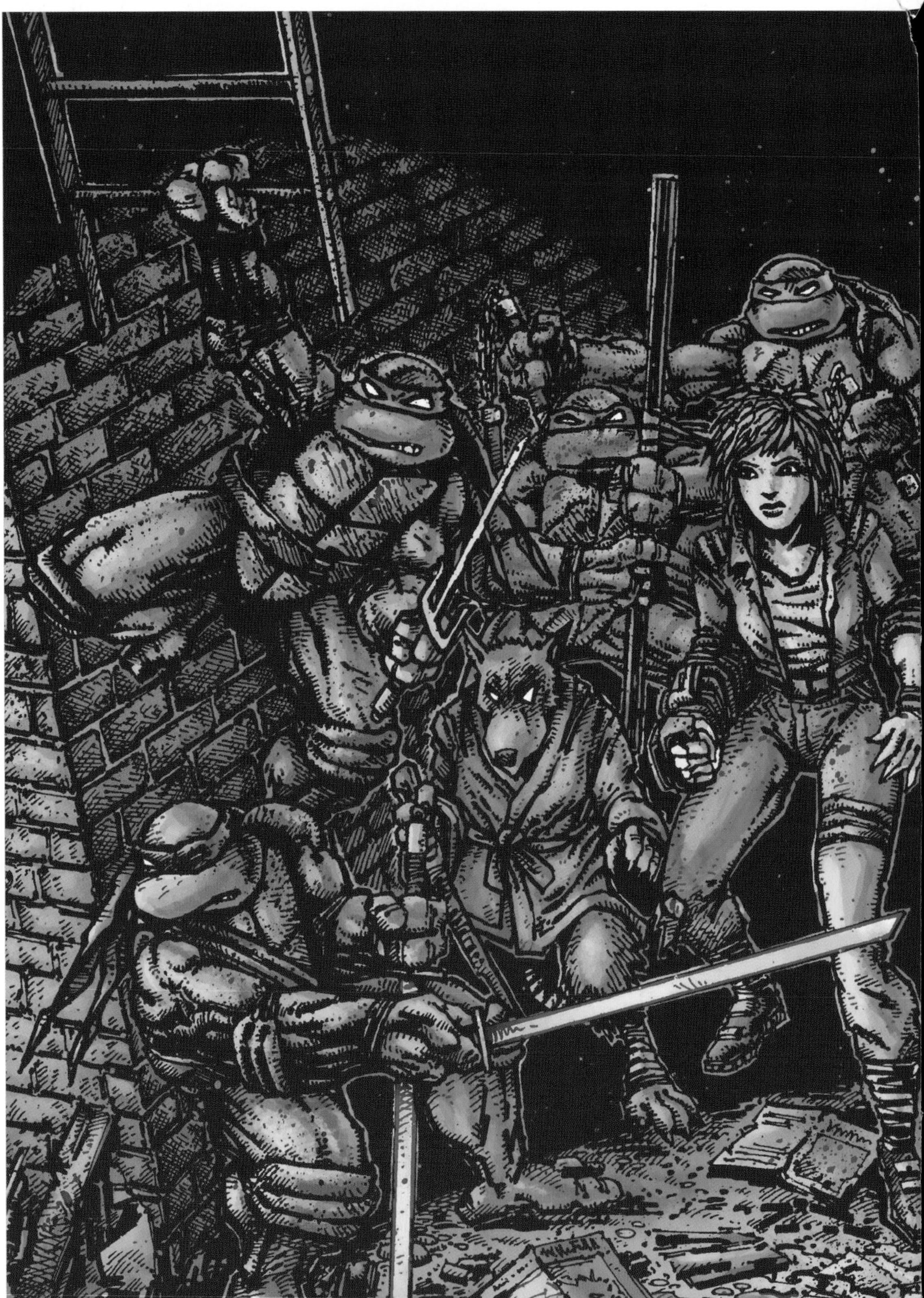
EASTMAN 2016

ART BY KEVIN EASTMAN · COLORS BY TOMI VARGA

OPPOSITE PAGE: ART BY ERIC JONES

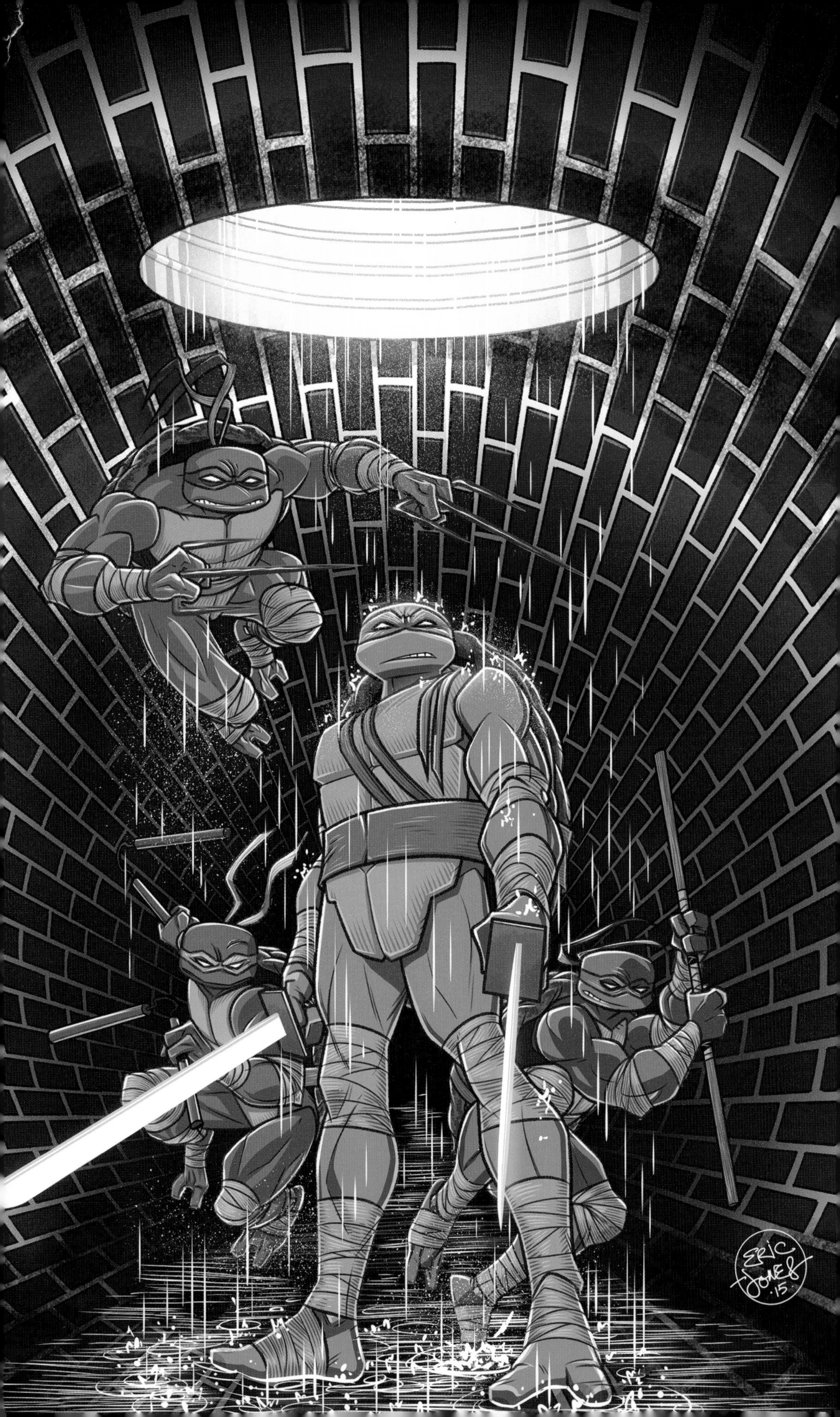
ERIC JONES '15

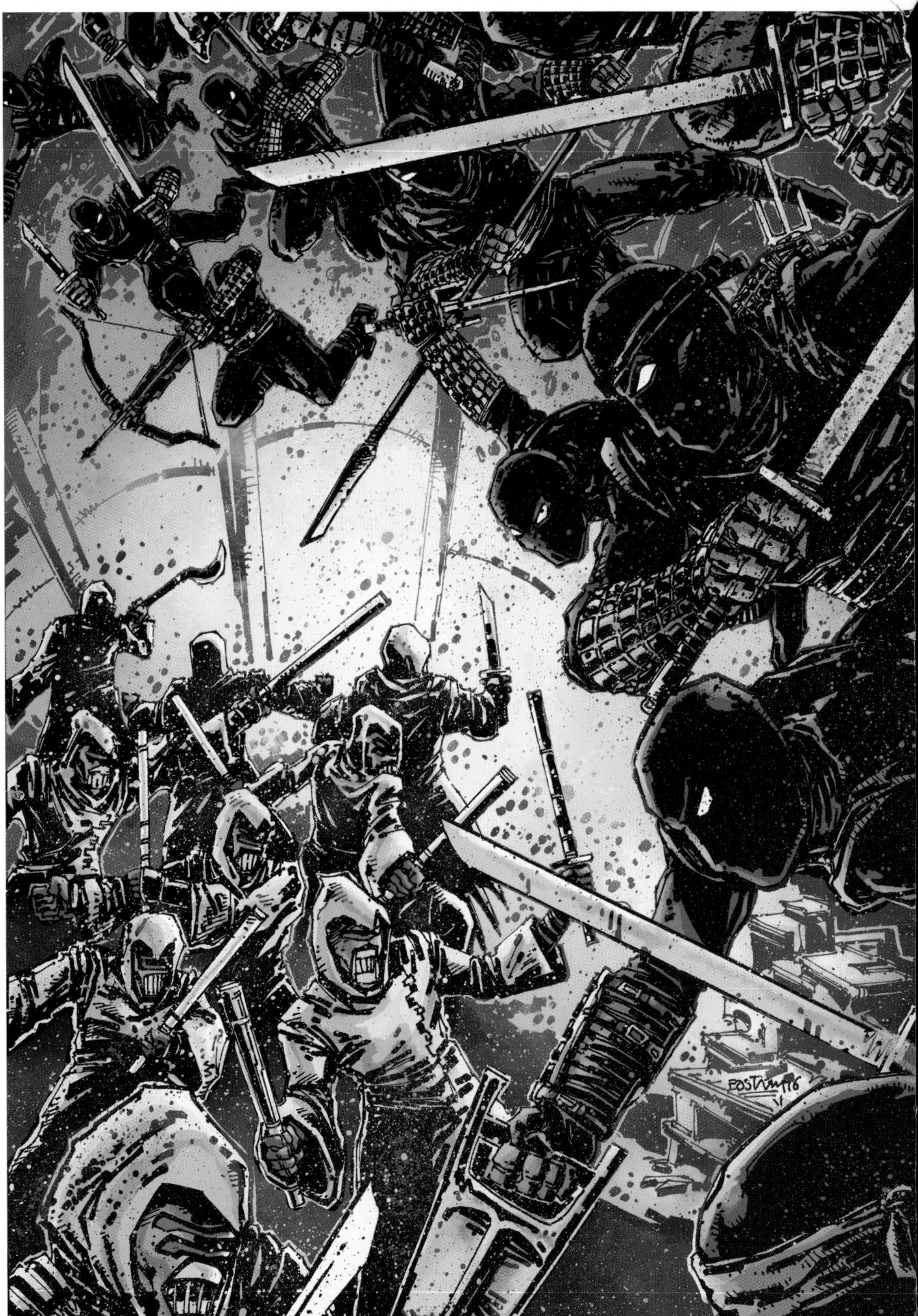
EASTMAN '16

ART BY KEVIN EASTMAN · COLORS BY TOMI VARGA

OPPOSITE PAGE: ART BY DAVE WACHTER

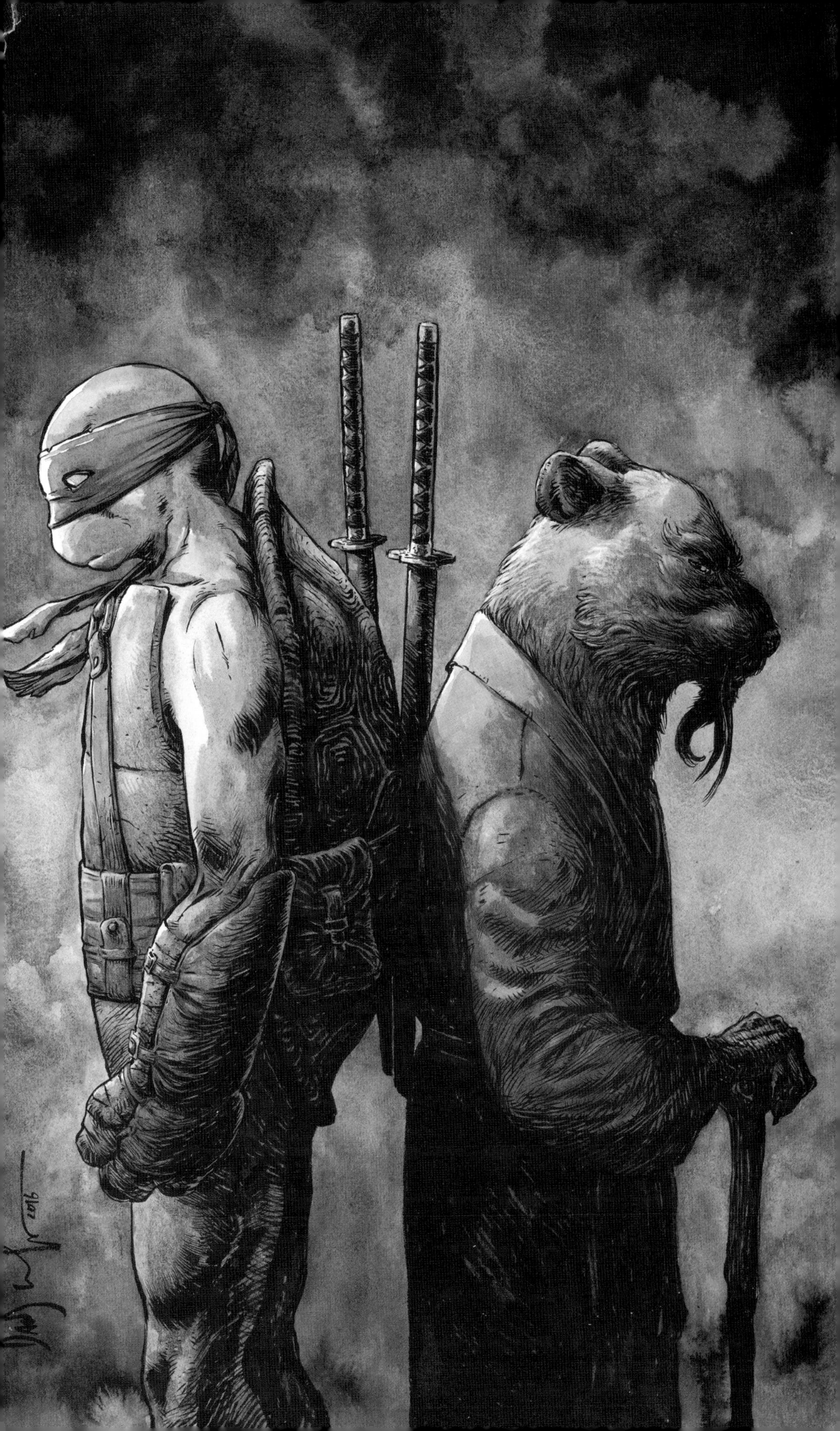

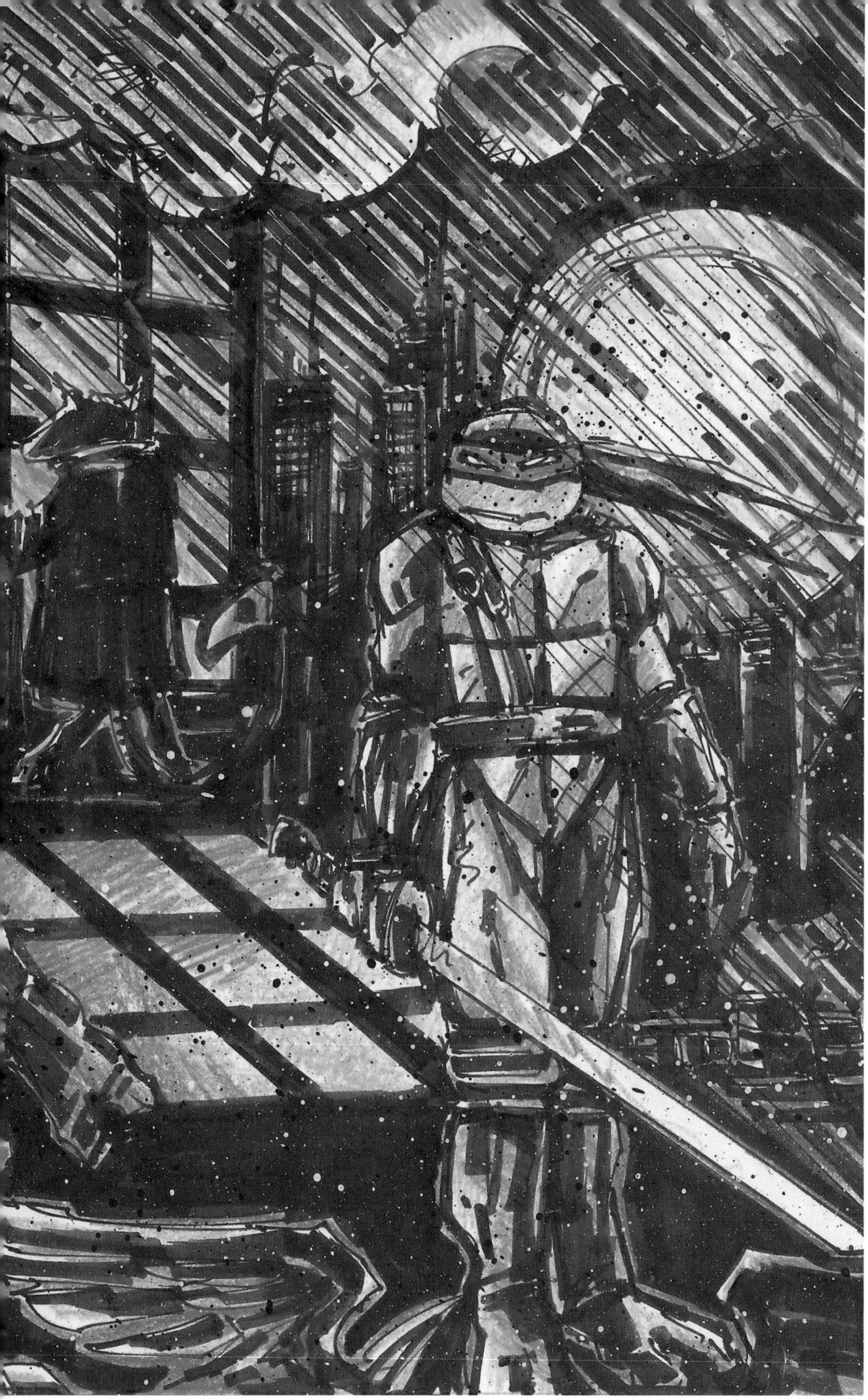

ART BY KEVIN EASTMAN

OPPOSITE PAGE: ART BY EDWIN HUANG

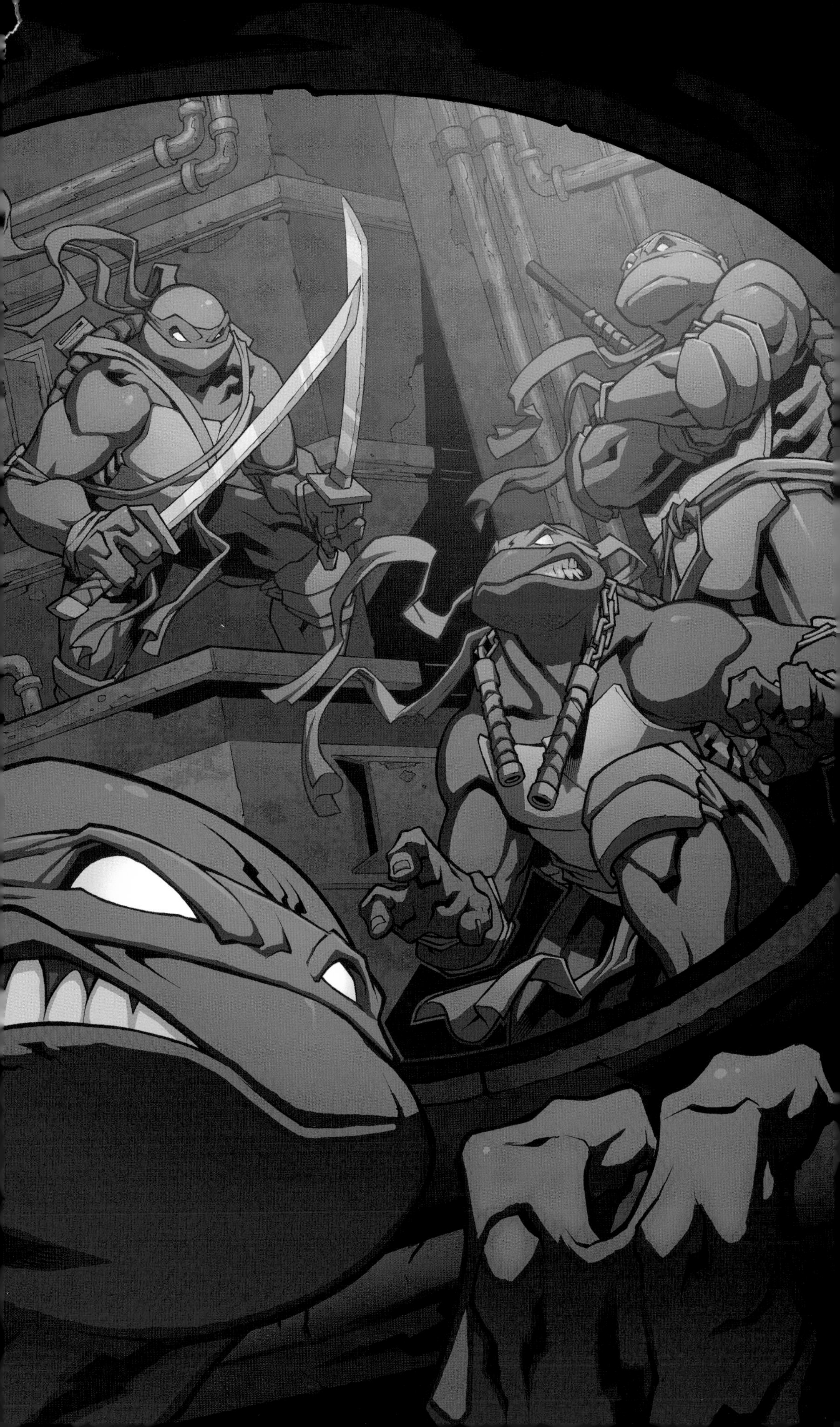

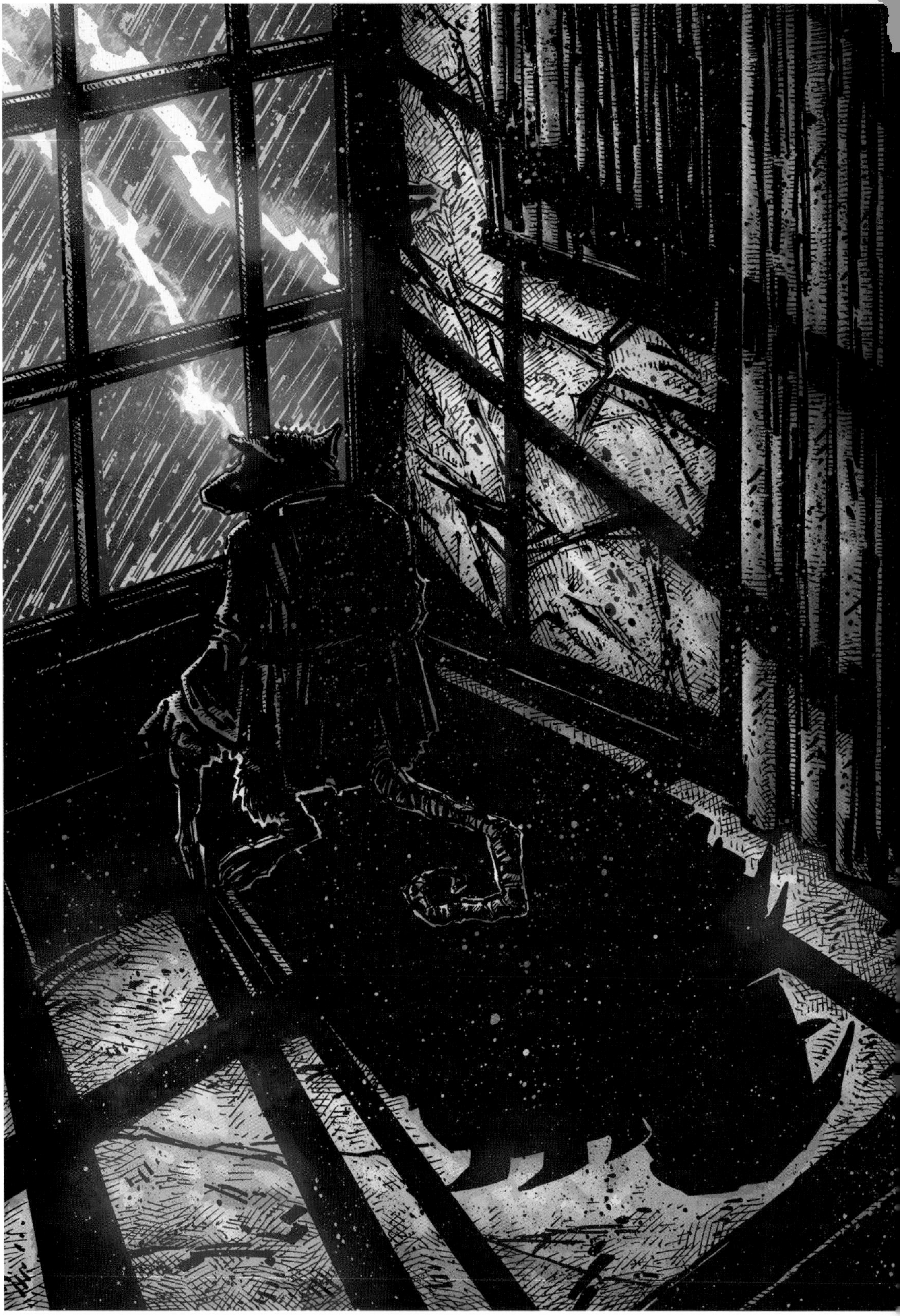

ART BY KEVIN EASTMAN · COLORS BY TOMI VARGA

OPPOSITE PAGE: ART BY MATEUS SANTOLOUCO

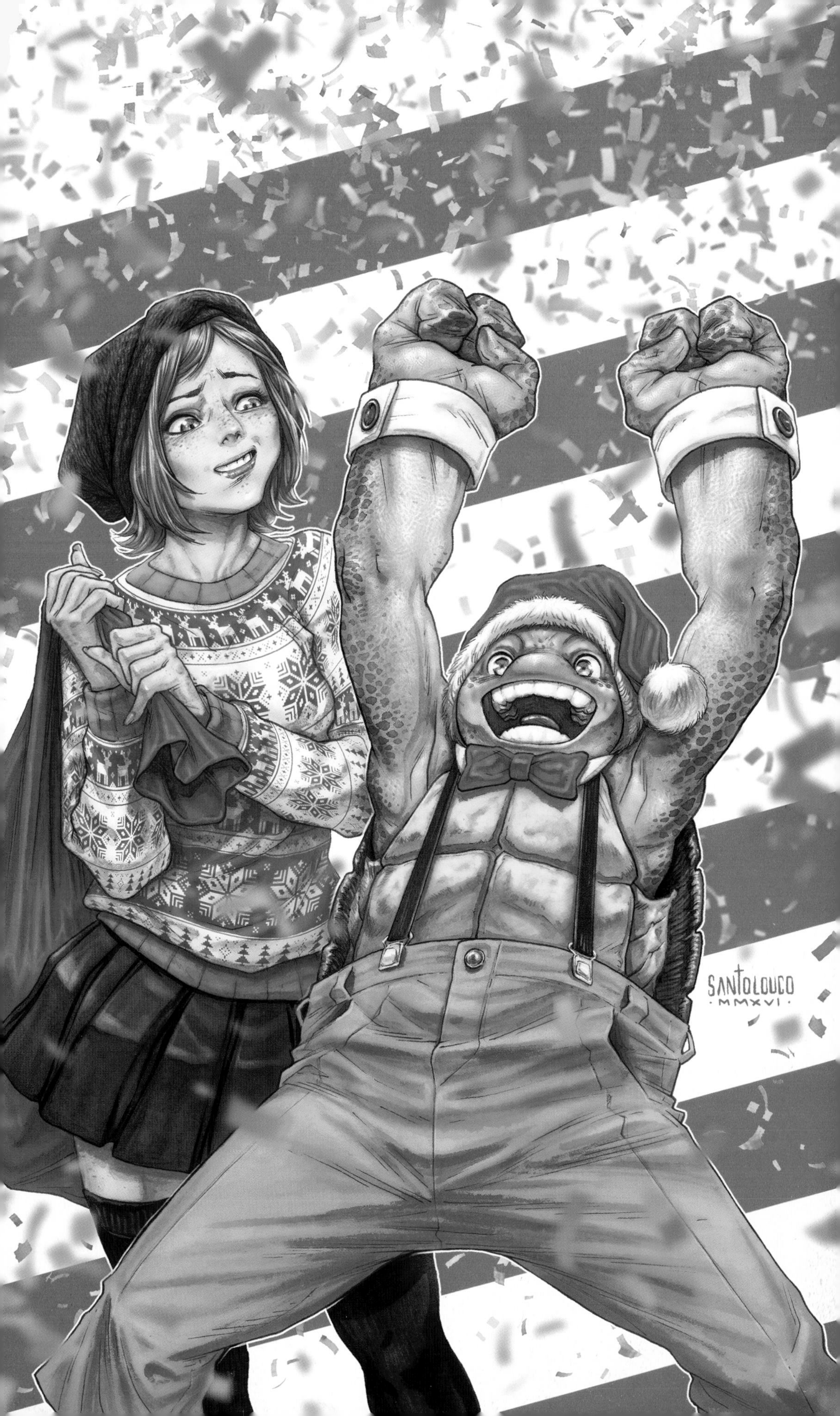
SANTOLOUCO
·MMXVI·

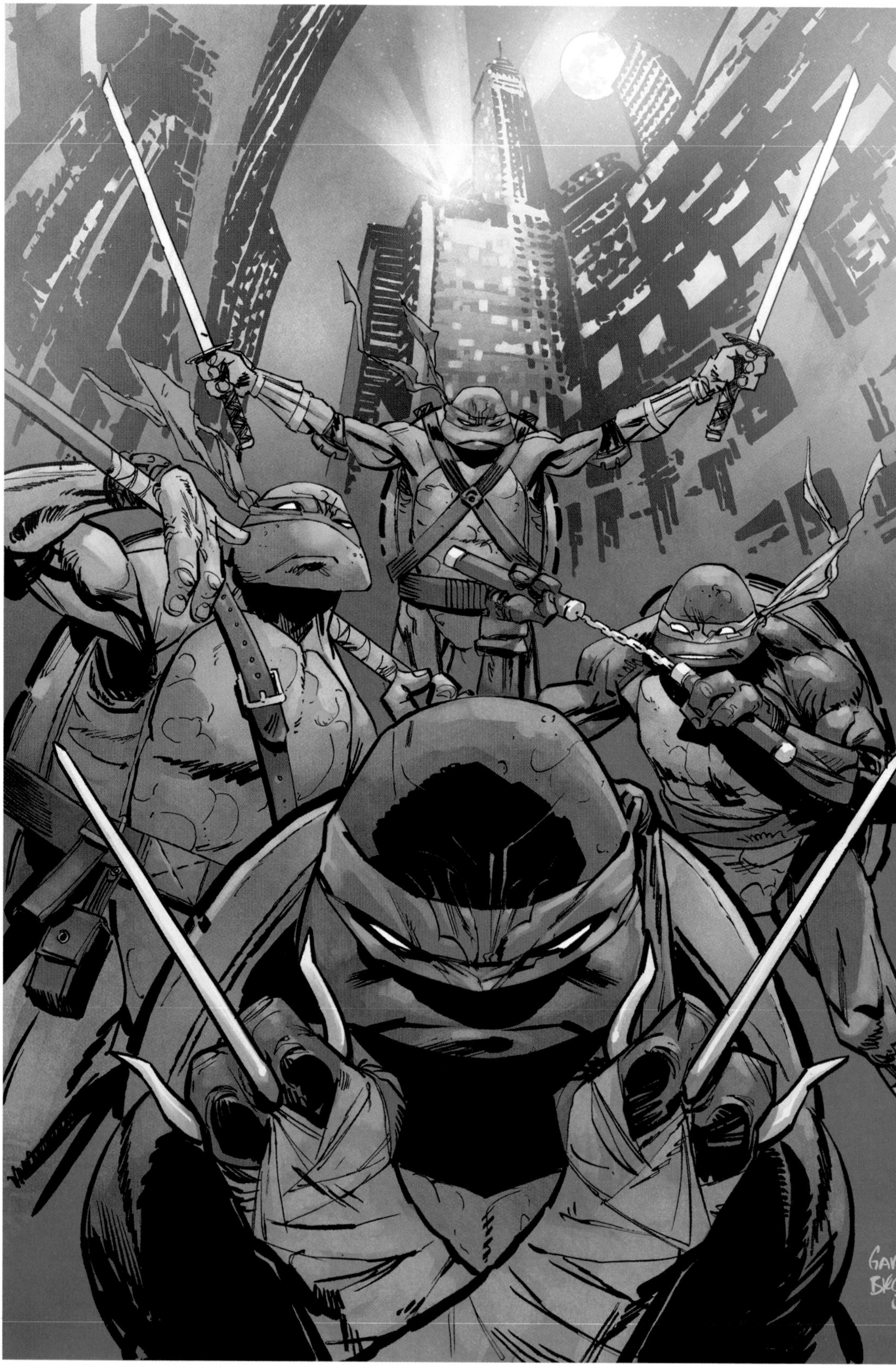

ART BY GARRY BROWN

OPPOSITE PAGE: ART BY KEVIN EASTMAN · COLORS BY TOMI VARGA

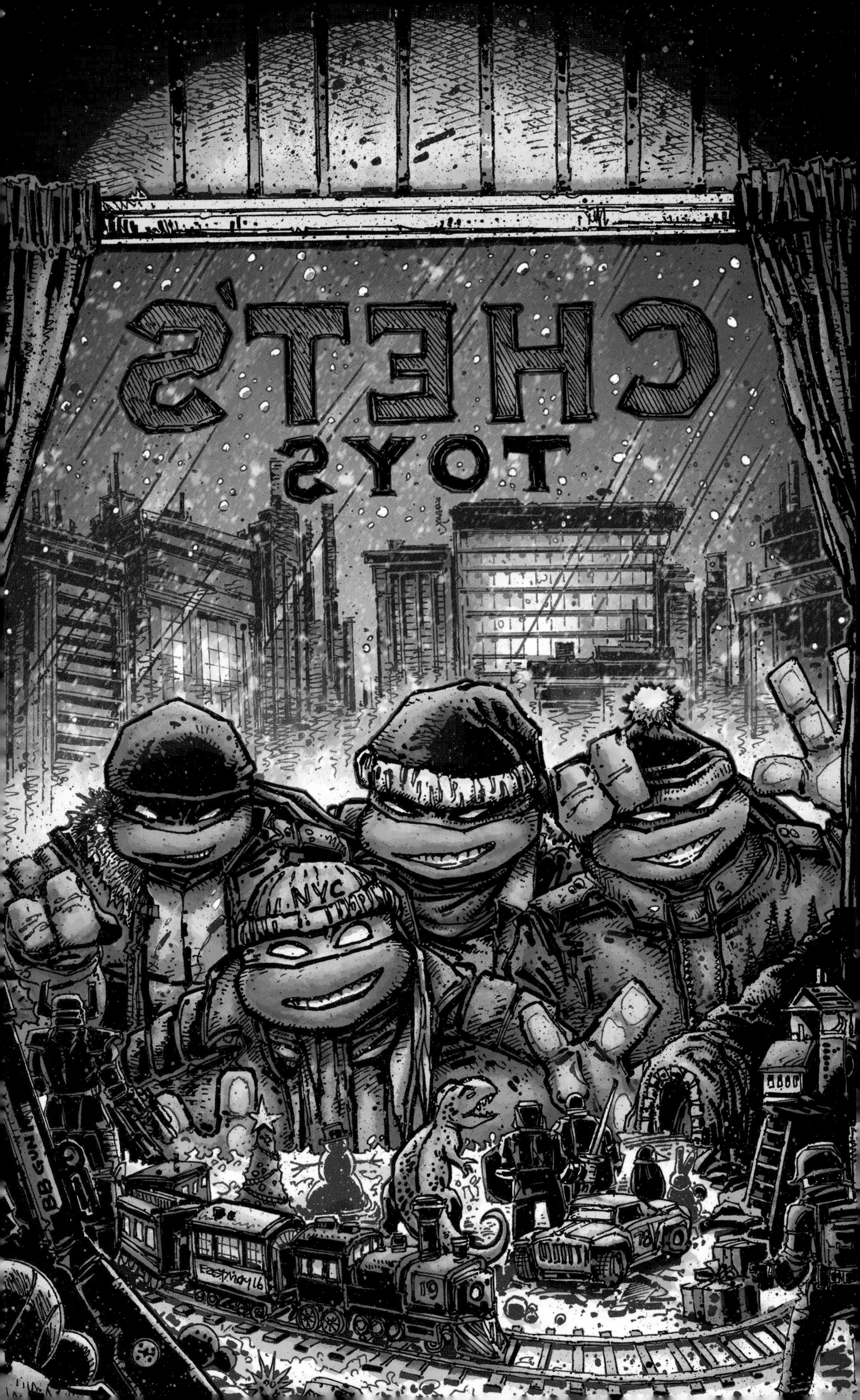
CHET'S
TOYS
NYC
BB GUN